Sidrah Reflections

A Guide to Sidrot and Haftarot

Rabbi Ronald H. Isaacs

KTAV Publishing House, Inc.
Hoboken, NJ

Contents

Book of Bamidbar

Book of Devarim

Readings and Haftarot for Special Occasions

Preface

The first five books of the Hebrew Bible comprise the Torah, and are regarded as Judaism's central document. Along with the stories about the patriarchs Abraham, Isaac, and Jacob, the matriarchs Sarah, Rebekah, Rachel, and Leah, and Moses and the exodus from Egypt, they contain the 613 commandments, the backbone of all of later Jewish law. The Torah has likely been the most influential book in human history. Both Judaism and Christianity consider it to be one of their major religious texts. Several of its central ideas—that there is One God for all people, one universal standard of morality, that people are obligated to care for the poor, widow, orphan, and stranger, that people should refrain from work one day a week and dedicate themselves to making that day holy, and that the Jews have been selected by God to spread His message to the world—have transformed both how men and women have lived, and how they have understood their existence.

The Torah influences the thought patterns of nonreligious as well as religious people. The idea that human beings are responsible for each other, crystallized by Cain's infamous question "Am I my brother's keeper?" (Genesis 4:9), has become part of the backbone of Western civilization. Our values in every area of life are suffused with images and concepts from the Bible.

This volume is intended to provide a user-friendly synopsis of the ideas, concepts, values, and religious obligations (mitzvot) in each of the Torah portions throughout the year, including the special readings for Jewish holy days. In addition, there is a synopsis of the accompanying Haftarot (prophetic portions) to each of the Torah portions.

The aim of the book is to present the Torah portions as a guide to Jewish living and as a timely stimulus for positive thought in terms of the challenges of contemporary life.

The Jewish people are called upon to walk in the light shed by the Torah. May this book help to enlighten you toward the performance of this sacred task.

Ronald H. Isaacs

How to Use This Book

The book includes all of the Torah portions throughout the year and the accompanying Haftarot. The Torah portions are organized in a similar manner and include these elements:

Summary הַסְכּוּם

This is a brief synopsis in outline form of the major points of information in the portion.

Key Concepts and Values מוּשָׂגִים

This includes the important concepts and values which are presented in the portion. Sources will include both biblical and rabbinic texts and commentary.

Notable Mitzvot מִצְווֹת

This includes a partial listing of the relevant mitzvot that may appear in the Torah portion.

Notable Quotations צִיטָטִים

This section relates the most noteworthy verses and quotations in the Torah portion, those most likely to have lasting value and significance.

Accompanying each Torah portion is a section entitled "The Haftarah Connection." The Haftarah (literally the "conclusion") is the prophetic section recited after the reading of the Torah on Sabbaths and festivals. Usually, though not always, the Haftarah contains some reference to an incident mentioned in the Torah reading. The custom of reading a Haftarah has been traced to the period of persecution preceding the Maccabean revolt, when it was introduced as a substitute for the Torah reading, which had been prohibited under the severe decrees of King Antiochus.

In the sections called "The Haftarah" you will find the following elements:

Summary   הַסְכּוּם

This is a brief summary of the story presented in the Haftarah.

The Haftarah Connection   הַקֶּשֶׁר

This section presents the thematic link between the Haftarah and the Torah portion to which it is connected.

Important Concepts   מוּשָׂגִים

This section briefly presents the major ideas and concepts in the Haftarah.

Notable Quotations   צִיטָטִים

The section presents the most noteworthy verses in the Haftarah, memorable passages that will likely continue to have a lasting significance in years to come.

בְּרֵאשִׁית

Bereshit (Genesis 1–6:8)

Summary הַסְכּוּם

1. **Origin of the universe and the human race**

   Creation of the world

   a. First day: *Light*

   b. Second Day: *Firmament*

   c. Third Day: *Sea, land, and vegetation*

   d. Fourth day: *Heavenly bodies*

   e. Fifth day: *Fish and birds*

   f. Sixth day: *Land animals and human beings*

   g. Seventh day: *Shabbat: Day of Rest*

2. **Freedom of choice.** Sin and Punishment. Adam and Eve eat of the forbidden fruit and are expelled from the Garden of Eden.

3. **Cain and Abel** קַיִן וְהֶבֶל. God accepts Abel's superior offering. Cain becomes jealous and kills his brother Abel. Cain learns of his punishment, which is to wander the earth.

Key Concepts and Values מוּשָׂגִים

1. **People are God's partners.** Literally the "Book of Instruction," the Torah is meant to offer guidance for living a Godly life. A basic concept in this Torah portion is that of God as the Creator. Creation is a continuous process, in which humans are partners with God. As such, one strives to become a better person by acquiring those personal qualities which are considered "Godly."

9

Rabbi Hamnuna said: "The person who prays on the eve of Shabbat (and recites 'the heaven and the earth were finished'), the Torah treats that person as though he or she had become a partner with the Blessed Holy One in the Creation" (Talmud Shabbat 119b).

2. Sin חֵטְא. Sin is a mistake, a deviation from the norms handed down to us by our parents, teachers, and society. Reward and punishment are a possibility in our every action. Each good deed is its own reward. Each sin, its own punishment. Every action that a person does will bear a consequence.

3. Freedom of choice בְּחִירָה חוֹפְשִׁית. Judaism holds that every person has been endowed with the freedom to choose between right and wrong. At the same time, Judaism teaches that God has advance knowledge of the choice each individual will make.

4. In God's image בְּצֶלֶם אֱלֹהִים. The Bible reports that humans were made in God's image. But God is imageless and without form. What can this possibly mean? Rabbinic authorities often define the verse to mean that people should follow the attributes of God. For instance, just as God clothed Adam and Eve (Genesis 3:21), so too we should try to clothe the needy who have no clothing. Just as God visited Abraham, who became ill after his circumcision, so too we should make it our duty to visit sick people (see Genesis 18:1). All acts of justice and goodness are closely connected with the concept of being in God's image (Genesis Rabbah 8:13).

5. Symbolic meaning of Hebrew letters. The very first Hebrew word in the Torah, בְּרֵאשִׁית ("in the beginning"), has special meaning. Each Hebrew letter stands for a word that has special meaning. When you put them together it can provide a wonderful pattern of life.

ב **Bet** stands for *bitachon*—faith. *Bitachon* means to believe in God, even in difficult times.

ר **Resh** stands for *ratzon*—will. People often find excuses for themselves, blaming things on others. Each person has a will, and with willpower, we can change our own lives for the better.

א **Aleph** stands for *ahavah*—love. When we do not love, we only think of our own needs and never of another's. To be able to love another person is a requisite of a life of fulfillment. Rabbi Akiva once said that the verse "Love your neighbor as yourself" is the most important verse in the entire Torah. All the rest is commentary.

שׁ **Shin** stands for *shetikah*—silence. There is in life a time to speak, and a time to be quiet. We must learn the times to be silent. If so, we will be much better listeners.

י **Yud** stands for *yirah*—reverence. Judaism teaches that everything a person does in life should reflect reverence for God. One should use words for healing and take actions for sustaining; even eating a meal that includes blessings can become an encounter with the divine.

ת **Tav** stands for *Torah*. Each of us has been given a blueprint of life through the Torah. It teaches us how to live with each other and with God. It teaches us to do justly and love mercy, to live a life of goodness.

Thus we have **BERESHIT** בְּרֵאשִׁית:

ב: Bitachon	בִּטָּחוֹן	*Faith*
ר: Ratzon	רָצוֹן	*Will*
א: Ahavah	אַהֲבָה	*Love*
שׁ: Shetikah	שְׁתִיקָה	*Silence*
י: Yirah	יְרָאָה	*Reverence*
ת: Torah	תּוֹרָה	*The Source of all of these qualities*

6. God the tailor. God's last act before sending Adam and Eve from the Garden of Eden was to make them clothing. This was an act of lovingkindness that God performed for them. God made

11

these outfits to protect them, and even took the time to put the clothing on both Adam and Eve. If humans are to strive to be like God, it is important for them to clothe those who do not have clothing. In pondering the meaning of "in God's image," we also learn that clothing is important to God, and that the type of clothing we wear and the way we look are concerns to God. Think about what God would think about the way you dress. Look at yourself in a mirror and see if you can see the "image of God."

7. God's unfinished world. After six days of creation we read the following: "And God saw everything that He had made, and it was very good" (Genesis 1:31). Note that God said that the world was very good, but not perfect.

There is the story of a young man who was depressed by evil and suffering in the world. He complained to his rabbi: "Why, I could make a better world than this myself." His rabbi answered quietly: "That is exactly the reason God put you in the world—to make it a better one. Now go ahead and do your part!"

God depends on people like us to help Him with His work. There are so many things that God does not do without us. We must work with God to complete the unfinished world. Even though God completed one stage of creation, creation goes on endlessly. We are never finished with our work, nor is God. There is no end to what we and God must do together!

8. God's concern for people. In our Torah portion, God asks Adam the unusual question "Where are You?" (Genesis 3:9). Since God is all-knowing, God surely knew where Adam was. Why then did God ask this question?

Some say that when God asked this question, God wanted Adam to realize where he was, to what point he had come, what he had done concerning the eating of the forbidden fruit and wherein resided his responsibilities.

Like Adam, we too often seek hideouts by evading our responsibilities. We must always be aware of where we are, who we are, and where we must go.

Notable Mitzvot מִצְוֹת

The most notable mitzvah in this Torah portion is that of "be fruitful and multiply, and fill the earth, and subdue it" (Genesis 1:28).

1. When a man reaches the age of eighteen he become subject to the mitzvah to marry and to have children.

2. According to rabbinic law, a man must beget at least one son and one daughter in order to fulfill the mitzvah of being fruitful.

Be fruitful   פְּרוּ

and multiply.   וּרְבוּ

Genesis 1:28

Notable Quotations   צִיטָטִים

And God blessed	וַיְבָרֶךְ אֱלֹהִים
the seventh day	אֶת־יוֹם הַשְּׁבִיעִי
and made it holy	וַיְקַדֵּשׁ אֹתוֹ
because God rested	כִּי בוֹ שָׁבַת
from all the work	מִכָּל־מְלַאכְתּוֹ
which He had been	אֲשֶׁר־בָּרָא אֱלֹהִים
creating.	לַעֲשׂוֹת.

Genesis 2:3

It is not good	לֹא־טוֹב
for a human to be alone.	הֱיוֹת הָאָדָם לְבַדּוֹ.

Genesis 2:18

Am I my brother's keeper?	הֲשֹׁמֵר אָחִי אָנֹכִי?

Genesis 4:9

God spoke	וַיִּקְרָא יְהוָה אֱלֹהִים
to Adam, saying to him:	אֶל־הָאָדָם וַיֹּאמֶר לוֹ:
"Where are you?"	„אַיֶּכָּה?"

Genesis 3:9

14

הַפְטָרַת בְּרֵאשִׁית

The Haftarah (Isaiah 42:5–43:10)

Summary הַסִכּוּם

The Haftarah of Bereshit is taken from the Book of Isaiah, a prophet who lived some 2,700 years ago. In the Haftarah Isaiah speaks to the exiled Israelites in Babylonia. Depressed and filled with despair, they wonder whether God has totally forsaken them. What has become of the covenant between God and the Israelites?

Isaiah brings a message of hope: God is the Creator and the Redeemer. He reminds the people of God's special mission for them, namely, to open the eyes of the blind, bring prisoners out from the dungeon, and serve as a light to the other nations. The Israelites are reminded at the Haftarah's conclusion that they are God's chosen people, and that they will not be forsaken.

The Haftarah Connection הַקֶּשֶׁר

Each Haftarah has a thematic connection to the Torah reading that precedes it. The connection here is clearly found in the opening words of the Haftarah (v. 5), which speak of God as the Creator of heaven and earth. The opening chapters of Genesis also speak of the creation of the world. Isaiah likewise proclaims that God is the Creator of the universe and will rescue Israel. In addition, Israel is reminded of its special duty and mission, namely, to enlighten all people who are blind to the truth, and to free those in both physical as well as spiritual bondage.

15

Important Concepts מוּשָׂגִים

1. Israel is God's chosen people.

2. God wants Israel to be a light for all of the nations of the world. The mission of Israel is to enlighten those who are blind to the truth and to free those who are in spiritual bondage.

3. Israel is to be a witness, testifying to all of the peoples of the world that there is One God, Creator of all that is.

Notable Quotations צִיטָטִים

I God,	אֲנִי יְהֹוָה
have called you in righteousness	קְרָאתִיךָ בְצֶדֶק
. . . to be a light to the nations.	. . . לְאוֹר גּוֹיִם

Isaiah 42:6

Fear not,	אַל־תִּירָא
for I am with you.	כִּי אִתְּךָ־אָנִי

Isaiah 43:5

You are My witnesses,	אַתֶּם עֵדַי
says God,	נְאֻם־יְהֹוָה
and My servant	וְעַבְדִּי
whom I have chosen.	אֲשֶׁר בָּחָרְתִּי

Isaiah 43:10

נֹחַ

Noah (Genesis 6:9–11:32)

Summary הַסְכּוּם

1. God decides to destroy the wicked world by means of a flood.

2. God chooses Noah, a righteous man, and his family to be saved.

3. Noah, his family, and the animals enter the ark and are saved from the flood.

4. The earth dries, and God promises, through the symbol of a rainbow, that the world will never again be destroyed in a flood.

5. The genealogical tables of the seventy nations are presented.

6. People build the Tower of Babel, whose construction is foiled by God by the confusion of their language.

Key Concepts and Values מוּשָׂגִים

1. Being righteous is a virtue. In explaining why the Torah adds the apparently superfluous words "Noah was in his generations a righteous man," some rabbis felt that this statement means that Noah was not an especially unusual human being. For only "in his generation" (of wickedness) did he appear righteous; had he lived in Abraham's generation, he would have not been considered so righteous. Other rabbis took the opposite view. Since everyone around Noah was wicked, it was far more difficult for him to live a righteous life. This is to Noah's credit (Talmud Sanhedrin 108a;

17

Genesis Rabbah, 30:18). The latter message implies that no matter what the conduct of others may be, we can emulate Noah by rising above our environment rather than conforming to society.

2. The rainbow is the sign of God's covenant הַקֶּשֶׁת. In ancient mythologies, a rainbow represented instruments used by gods in battle. The bows would be hung in the sky as symbols of victory. Today the rainbow has come to remind people of God's promise that never will the world again be destroyed by a flood. There is a special blessing when seeing a rainbow. It is: "Praised are You, Adonai our God, Sovereign of the universe, Who remembers His covenant, is faithful to it, and keeps His promise."

3. Embarrassing another person is a transgression. Commenting on the verse "he who sheds man's blood, by man shall his blood be shed," the Chafetz Chayim interprets it to mean embarrassment of one's fellow human being: "One who embarrasses his fellow human being, it is as if one shed that person's blood." Interestingly, the Hebrew word for embarrass, *l'halbin*, means "to make white," or "to drain the blood."

4. Avoid self-aggrandizement. According to many rabbinic interpreters, the Tower of Babel represents the human tendency to reach too high, attempting to equal if not displace God. Having a common dwelling place and a unified language encouraged the designs of the people who built the Tower. Once these elements were removed, their pompous enterprise collapsed.

Notable Mitzvot מִצְוֹת

Jewish tradition holds that non-Jews are bound by seven laws, presumed to date from the time of that most righteous of gentiles, Noah. These have come to be known as the Seven Noahide Laws and are based on rabbinic interpretation of Genesis 9:1–6. In all, there are six negative laws and one positive one:

1. Not to deny God (e.g., through idolatry).

2. Not to blaspheme God.

3. Not to murder.

4. Not to engage in incestuous or adulterous relationships.

5. Not to steal.

6. Not to eat the limb from a living animal.

7. To set up courts to ensure obedience to the other six laws. (Talmud Sanhedrin 56a)

Judaism regards any non-Jew who keeps these laws as a righteous person who is a guaranteed a place in the world-to-come.

Notable Quotations צִיטָטִים

With God	אֶת־הָאֱלֹהִים
Noah walked.	הִתְהַלֶּךְ־נֹחַ.

Genesis 6:9

I have set My rainbow in the cloud,	אֶת־קַשְׁתִּי נָתַתִּי בֶּעָנָן
and it shall be for a sign of	וְהָיְתָה לְאוֹת
a covenant between Me	בְּרִית בֵּינִי
and the earth.	וּבֵין הָאָרֶץ.

Genesis 9:13

Anyone who sheds human blood,	שֹׁפֵךְ דַּם הָאָדָם
by man will his blood be shed,	בָּאָדָם דָּמוֹ יִשָּׁפֵךְ
for in the image of God	כִּי בְּצֶלֶם אֱלֹהִים
He made man.	עָשָׂה אֶת־הָאָדָם.

Genesis 9:6

הַפְטָרַת נֹחַ

The Haftarah (Isaiah 54–55:5)

Summary הַסְכּוּם

The Haftarah of Noah is taken from the Book of Isaiah. In it, Isaiah speaks to those Jews who had been exiled to Babylon after the destruction of the Jerusalem Temple in 586 B.C.E. The people are obviously in a state of shock and deep despair, and Isaiah attempts to comfort them.

The Israelites are reminded that God's kindness will never depart from them, and that all weapons that may be directed at them will never prosper. The Haftarah's concluding theme is that the return to Zion should also be a return to God. It is a call to rich and poor alike to participate in the blessings of the new era, by coming to the source from which the knowledge of duty springs— namely, the word of God.

The Haftarah Connection הַקֶּשֶׁר

The reference in verse 9 of chapter 54 to "the waters of Noah" provides the literal connection with the Torah portion. The flood was clearly an act of destruction, yet by wiping out an evil world, it paved the way for a new humanity. Similarly, the prophet Isaiah declares that from its suffering after the destruction of the Temple, Israel is becoming stronger in loyalty to God. Again, God's covenant with Noah ("I will establish My covenant with you . . . neither shall there any more be a flood to destroy the earth") is paralleled

20

by the Covenant of Peace into which, in God's eternal mercy, Israel now enters.

Important Concepts מוּשָׂגִים

1. God's relationship to Israel is like that of husband and wife (Isaiah 54:5).

2. God's kindness toward Israel is eternal and everlasting (Isaiah 54:7).

3. God's covenant of peace with Israel is eternal (Isaiah 54:10).

4. Peace will increase when all children are taught about God (Isaiah 54:13).

Notable Quotations צִיטָטִים

For the mountains may depart,	כִּי הֶהָרִים יָמוּשׁוּ
and the hills be removed.	וְהַגְּבָעוֹת תְּמוּטֶנָה
But My kindness will not leave you	וְחַסְדִּי מֵאִתֵּךְ לֹא־יָמוּשׁ
and My covenant of peace	וּבְרִית שְׁלוֹמִי
will not be withdrawn,	לֹא תָמוּט
says your compassionate God.	אָמַר מְרַחֲמֵךְ יְהוָה.

Isaiah 54:10

All your children shall know God	וְכָל־בָּנַיִךְ לִמּוּדֵי יְהוָה
and great shall be the peace	וְרַב שְׁלוֹם
of your children.	בָּנָיִךְ.

Isaiah 54:13

This is like the waters of Noah	כִּי־מֵי נֹחַ
for me, since I have sworn that	זֹאת לִי אֲשֶׁר נִשְׁבַּעְתִּי
never will Noah's waters flood	מֵעֲבֹר מֵי־נֹחַ עוֹד
over the earth again,	עַל־הָאָרֶץ
so have I foresworn	כֵּן נִשְׁבַּעְתִּי
raging against you	מִקְּצֹף עָלַיִךְ
and rebuking you.	וּמִגְּעָר־בָּךְ.

Isaiah 54:9

21

לֶךְ־לְךָ

Lech Lecha (Genesis 12:1–17:27)

Summary   הַסְכּוּם

1. Abram is called to leave his family and the city of Haran in Mesopotamia.

2. God appears to Abram in Canaan and tells him that this land will be assigned to him and his heirs.

3. Because of a famine in Canaan, Abram goes to Egypt, and for a time lives there.

4. Abram separates from his nephew Lot by remaining in the land of Canaan, while Lot journeys eastward, ultimately settling near the wicked city of Sodom.

5. Lot becomes involved in a war with enemy chieftains, and Abram comes to Lot's rescue.

6. God makes a covenant with Abram in which God promises him that Canaan shall be the land of the generations of Hebrews to come.

7. Because Abram has no children with his wife Sarai, he takes Hagar too as his wife and with her bears a child named Ishmael.

8. God makes a covenant (requiring circumcision of every male on the eighth day) with Abram, whose name is changed to Abraham, meaning "father of a multitude of nations."

9. God changes Sarai's name to Sarah, meaning "princess," and she is told that she will bear a son.

10. Abraham circumcises himself in his ninety-ninth year, while his son Ishmael is circumcised at age thirteen.

Key Concepts and Values מוּשָׂגִים

1. The call to Abram. Abram is called to leave his country, his family, his father's house, and go to a new land that God will show him (Genesis 12:1). The great medieval commentator Rashi explains that *lech lecha* ("get you out") means "for your pleasures and for your good." He explains that Abraham will not only enjoy the new land in which he is to settle, but that he will also realize that it is to his personal benefit to settle there.

In our own personal lives it would be beneficial for us to pursue that which is of advantage to our moral and spiritual growth, in the knowledge that only such striving leads to true health, wealth, and joy.

2. Peace is a value toward which humanity must strive שָׁלוֹם. In Genesis 13:8, Abraham says to his nephew Lot, "Let there be no strife, I pray you, between me and you . . . for we are brothers." Our rabbis comment that since strife and confrontation are forbidden even among strangers, how much more ought we to try to establish peace and harmony between ourselves, our families, relatives and friends (cf. Genesis Rabbah 41:7).

Psalms 34:13 states: "Seek peace and pursue it." The Torah does not obligate us to pursue the mitzvot, but only to fulfill them at the proper time, on the appropriate occasion. Peace, however, must be sought at all times; at home and away from home we are obliged to seek peace and to pursue it (Numbers Rabbah 19:27).

3. The Covenant of Abraham (circumcision) בְּרִית מִילָה. In verse 10 of chapter 17 of Genesis, we are informed that circumcision is to be the external sign of the covenant between God and Abraham. Jewish men and women have in all ages been

23

ready to lay down their lives in its defense. The Maccabean martyrs died for it. The officers of King Antiochus punished mothers who initiated their children into the covenant of circumcision by putting them to death and hanging their babies about their necks (I Maccabees 1:61).

4. The importance of a person's name. For Jewish people, a name is a complicated gift. Not only does it bestow identity, but also it can reflect religious and spiritual dimensions. First Samuel 25:25 says, "As his name, so the man." Proverbs 22:1 says that "a good name is preferable to great riches." And the Ethics of the Fathers 4:17 teaches that "there are three crowns: the crown of Torah, the crown of priesthood, and the crown of royalty, but the crown of a good name excels them all."

The Torah portrays naming as the first independent act, when Adam gives names to the animals. It also underscores the importance of names in its attention to dramatic name changes. In our Torah portion, Abram's name is changed to Abraham ("father of a multitude of nations"), and Sarai's name is changed to Sarah ("princess"). These new names emphasize the missions of Abraham and Sarah to the Jewish people. Abraham's task is to bring all people under the wings of God, and Sarah is to be the complement to her husband's work.

Notable Mitzvot מִצְוֹת

The major mitzvah in this Torah portion is circumcision. Genesis 17:10 states that "every male among you shall be circumcised." Here are some of the basic laws related to circumcision.

1. It is incumbent on the father to circumcise his son. If the father cannot perform this act himself, he may appoint a mohel (ritual circumciser) to perform the mitzvah for him. Today, a woman is allowed to serve as a mohelet in some communities.

2. Circumcision must take place as early as possible on the eighth day after the infant's birth.

3. If the child is physically unfit for circumcision, the ceremony must be postponed until he is in good health.

4. A convert to Judaism who was circumcised before his conversion must undergo, according to Jewish law, a symbolic circumcision. This is done by drawing one drop of blood from the place where circumcision is ordinarily performed.

5. Participants in a circumcision ceremony include the following: the kvater קְװאָטֶר (godfather) and kvaterin קְװאָטֶרין (godmother), who bring the baby into the room where the circumcision is to be performed; the sandek סַנְדֵק, who holds the baby while the circumcision is being performed; the mohel מוֹהֵל or mohelet מוֹהֶלֶת, who performs the circumcision; the rabbi רַב or cantor חַזָן, who often names the baby in Hebrew following the surgical procedure; and the parents.

You shall circumcise   הִמּוֹל לָכֶם

every male.   כָּל־זָכָר. ·

Genesis 17:10

Notable Quotations   צִיטָטִים

Go from your country,	. . . לֶךְ־לְךָ מֵאַרְצְךָ
and from your family,	וּמִמּוֹלַדְתְּךָ
and your father's house,	וּמִבֵּית אָבִיךָ
to a land that I will show you.	אֶל־הָאָרֶץ אֲשֶׁר אַרְאֶךָּ:

Genesis 12:1

Your name shall no longer be called Abram.	וְלֹא־יִקָּרֵא עוֹד אֶת־שִׁמְךָ אַבְרָם
Your name shall be Abraham,	וְהָיָה שִׁמְךָ אַבְרָהָם
for the father of a multitude	כִּי אַב־הֲמוֹן
of nations have I made you.	גּוֹיִם נְתַתִּיךָ

Genesis 17:5

25

הַפְטָרַת לֶךְ-לְךָ

The Haftarah (Isaiah 40:27–41:16)

Summary הַסְכּוּם

The Haftarah of Lech Lecha is taken from the Book of Isaiah. It is a message by the prophet to the exiled Jews in Babylon who find themselves in an unhappy state of depression and confusion. Isaiah, being the prophet of consolation and comfort, attempts to assure the Israelites that God has not forgotten them. Asking them to be patient, he reassures the Israelites that having patience and faith in God's goodness and good judgment will eventually end in their return to their homeland. God, he says, must have good reason for delaying the forthcoming redemption.

In Isaiah's second message (chap. 41) he summons the nations to a trial before God. Cyrus, the ruler of Persia, is going to be used as the vehicle through which God will bring about the redemption of the exiled Israelites. All of the nations that were once enemies of Israel will see the redemption happening and will become confused and embarrassed. And God will ultimately bring victory to the Israelites.

The Haftarah Connection הַקֶּשֶׁר

The connection of this Haftarah to the Torah portion of Lech Lecha can be found in chapter 41:8 of the Haftarah: "But you, Israel, My servant, Jacob whom I have chosen, the seed of Abraham My friend." God had made a covenant with Abraham more than a

26

thousand years prior to the time of the prophet Isaiah. The covenant assured Abraham that he would be the father of a nation that would be as numerous as the stars in the sky. In the Haftarah, Isaiah reminds the Israelites of that special agreement, in an attempt to comfort them and offer them assurance that redemption was on the horizon and that God would bring them ultimate victory. Isaiah's prophecy came true when, in 539 B.C.E., Cyrus conquered Babylon, permitting the Israelites to return to their homeland. The returning exiles carried with them the plundered vessels of the Temple and funds for its reconstruction. Both were gifts from Cyrus.

Important Concepts מוּשָׂגִים

1. Having faith in God will help renew one's strength.

2. Abraham and God are forever bound in an eternal covenantal relationship.

3. Israel is God's chosen people.

4. Israel's enemies will be confounded.

Notable Quotations צִיטָטִים

Those who wait for God	וְקֹוֵי יְהֹוָה
will renew their strength.	יַחֲלִיפוּ כֹחַ.

Isaiah 40:31

I the Lord am the first	אֲנִי יְהֹוָה רִאשׁוֹן
and will be with the last	וְאֶת־אַחֲרֹנִים
I am he.	אֲנִי־הוּא.

Isaiah 41:4

You are My servant.	וָאֹמַר לְךָ עַבְדִּי־אַתָּה
I have chosen you	בְּחַרְתִּיךָ
and will not reject you .	וְלֹא מְאַסְתִּיךָ.

Isaiah 41:9

וַיֵּרָא

Vayera (Genesis 18:1–22:24)

Summary הַסְכּוּם

1. Abraham greets three visiting strangers and shows them hospitality.

2. Abraham intercedes for the city of Sodom, but is unsuccessful.

3. Lot escapes destruction, but his wife turns into a pillar of salt.

4. Alliance between Abraham and Avimelech.

5. Isaac is born to Abraham and Sarah.

6. Sarah asks Abraham to send Ishmael away, due to his bad influence on Isaac.

7. Abraham is tested by God, asked to sacrifice his beloved son Isaac.

Key Concepts and Values מוּשָׂגִים

1. Hospitality הַכְנָסַת אוֹרְחִים. Hospitality (*hachnasat orchim*) is an important value in Judaism. A graphic description of hospitality to strangers is displayed by Abraham, who runs from the entrance of his tent to greet his three visitors, providing them with food and water. Ethics of the Fathers 1:5 reminds us of this important value when it states: "Let your house be wide open; treat the poor as members of your own family.

Justice and compassion צֶדֶק וְרַחֲמִים. Justice is not only the ethical quality in God or man, but the basis for all the other qualities. The virtue of compassion also ranks very high in the scale of

Jewish values. In this Torah portion Abraham challenges God's justice, hoping to convince God not to destroy the Sodomites if enough righteous persons can be found. God says that He will not destroy the city for the sake of ten persons. The number 10 has become the minimum number of persons to constitute a community, and thus a minyan for purposes of worship consists of ten persons.

We see from this Torah portion that we have the freedom to question what God does, although we will have to submit to God's judgment in the end.

3. Merit of the few זְכוּת. Abraham does not plead merely for the innocent but for the sinners as well, through the merit of the few righteous. The story thereby introduces the concept of merit (*zechut*), stipulating that a handful of concerned, decent, and righteous people could have averted Sodom's calamity by their merit.

The story also suggests that there are limits to the influence of even the best people. Unless they find a minimum of like-minded associates, they will be ineffective. Eventually, if they persist in living in such a society, they will perish with it.

4. God tests people. Abraham is tested by God, being asked to sacrifice his beloved son Isaac. The Torah does not state precisely why God is testing Abraham. Is it to test Abraham's faith that God will not go back on His promise? Or is it to test Abraham's unquestioning obedience to the divine will, his faithfulness rather than his faith? Perhaps the test is both for faith and faithfulness, which together represent the quality of *emunah*, obedience with complete trust.

Maimonides writes that God tested Abraham precisely because He knew that he would pass the test. Abraham's faith would therefore become a beacon to the nations. The philosopher Franz Rosenzweig sees in the test a temptation by God. According to his view, God purposely conceals His true purpose, giving Abraham an opportunity to ground his faith in trust and freedom.

Notable Mitzvot מִצְווֹת

Two mitzvot which are rabbinically deduced from this Torah portion are those of visiting the sick (*bikkur cholim*) and hospitality to strangers (*hachnasat orchim*).

Visiting the sick בְּקוּר חוֹלִים. The mitzvah of visiting the sick is derived from the fact that God appeared to Abraham (Genesis 18:1) to pay him a sick call after he had just been circumcised.

1. Visiting the sick is one of the commandments for which a person is rewarded both in this world and the world-to-come (Talmud Shabbat 127a).

2. When one visits the sick, one helps a person to recover (Talmud Nedarim 40a).

Hospitality הַכְנָסַת אוֹרְחִים. This mitzvah is derived from the hospitality that Abraham demonstrated to the three strangers.

1. It is the duty of a host to be cheerful during meals, thus making his guests feel at home (Talmud Derech Eretz Zutah 9).

2. It is commendable that the host personally serve at the table, thereby showing willingness to satisfy the guests.

3. A guest should comply with every request that a host makes (Talmud Derech Eretz Rabbah 6).

4. Guests should acknowledge the hospitality of their host by including a special section of the Blessing after the Meal in the host's honor.

Notable Quotations   צִיטָטִים

Is anything too miraculous for God?   הֲיִפָּלֵא מֵיְהֹוָה דָּבָר?
Genesis 18:14

Shall the Judge of the entire earth   הֲשֹׁפֵט כָּל־הָאָרֶץ
not act justly?   לֹא יַעֲשֶׂה מִשְׁפָּט?
Genesis 18:25

The angel of God called to him   וַיִּקְרָא אֵלָיו מַלְאַךְ יְהֹוָה
from the heavens   מִן־הַשָּׁמַיִם
and said: "Abraham,   וַיֹּאמֶר "אַבְרָהָם,
Abraham,"   אַבְרָהָם,"
And he said: "Here I am."   וַיֹּאמֶר "הִנֵּנִי."
Genesis 22:11

הַפְטָרַת וַיֵּרָא

The Haftarah (II Kings 4:1–37)

Summary הַסְכּוּם

The Haftarah tells of an event in the life of the prophet Elisha, who lived in the ninth century B.C.E. Elisha was known for his compassion and for his ability to perform acts of kindness. This Haftarah presents several incidents in his life that allowed him the opportunity to do good for others.

In the first story, Elisha is approached by a poor widow whose two children are about to be taken from her because she cannot pay her debts. Elisha is able to perform a miracle, supplying the woman with oil, which she in turn sells in order to pay her creditors. Thus the woman's children are saved.

In the second story Elisha is given shelter in the house of a woman in the town of Shunem. In return for her graciousness and hospitality, Elisha informs the woman that she will soon be blessed with a child. Several years later, the child suffers a sunstroke. The child is close to death, but the mother brings him to Elisha, who applies mouth-to-mouth resuscitation. The child is revived.

The Haftarah Connection הַקֶּשֶׁר

The parallel between the Torah portion and the Haftarah is a clear one. The prophet Elisha, like Abraham, seeks every opportunity to practice lovingkindness and bring relief and blessing wherever he goes in the course of his ministrations. Even more does the

story of the Shunemmite woman and her child recall the story of
Sarah. Both occurrences were "divine" happenings.

Important Concepts מוּשָׂגִים

The major concept in this Haftarah relates to the important
Jewish value called גְּמִילוּת חֲסָדִים—deeds of lovingkindness.
Elisha is the man par excellence who spends a lifetime searching
for opportunities to perform kindnesses for others.

Notable Quotations צִיטָטִים

What shall I do for you?	מָה אֶעֱשֶׂה־לָּךְ?

II Kings 4:2

And he went up,	וַיַּעַל
stretched himself over the child,	וַיִּשְׁכַּב עַל־הַיֶּלֶד,
put his mouth upon his mouth	וַיָּשֶׂם פִּיו עַל־פִּיו
and his eyes upon his eyes.	וְעֵינָיו עַל־עֵינָיו

II Kings 4:34

חַיֵּי שָׂרָה

Chaye Sarah (Genesis 23:1–25:18)

Summary הַסִכּוּם

1. Death and burial of Sarah in the Cave of Machpelah.

2. Abraham sends his servant Eliezer in search of a wife for Isaac.

3. Eliezer prays to God for assistance in his search.

4. Eliezer finds Rebekah, whom Isaac chooses to be his wife.

4. Death of Abraham, who is buried next to Sarah in Cave of Machpelah.

5. Descendants of Ishmael.

Key Concepts and Values מוּשָׂגִים

1. Met mitzvah: the religious obligation to bury one's dead מֵת מִצְוָה. Abraham's concern about a grave for his wife Sarah is the first reference in the Bible to burial. Prompt and reverent care for the dead is an important religious obligation. Jewish law defines in detail what must be done for the dead and how they must be buried. In this portion Abraham wishes to be sure to buy and thus legally own a burial place for his wife. In addition, he does not want a free piece of land, but insists on paying the full price.

2. Ahavat ha'umah: love for one's people and marrying within the faith אַהֲבַת הָאוּמָה. Concern for the integrity of family and nation is illustrated by Abraham's insistence that Isaac not marry a woman of alien origin. Judaism has always strongly opposed intermarriage, stressing the importance of marrying within the faith and preserving its heritage of culture and traditions. In our

34

Torah portion we have the very first biblical reference on the subject of opposition to mixed marriage.

3. Tza'ar ba'alei chayim: prevention of cruelty to animals צַעַר בַּעֲלֵי חַיִּים. Kindness to animals is an important religious obligation in Judaism. Rebekah's insistence that Eliezer's camels also receive water was one of the conditions for her being chosen as the eventual wife of Isaac. It clearly displayed her sensitivity and compassion toward animals.

4. Meditation חֶשְׁבּוֹן הַנֶּפֶשׁ. Isaac went out to meditate in the field (Genesis 24:63) Our rabbis tells us that Isaac was not merely meditating and communing with nature, but was engaging in prayer, for he had instituted the tradition of the Minchah afternoon prayer service (Talmud Berachot 25a). The afternoon prayer service is the shortest of the three daily prayer services. Often popularly called "the pause that refreshes," it is a service during the middle of the day that affords the worshipper an additional opportunity to cultivate a genuine appreciation of the true blessings of life.

5. Prayer תְּפִילָה. One of the first references to a prayer in the Torah is the spontaneous prayer of Eliezer, who says, "O God, the God of my master Abraham, send me, I pray You, good speed this day, and show kindness to my master Abraham" (Genesis 24:12). To further emphasize the importance of this prayer, the cantillation note called the *shalshelet* is placed over the Hebrew word *vayomar* ("and he said"). This musical note is considered one of the most dramatically melodic ones, appearing only in a few places in the entire Torah.

Notable Mitzvot מִצְווֹת

1. Being kind to animals צַעַר בַּעֲלֵי חַיִּים. The Bible has many laws related to being kind to animals. For example, an ox and a donkey are not to be used to plow in the same yoke

(Deuteronomy 22:10) because of the unequal strength of these two animals. In the Ten Commandments we learn that animals were to rest on the holy Sabbath (Exodus 20:10). One of the most insightful instructions concerning the treatment of animals is found in this profoundly simple statement: "You must not eat your own meal until you have seen to it that all your animals have been fed" (Talmud Berachot 40a).

2. Met mitzvah: honoring the dead and comforting the mourners מֵת מִצְוָה. Burying the dead and comforting the bereaved is a true act of kindness. There are many citations related to burial in the Torah. In addition to the one in this Torah portion, we read in Deuteronomy that "a person must not let a human body remain on the stake overnight, but must bury it the same day" (Deuteronomy 21:23). From this verse the rabbis deduced that it is preferable to bury a person within twenty-four hours of the time of death.

There are a whole array of customs and traditions related to caring for the human body following death. These include watching the body and reciting psalms, and ritually washing and dressing the body in white linen shrouds, an act performed by members of the Chevra Kaddisha, the Holy Burial Society. Following the burial, the mourners customarily return to the home of the deceased to sit shivah. During this period the family of the deceased stays together, and friends and community members come to pay their respects and offer words of comfort.

Notable Quotations צִיטָטִים

You shall not take a wife	... לֹא־תִקַּח אִשָּׁה
for my son from the daughters of	לִבְנִי מִבְּנוֹת
the Canaanites	הַכְּנַעֲנִי
among whom I dwell.	אֲשֶׁר אָנֹכִי יוֹשֵׁב בְּקִרְבּוֹ.

Genesis 24:3

O God, the God of	יְהֹוָה אֱלֹהֵי
my master Abraham,	אֲדֹנִי אַבְרָהָם
be with me today,	הַקְרֵה־נָא לְפָנַי הַיּוֹם
and be kind to	וַעֲשֵׂה־חֶסֶד עִם
my master Abraham.	אֲדֹנִי אַבְרָהָם.

Genesis 24:12

| Isaac went out to meditate | וַיֵּצֵא יִצְחָק לָשׂוּחַ |
| in the field in the evening. | בַּשָּׂדֶה לִפְנוֹת עָרֶב. |

Genesis 24:63

הַפְטָרַת חַיֵּי שָׂרָה
The Haftarah (I Kings 1:1–31)

Summary הַסְכּוּם

Taken from the First Book of Kings, the Haftarah tells of King David's approaching death and his plans for choosing a successor. There is substantial plotting going on in the royal court, and Adoniyah, King David's fourth son, is so eager to succeed his father that he cannot even wait for his death. Adoniyah prepares a banquet at which he plans to crown himself king. When David is told of Adoniyah's plot by Bat-Sheba, his wife, and Nathan the prophet, he takes an oath that Solomon will succeed him as king. When David dies, Solomon becomes Israel's third king.

The Haftarah Connection הַקֶּשֶׁר

The connection between the Torah reading and the Haftarah is readily seen. The Torah reading portrays Abraham's old age, and the Haftarah, King David's old age. The Torah reading depicts Abraham's concern for the piety of his house, and the Haftarah depicts King David's anxiety for the right succession in his royal court. There is contrast in the characters of the two sons portrayed in the Torah and in the Haftarah. Isaac allows himself to be guided by his father Abraham in a great decision, in spite of being forty years old. Adoniyah, in the Haftarah, cannot wait for the death of his father to proclaim himself king.

Important Concepts מוּשָׂגִים

1. All leaders must carefully choose a successor.
2. Sibling rivalry is common in family life.

Notable Quotations צִיטָטִים

Solomon your son	כִּי־שְׁלֹמֹה בְנֵךְ
shall reign after me.	יִמְלֹךְ אַחֲרָי.

I Kings 1:17

Let my lord King David live	יְחִי אֲדֹנִי הַמֶּלֶךְ דָּוִד
forever.	לְעֹלָם.

I Kings 1:31

תוֹלְדוֹת

Toledot (Genesis 25:19–28:9)

Summary הַסְכּוּם

1. Isaac prays for the barren Rebekah, who gives birth to Esau and Jacob.

2. Esau grows up a hunter, and Jacob, an upright dweller in tents.

3. Esau, the elder, sells his birthright to Jacob for a pot of lentil soup.

4. Rebekah, who favors her younger son Jacob, arranges for Jacob to secure his father's coveted blessing instead of Esau.

5. Jacob, disguised as his brother Esau, is able to secure his father Isaac's blessing.

6. Isaac bids Jacob to marry one of his uncle Laban's daughters.

Key Concepts and Values מוּשָׂגִים

1. Sibling rivalry. The Torah tells us that even before Esau and Jacob were born, their mother Rebekah felt them battling with each other in her womb. For many Jewish commentators, Esau and Jacob were more than brothers. They were two different nations at war with each other. Their personalities were very different, and their descendants became enemies throughout all history. They were not only Esau and Jacob, but Israel and Edom, then Israel and Rome, then Israel and all who plotted the destruction of the Jewish people.

40

2. Parental favoritism. The Torah portion takes us into the biblical home of Rebekah and Isaac. To complicate family matters, we are told that each parent has chosen a favorite son. Isaac prefers Esau "because he had a taste for freshly killed game," while "Rebekah loved Jacob." While most Bible commentators agree that Esau and Jacob had very different personalities, there are some who suggest that the distrust and hatred that developed between them was the fault of their parents. Psychologist Chaim G. Ginott points out that the competition and jealousy between them was sparked by parental favoritism and preferential treatment. Good parenting includes the fair treatment of siblings.

Intermarriage. The subject of marriage is raised twice in the Torah portion. We are told that when Esau was forty years old he married two Hittite women, and that the marriages were a source of bitterness to Isaac and Rebekah (Genesis 26:34). Then, near the end of the Torah portion, it is reported that Rebekah tells Isaac that she is worried that Jacob, like Esau, will marry a woman from among the Canaanites rather than someone from their ancestral home. Isaac agrees with her, and sends for Jacob, instructing him to go to find a bride among the daughters of Laban, Rebekah's brother. As the Torah portion indicates, the subject of intermarriage between Jews and non-Jews has been a concern since the beginning of Jewish history. We are not explicitly told what it is that "displeases" Isaac and Rebekah about Esau's Hittite wives. Yet it is clear that they are troubled by what Esau has done, and therefore warn Jacob not to marry from among the Canaanites, but tell him to find a wife among his own tribal family.

Notable Mitzvot מִצְווֹת

Family blessings בִּרְכַּת הַמִשְׁפָּחָה Blessing one's children is a sacred duty in Judaism. The custom is to bless children before

41

eating the Friday evening Shabbat meal. The blessing for boys invokes the shining examples of Jacob's grandchildren Ephraim and Manasseh, who, although raised in Egypt, did not lose their identity as Jews. The blessing for girls refers to the four matriarchs, Sarah, Rebekah, Rachel, and Leah, all of whom were known for their concern and compassion for others.

Notable Quotations צִיטָטִים

Two nations are in your womb . . .	שְׁנֵי גוֹיִם בְּבִטְנֵךְ
and the elder	וְרַב
shall serve the younger.	יַעֲבֹד צָעִיר.

Genesis 25:23

The voice	הַקֹּל
is the voice of Jacob,	קוֹל יַעֲקֹב,
but the hands	וְהַיָּדַיִם
are the hands of Esau.	יְדֵי עֵשָׂו.

Genesis 27:22

הַפְטָרַת תּוֹלְדוֹת

The Haftarah (Malachi 1–2:7)

Summary הַסְכּוּם

Malachi was the last of the prophets. Nothing is known of his life, except that which can be gleaned from his prophecies, which seem to have been spoken about the year 450 B.C.E. The Second Temple had been rebuilt, but the high hopes of the returned exiles had not been fulfilled. Sacred things were being treated with total indifference. Israel began to have its doubts about God, and Malachi in his message affirms the divine election of Israel. Malachi gives eternal expression to the brotherhood of man: "Have we not one father? Has not one God created us? Why do we deal treacherously every person against his brother?" (Malachi 2:10).

The Haftarah Connection הַקֶּשֶׁר

The connection with the Torah portion lies chiefly in the opening verses. The difference in the treatment of the two nations descended from Jacob and Esau is due to the differences in character and life between these nations. The Edomites were fierce and cruel, and that is why so much disdain for this people was displayed.

Important Concepts מוּשָׂגִים

1. The Edomites are descended from Esau. Esau is not worthy of his birthright, and his unruly behavior gives birth to the Edomites, known for their cruelty and turbulent characters.

2. Reverential awe is one of the first essentials for one who is a part of the Jewish priesthood.

43

Notable Quotations צִיטָטִים

From the rising of the sun	מִמִּזְרַח־שֶׁמֶשׁ
to its setting,	וְעַד־מְבוֹאוֹ
My name is honored	גָּדוֹל שְׁמִי
among the nations.	בַּגּוֹיִם.

Malachi 1:11

They shall seek the law	וְתוֹרָה יְבַקְשׁוּ
from his mouth,	מִפִּיהוּ,
since a messenger	כִּי מַלְאַךְ
of the Lord of Hosts is he.	יְהוָֹה־צְבָאוֹת הוּא.

Malachi 2:7

וַיֵּצֵא

Vayetze (Genesis 28:10–32:3)

Summary הַסְכּוּם

1. Jacob's heavenly-ladder dream.

2. Jacob becomes a member of Laban's family.

3. Jacob marries Leah, and works for seven more years in order to acquire Rachel for a wife.

4. Jacob's flight from Laban.

Key Concepts and Values מוּשָׂגִים

1. Yirah: the awe of God יִרְאָה. When Jacob awakens from his heavenly dream, his first words are: "Surely God is in this place, and I did not know it" (Genesis 28:16). Our rabbis tell us that no vision in life will ever come to successful fruition unless we can say: "Surely God is in this place" (*panim yafot*). Jacob had a spiritual experience and felt the Presence of God. Some say that the ladder in Jacob's dream, called in Hebrew a *sulam*, was a symbol of Sinai. In gematria, the words *sulam* and *Sinai* both have the same numerical value, 130.

2. Bargaining with God. The Torah tells us that just after Jacob awoke from his dream, he made a promise to God in the form of a prayer: "If God remains with me, if God protects me on this journey and gives me bread to eat and clothing to wear, and if I return safely to my father's house—the Lord shall be my God . . . and of all that You give me I will always set aside a tithe for you" (Genesis 28:20–22). Biblical commentators have been bothered by

45

the fact that Jacob in this vow seems to be bargaining with God. Rather than promising what he will or will not do, which is the accepted form of a vow, Jacob laces his commitment with conditions. This is not a "proper" prayer.

Nechama Leibowitz, a noted Bible scholar, writes that no deal is involved in Jacob's vow. What Jacob meant was that if God did not grant him to return to his father's house, how would he be able to erect a temple on the spot? All that Jacob's vow implied was: "Give me the possibility of serving You, O God."

3. Ma'aser: tithing מַעֲשֵׂר. Jacob promised to give to God one-tenth of all the wealth that God would bestow upon him (Genesis 28:22). This pledge later became the basis for the tithe given to the Temple, to the priests, and to the poor.

4. Sinnat chinam: causeless hatred שִׂנְאַת חִנָּם. Hatred without just cause between individuals and nations is exemplified by Esau's hatred for his brother Jacob, and later by the hostility shown by the Edomites for the people of Israel. According to the sages, the Messianic era can only begin when causeless hatred has vanished from the earth. Years ago they wrote: "What is hateful to you, do not do to others" (Talmud Shabbat 31a). They also said that "hatred without cause is as wicked as idolatry, adultery, and murder combined" (Talmud Yoma 9).

Notable Mitzvot מִצְוֹת

1. Ma'aser: tithing מַעֲשֵׂר. It is a mitzvah to give a tenth of one's yearly income to tzedakah. Three categories of tithes are mentioned in the Torah: first tithe, which must be given to the Levites, who, in their turn must give a tenth of it as a contribution to the priest; second tithe, which the owner must consume in Jerusalem (Deuteronomy 14:22–27); poor man's tithe, which takes the place of the second tithe in the third and sixth years of the seven-year cycle culminating in the Sabbatical year. Today, in what is essentially a nonagricultural society, the mitzvah of tithing has come to be understood as one-tenth of one's gross annual income.

Notable Quotations צִיטָטִים

Truly God is in this place	יֵשׁ יְהוָֹה בַּמָּקוֹם הַזֶּה
and I,	וְאָנֹכִי
I did not know.	לֹא יָדָעְתִּי.

Genesis 28:16

How awe-inspiring this place is!	מַה־נּוֹרָא הַמָּקוֹם הַזֶּה!
This is nothing less	אֵין זֶה כִּי
than the House of God	אִם־בֵּית אֱלֹהִים
and this is the gate to heaven.	וְזֶה שַׁעַר הַשָּׁמָיִם.

Genesis 28:17

Everything that you give me,	וְכֹל אֲשֶׁר תִּתֶּן־לִי
I will donate a tenth to You.	עַשֵּׂר אֲעַשְּׂרֶנּוּ לָךְ.

Genesis 28:22

הַפְטָרַת וַיֵּצֵא

The Haftarah (Hosea 12:13–14:10)

Summary הַסְכּוּם

Hosea, the author of this Haftarah, was the prophet of the decline of the Northern Kingdom. The reign of Jeroboam II, a time of prosperity, luxury, and idolatry in the Northern Kingdom, closed in the year 740 B.C.E. Because of bad leadership, Israel amused itself with international intrigues. There is a coming threat on the horizon: the powerful kingdom of Assyria. Hosea, sensing the doom that this powerhouse will bring, tries to alert the Israelites to their wrongdoing against God, and to the penalties they will have to pay unless they change their ways. Hosea concludes with a desperate call to repentance, asking the people to repent and return to God. Interestingly, the last part of this Haftarah is also chanted on the Sabbath that falls between Rosh Hashanah and Yom Kippur, called the Sabbath of Repentance.

The Haftarah Connection הַקֶּשֶׁר

The connection between the Haftarah and the Torah reading appears in the opening verse of the Haftarah: "Jacob fled into the field of Aram, and Israel searched for a wife." This reference to Jacob takes the people back to their beginning, to their ancestor Jacob, the subject of the Torah reading. Hosea attempts to convince the Israelites that just as Jacob, in his hard life, found God his support, guide, and redeemer, so too the people should remember that God is their only redeemer.

48

Important Concepts מוּשָׂגִים

God will forgive authentic repentance.

Notable Quotations צִיטָטִים

Any God besides Me	וֵאלֹהִים זוּלָתִי
you shall not know;	לֹא תֵדָע;
beside Me there is no savior.	וּמוֹשִׁיעַ אַיִן בִּלְתִּי.

Hosea 13:4

Return, O Israel,	שׁוּבָה יִשְׂרָאֵל
to the Lord your God	עַד יְהֹוָה אֱלֹהֶיךָ
for you have stumbled into sin.	כִּי כָשַׁלְתָּ בַּעֲוֹנֶךָ.

Hosea 14:2

The ways of God are right,	כִּי־יְשָׁרִים דַּרְכֵי יְהֹוָה
and the righteous walk in them.	וְצַדִּקִים יֵלְכוּ בָם

Hosea 14:10

וַיִּשְׁלַח

Vayishlach (Genesis 32:4–35:29)

Summary הַסְכּוּם

1. Jacob wrestles with a man-angel who changes his name to Israel.

2. Jacob and Esau meet and part peacefully.

3. Dinah, the daughter of Leah and Jacob, is violated by Shechem.

4. Jacob takes revenge by murdering all the males of Shechem and plundering the city.

5. Rachel dies giving birth to Benjamin and is buried near Bethlehem.

6. Isaac dies and is buried in Hebron near his parents Abraham and Sarah.

7. Listing of the genealogy of Jacob and Esau.

Key Concepts and Values מוּשָׂגִים

1. Importance of a person's name. For Jews, a name is a complicated gift. Not only does it bestow identity, but it can also reflect religious and spiritual dimensions. The Torah portrays naming as the first independent human act. Jacob, after conquering the unnamed adversary, is given the new name Israel, meaning "champion of God." The struggle he fought during his sleepless night was an inner battle that profoundly influenced his spiritual and emotional growth. That night he ceased to be the "quiet man, dwelling in tents" (Genesis 25:27) and assumed the quality of Israel, God's champion.

2. Reconciliation. Judaism has always emphasized the importance of making peace with one's fellow human being after an argument or fight. In our Torah portion Jacob reunites with his brother Esau, whose birthright he has stolen. Jacob's strategy in this reconciliation (sending a delegation to represent him, humility, prayer, and gifts to reduce his brother's hostility) has been praised by many biblical interpreters.

Notable Mitzvot מִצְווֹת

1. Keeping kosher כַּשְׁרוּת. The struggle of Jacob and the adversary leaves its mark on Jacob, who limps away with a wounded thigh. The portion goes on to say that the children of Israel must not eat the sinew of the thigh-vein, one of the Jewish dietary laws. This precept is a constant reminder of Divine Providence to the Israelites, as exemplified in the experience of Jacob the patriarch.

Notable Quotations צִיטָטִים

I am unworthy	קָטֹנְתִּי
of all the kindnesses	מִכֹּל הַחֲסָדִים
and all the trust	וּמִכָּל־הָאֱמֶת
that you have shown	אֲשֶׁר עָשִׂיתָ
for your servant.	אֶת־עַבְדֶּךָ.

Genesis 32:11

I will make your seed	וְשַׂמְתִּי אֶת־זַרְעֲךָ
as the sand of the sea,	כְּחוֹל הַיָּם
so many will they be.	אֲשֶׁר לֹא־יִסָּפֵר מֵרֹב.

Genesis 32:13

You contended with God   כִּי־שָׂרִיתָ עִם־אֱלֹהִים
and with man,   וְעִם־אֲנָשִׁים
and you have prevailed.   וַתּוּכָל.

Genesis 32:29

I have plenty, my brother.   יֶשׁ־לִי רָב אָחִי
Let what is yours remain yours.   יְהִי לְךָ אֲשֶׁר־לָךְ.

Genesis 33:9

הַפְטָרַת וַיִּשְׁלַח

The Haftarah (Obadiah 1:1–21)

Summary הַסְכּוּם

The Haftarah is from the book of the prophet Obadiah, the Bible's shortest book, consisting of only a single chapter. Obadiah predicts the destruction of Edom, representing the forces of evil. He severely condemns the Edomites for having refused to assist Jerusalem in the day of calamity, and expresses the conviction that they will be treated measure for measure for having helped the Babylonians to bring about the downfall of Judea. From their mountainous strongholds south of the Dead Sea, the cruel Edomites, archenemies of the Israelites, looked down upon their neighbors in Jerusalem. Obadiah predicts Israel's triumph over this enemy, stating that the forces of evil will never destroy the Israelites because of their eternal faith.

The Haftarah Connection הַקֶּשֶׁר

What especially angered the prophet Obadiah about Edom was the fact that this warlike nation was descended from Esau. Herein lies the thematic link between the Haftarah and the Torah portion. It is the struggle between Jacob and Esau, and later between their descendants.

Important Concepts מוּשָׂגִים

The forces of evil will never destroy Israel, because Israel's faith and the truth enshrined in it are eternal.

53

Notable Quotations   צִיטָטִים

Because of the violence against   מֵחֲמַס
your brother Jacob   אָחִיךָ יַעֲקֹב
you shall be covered in shame.   תְּכַסְךָ בוּשָׁה.

Obadiah 1:10

Saviors shall climb Mount Zion   וְעָלוּ מוֹשִׁעִים בְּהַר צִיּוֹן
to judge the Mount of Esau.   לִשְׁפֹּט אֶת־הַר עֵשָׂו
And God shall possess   וְהָיְתָה לַיהוָה
the kingdom.   הַמְּלוּכָה.

Obadiah 1:21

וַיֵּשֶׁב

Vayeshev (Genesis 37:1–40:23)

Summary הַסְכּוּם

1. Joseph's dreams cause jealousy among his brothers.
2. Joseph is sold to a caravan of Ishmaelites.
3. Judah and Tamar.
4. Joseph rejects Potiphar's wife.
5. Joseph is thrown into prison, and interprets dreams of Pharaoh's chief cupbearer and chief baker.

Key Concepts and Values מוּשָׂגִים

1. Dreams חֲלוֹמוֹת. From ancient times, dreams have tantalized people with their secrets. Today dreams are used to explore the inner chambers of the dreamer's mind. In biblical times, however, dreams were thought to be signs from divine powers exposing their intent. Professional dream interpreters were prominent in both Mesopotamia and Egypt. In the Torah portion, six dreams (two by Joseph, two by the prisoners, and two by Pharaoh) lend suspense to the story. Joseph attributes his ability to interpret dreams to God, the ultimate Interpreter (Genesis 40:8).

2. Adultery is a transgression זְנוּת. In his response to Potiphar's wife, Joseph says that yielding to her invitation to commit adultery would be a "sin before God" (Genesis 39:9). On the Hebrew word for "he refused" (*vayema'en*), the *shalshelet* musical notation is placed, indicating the importance of Joseph's refusal to commit adultery. Joseph speaks in the true accents of the Bible, which regards marriage as more than a relationship of civil law, but a

55

sanctified covenantal bond. Jewish tradition considers the command against adultery as one of the Noahide laws that every human being is bound to observe.

3. Bitachon: trust בִּטָּחוֹן. Throughout the trials of slavery and imprisonment, Joseph never lost his trust in God and in a better future. The Hebrew word *emunah* ("faith") is related to *emet* ("truth"). Trust is a vital prerequisite in any close relationship.

Notable Mitzvot מִצְווֹת

1. Nichum aveilim: comforting mourners נִחוּם אֲבֵלִים. It is a religious duty to visit mourners and to offer comfort and consolation to one who has lost a loved one. In our Torah portion, when Jacob believes that his son Joseph has died, he rends his garment and mourns for his son for many days. All of his sons and daughters rose up to offer him comfort (Genesis 37:35).

When comforting a mourner, you are not permitted to open the conversation before the mourner has spoken, and if you perceive that the mourner wants you to leave, you must do so. The traditional phrase of comfort that one addresses to a mourner is:

"May God comfort you	הַמָּקוֹם יְנַחֵם אוֹתְךָ
along with the rest	בְּתוֹךְ שְׁאָר
of the mourners of Zion."	אֲבֵלֵי צִיוֹן וִירוּשָׁלָיִם.

Notable Quotations ציטטים

He made him	וְעָשָׂה לוֹ
a coat of many colors.	כְּתֹנֶת פַּסִּים.

Genesis 37:3

Will you indeed rule over us?	הֲמָלֹךְ תִּמְלֹךְ עָלֵינוּ?

Genesis 37:8

Look, the dreamer	הִנֵּה בַּעַל הַחֲלֹמוֹת
is coming.	הַלָּזֶה בָּא:

Genesis 37:19

Doesn't God provide interpretations?	הֲלוֹא לֵאלֹהִים פִּתְרֹנִים?

Genesis 40:8

הַפְטָרַת וַיֵּשֶׁב

The Haftarah (Amos 2:6–3:8)

Summary הַסִּכּוּם

Amos, a shepherd, felt the stirring of the spirit of God while pursuing his calling amid the Judean hills. Amos is the older contemporary of Hosea and the first of the so-called literary prophets. The master-word of existence to Amos is "righteousness," which to him means holiness of life in the individual and the triumph of right in the world. Amos points out all of the wrongdoing of the people of the Northern Kingdom, including their inhumanity to one another. For this, Amos says, they will be punished.

The Haftarah Connection הַקֶּשֶׁר

The connection between the Haftarah and the Torah reading occurs in the opening verse of the Haftarah: "For three transgressions of Israel, yea, for four, I will not reverse it. Because they sell the righteous for silver, and the needy for a pair of shoes." In this verse we are told that the innocent are declared guilty for a bribe, with the rich selling into slavery poor but honest people whose only crime was that they were in debt to them, sometimes only for the value of a pair of shoes. This sale of the innocent man (*tzaddik* in Hebrew) provides the connection with the story of Joseph in the Torah portion. The rabbis often spoke of Joseph as a tzaddik, the innocent victim of hatred and slander.

Important Concepts מוּשָׂגִים

1. Righteousness is the basis of national as well as individual life.

58

2. Humanity's greatest sin is when one person is inhumane to another.

3. God judges us according to our actions.

Notable Quotations צִיטָטִים

עַל־שְׁלֹשָׁה פִּשְׁעֵי יִשְׂרָאֵל,

וְעַל־אַרְבָּעָה,

לֹא אֲשִׁיבֶנּוּ.

For three offenses of Israel,
or for four,
I will not reverse my decree.

Amos 2:6

אִם־תִּהְיֶה רָעָה בְּעִיר,

וַיהוָה לֹא עָשָׂה?

Can evil come to a city,
if God has not sent it?

Amos 3:6

מִקֵּץ

Mikketz (Genesis 41:1–44:17)

Summary הַסְכּוּם

1. Joseph interprets Pharaoh's two dreams.

2. Joseph is rewarded by being put in charge of the land.

3. Famine strikes, and Jacob sends his sons, except Benjamin, to Egypt.

4. Joseph seizes Simeon and tells the brothers that he will not go free until they return with the youngest brother.

5. Joseph tests his brothers to see how they feel about their wrongdoing of long ago.

Key Concepts and Values מוּשָׂגִים

1. Responsibility אַחֲרָיוּת. Judah makes himself responsible for the welfare of his youngest brother, Benjamin. A sense of responsibility for individuals in need of special care is one of the marks of maturity. It also stresses, in the rabbinic adage that *kol yisrael arevim zeh lazeh* ("all Israelites are responsible for one another"), the sense of solidarity that should and does link the Jewish people throughout the entire world.

2. Admitting one's mistakes. Only when we admit our thoughtlessness, injustice, and unkind behavior toward others can we correct our flaws and thereby develop our own character. When Joseph's brothers first said to him, "We are upright men" (Genesis 42:11), Joseph pretended not to know them and acted angry. However, when Joseph overheard them confessing among themselves, "We are truly guilty" (Genesis 42:21), he broke down in tears and showed them compassion and tenderness. Judaism advises us to acknowledge our mistakes and make amends.

Notable Mitzvot מִצְווֹת

Doing teshuvah: repenting תְּשׁוּבָה. In this Torah portion Joseph is able to awaken remorse in the hearts of his brothers who had wronged him by selling him to a group of Ishmaelites. When they finally admit their guilt by saying, "We are truly guilty concerning our brother" (Genesis 42:21), they begin their road to doing repentance. Repentance requires a determined desire on the part of the sinner to break with the past. True repentance means giving up the sin, removing it from one's mind, and determining in one's heart never to repeat the evil action.

Notable Quotations צִיטָטִים

God will answer
with the peace of Pharaoh.

אֱלֹהִים יַעֲנֶה
אֶת־שְׁלוֹם פַּרְעֹה.

Genesis 41:16

There is none so discreet
and wise as you.

אֵין־נָבוֹן
וְחָכָם כָּמוֹךָ.

Genesis 41:39

He began with the oldest
and ended with the youngest.

וַיְחַפֵּשׂ בַּגָּדוֹל הֵחֵל
וּבַקָּטֹן כִּלָּה.

Genesis 44:12

הַפְטָרַת מִקֵּץ

The Haftarah (I Kings 3:15–4:1)

Summary הַסְכּוּם

The Haftarah tells of the wisdom of Solomon, Israel's third king. The first part of the Haftarah tells about the dream in which God asks Solomon what he would want most at this time in his life. Solomon asks for an "understanding heart" with which to judge the people fairly.

In the second part of the Haftarah Solomon is presented with a real-life dilemma. Two women who live together have given birth at the same time, and one infant dies during the night. Each woman claims that the only remaining living child is hers. Solomon has to decide to whom the living baby belongs. He orders the living infant cut in half, each woman to receive one half of it. One of the women quickly cries out that she withdraws her claim, and that the child should be given whole to the other woman. The second woman agrees to have the child divided. Solomon decides that the child must belong to the woman who showed a true mother's love, namely the one who chose to let it live at any cost.

The Haftarah Connection הַקֶּשֶׁר

Dreams are the thematic link between the Torah portion and the Haftarah. Joseph is able to interpret Pharaoh's dreams, while in the Haftarah Solomon asks God for an understanding heart. In the Torah portion, Joseph unravels the mystery to Pharaoh, after humbly ascribing his power of understanding to God, the source of all

62

wisdom. In the Haftarah, all Israel join the king in acknowledging that the wisdom which Solomon possesses is of God.

Important Concepts מוּשָׂגִים

Wisdom is a gift from God, and if used wisely it has the power to save lives.

Notable Quotations צִיטָטִים

Divide the living child	גִּזְרוּ אֶת־הַיֶּלֶד הַחַי
in two,	לִשְׁנָיִם,
and give half to the one,	וּתְנוּ אֶת־הַחֲצִי לְאַחַת,
and half to the other.	וְאֶת־הַחֲצִי לְאֶחָת.

I Kings 3:25

For they saw that God's wisdom	כִּי רָאוּ כִּי־חָכְמַת אֱלֹהִים
was in him,	בְּקִרְבּוֹ,
to promote justice.	לַעֲשׂוֹת מִשְׁפָּט.

I Kings 3:28

63

וַיִּגַּשׁ

Vayiggash (Genesis 44:18–47:27)

Summary הַסִכּוּם

1. Confrontation between Judah and Joseph, whose identity is still unknown to his brothers.

2. Judah pleads with Joseph to take him as a slave in place of Benjamin.

3. Joseph reveals his identity to his brothers.

4. Jacob arrives in Egypt for an emotional reunion with Joseph.

5. Jacob and his family increase in numbers and wealth in the area of Goshen.

Key Concepts and Values מוּשָׂגִים

1. Speaking out for justice. The Torah portion begins with Judah's plea for justice before the Egyptian head of state (Joseph), who has announced his plan to enslave Benjamin. The brothers are still unaware of Joseph's identity, but they know that if they return to Canaan without Benjamin, the loss will surely kill their father, Jacob. Every point that Judah made to Joseph was supported by facts and impossible to refute. His plea for justice was so compelling that it ultimately forced Joseph to reveal his true identity. Interestingly, when Judah pleads with Joseph on behalf of Benjamin, he tells him that Jacob's soul is "bound up with the lad's soul" (Genesis 44:30). The same phrase (in Hebrew, נַפְשׁוֹ קְשׁוּרָה בְנַפְשׁוֹ) is used in the First Book of Samuel to describe the relationship between David and Jonathan. It implies true love and empathy, a genuine intertwining of souls.

64

2. Reconciliation. The scene in which Joseph reveals himself to his brothers is a most memorable one. Overcome with tears, he tells his brothers, "I am Joseph," and asks, "Is my father still alive?" His brothers, quite astonished, are totally speechless. Reconciliation is an important value in Judaism. Rabbi Samuel Nachmani claims that Joseph acted with great sensitivity and wisdom. He did not fear his brothers. After overhearing them speaking to one another, he knew that they felt very guilty for selling him into slavery. Seeing how much they regretted what they had done to him, and how they fear now for the welfare of both Benjamin and their father, he was right to trust them (Midrash Genesis Rabbah 93:9).

Notable Mitzvot מִצְווֹת

None.

Notable Quotations צִיטָטִים

And if harm should come to him,	וּקְרָאָהוּ אָסוֹן,
on the road on which you travel	בַּדֶּרֶךְ אֲשֶׁר תֵּלְכוּ־בָהּ
then you will send down	וְהוֹרַדְתֶּם
my gray hairs	אֶת־שֵׂיבָתִי
in sorrow to the grave.	בְּיָגוֹן שְׁאוֹלָה.

Genesis 42:38

In order to preserve life	הִנֵּה כִּי לְמִחְיָה
God has sent me	שְׁלָחַנִי אֱלֹהִים
before you.	לִפְנֵיכֶם.

Genesis 45:5

And Joseph said to his brothers:	וַיֹּאמֶר יוֹסֵף אֶל־אֶחָיו:
"I am Joseph;	„אֲנִי יוֹסֵף;
is my father still alive?"	הַעוֹד אָבִי חָי?"

Genesis 45:3

הַפְטָרַת וַיִּגַּשׁ

The Haftarah (Ezekiel 37:15–28)

Summary הַסְכּוּם

Ezekiel, the son of a priest, was among those who were carried off into exile in Babylon. One of the main focal points of his teaching was his insistence on individual responsibility. The exiled Israelites, forced to live in a foreign land, were very unhappy. They wonder how much longer God will forsake them. Ezekiel promises the people a much better time ahead, if they renew their faith in God and decide to become more responsible for their actions. Ezekiel presents the symbol of two sticks which are unified. This represents the idea that the Israelites will return to the Promised land, where they will reacquaint themselves with God and live in peace.

The Haftarah Connection הַקֶּשֶׁר

The connection between the Torah portion and the Haftarah is the theme of reunification. Joseph is reunited with his brothers, and the Israelites will again return to the Holy Land, where both the Northern Kingdom and the Southern Kingdom will reunite.

Important Concepts מוּשָׂגִים

1. We are all responsible for our own actions.
2. God's Divine Presence will dwell among us when we are true to our vocation as a Holy People.

Notable Quotations   צִיטָטִים

Join one stick   וְקָרַב אֹתָם אֶחָד
to the other,   אֶל־אֶחָד לְךָ
so that they will become one   לְעֵץ אֶחָד, וְהָיוּ לַאֲחָדִים
in your hand.   בְּיָדֶךָ.

Ezekiel 37:17

I will be their God,   וְהָיִיתִי לָהֶם לֵאלֹהִים,
and they shall be My people.   וְהֵמָּה יִהְיוּ־לִי לְעָם.

Ezekiel 37:27

וַיְחִי

Vayechi (Genesis 47:28–50:26)

Summary הַסְכּוּם

1. The last years and death of Jacob.

2. Jacob blesses his son Joseph and his grandsons Manasseh and Ephraim.

3. Jacob then blesses all of his sons.

4. Joseph reassures his brothers that they will be safe, and promises to care for them and their families.

5. Joseph dies at age 110. He instructs his family before he dies to return his bones to the Holy Land.

Key Concepts and Values מוּשָׂגִים

1. Burial and mourning customs קְבוּרָה. The Torah portion provides an important description of burial and mourning practices. Jacob requests that he not be buried in Egypt but rather in Hebron with Abraham, Isaac, Sarah, and Rebekah. Joseph and his brothers mourn for their father a period of seven days. Today, the mourning period of shivah is also a seven-day period. During this time mourners are encouraged to remain at home (except on Shabbat or festivals, when they should join the congregation in prayer), to refrain from their ordinary pursuits and occupations, and to participate in daily services in the home.

2. Family blessings בְּרְכַּת הַמִשְׁפָּחָה Before he dies, Jacob calls his sons to gather about his bed for a blessing. Today it is customary for parents to bless their children before sitting down to the evening Sabbath meal. This provides them with a privileged opportunity to express appreciation for their children. The blessing for boys invokes the shining examples of Jacob's grandchildren Ephraim and Manasseh, who, although raised in Egypt, did not lose their identity as Jews (Genesis 48:20). The blessing for girls refers to the four matriarchs, Sarah, Rebekah, Rachel, and Leah, all of whom were known for their concern and compassion for others. The brief ceremony concludes with the priestly benediction (Numbers 6:24–26) invoking God's protection and peace.

Notable Mitzvot מִצְווֹת

1. **Burial of the dead** קְבוּרָה. It is a religious obligation to bury the dead. The proper burial of the dead is regarded as a sacred religious duty resting upon the entire community. Irrespective of their social status in life, all Jews are regarded as equal in death. Traditionally, white linen shrouds and a plain wood coffin are used for all. In ancient times families were buried together, as they are frequently today. Before his death, Jacob asks Joseph to "deal kindly and truly with me" (Genesis 47:29) and not to bury him in Egypt. Faithful compliance with the wishes of a dying person with regard to burial is described in Hebrew as *chesed shel emet* חֶסֶד שֶׁל אֱמֶת, a true lovingkindness, a final favor which the recipient cannot repay. The earliest mention of shivah, the seven-day mourning period observed after the death of a close relative, is found in the biblical account of the death of Jacob (Genesis 50:10).

Notable Quotations צִיטָטִים

Deal with me kindly and truly.
וְעָשִׂיתָ עִמָּדִי חֶסֶד וֶאֱמֶת
Genesis 47:29

May God make you
like Ephraim and Manasseh.
יְשִׂמְךָ אֱלֹהִים
כְּאֶפְרַיִם וְכִמְנַשֶּׁה.
Genesis 48:20

Am I in the place of God?
כִּי הֲתַחַת אֱלֹהִים אָנִי?
Genesis 50:19

You shall carry up
my bones from here.
וְהַעֲלִתֶם
אֶת־עַצְמֹתַי מִזֶּה.
Genesis 50:25

Note: This Torah portion ends the Book of Genesis. When the final words of one of the Five Books of Moses are read aloud in the synagogue, it is customary for the congregation to recite after the cantor the Hebrew phrase חֲזַק חֲזַק וְנִתְחַזֵּק ("Be strong, be strong, and let us strengthen one another"). It is a wish for the strength to apply to daily living the moral and religious teachings contained in the book that has just been completed.

YOU HAVE NOW FINISHED THE BOOK OF BERESHIT

חֲזַק חֲזַק וְנִתְחַזֵּק

Masoretic Notes:

The Book of Bereshit contains: 1534 verses

43 chapters

12 Sidrot

הַפְטָרַת וַיְחִי

The Haftarah (I Kings 2:1–12)

Summary הַסְכּוּם

In the Haftarah, David, feeling that the end of his life is near, gives his son Solomon the best of blessings in words which point the way of life for every child of Israel. He says, "Be strong, and show yourself a man. Keep the charge of God, to walk in God's ways and keep the statutes and commandments" (I Kings 2:2– 3). David has been ruler for some forty years (1000–960 B.C.E.). His life has seen many accomplishments, including the crowning of Jerusalem as the capital of Israel. Now, as David lies dying and bids farewell to his Solomon, his successor, he has many fears. He knows that others will oppose Solomon, supporting another heir to the throne, and therefore warns Solomon about them.

The Haftarah Connection הַקֶּשֶׁר

The connection between the Torah portion and the Haftarah is that of the old age of the dying Jacob and the dying David. Just as Jacob gave his last words of guidance, blessing, and advice to his children, so too does King David bless and offer advice to his son Solomon.

The offering of advice to sons in biblical times appears to have paved the way for the beautiful Jewish custom of writing an ethical will. Parents and grandparents would write letters to their children and grandchildren expressing their hopes for the future and the values they were bequeathing to their descendants. This custom appears to be the successor to the giving of advice by one about to die to one's sons, as in the instances of Jacob and King David.

Important Concepts מוּשָׂגִים

1. All parents have a sacred duty to bestow blessings on their children.

2. Always cherish tender gratitude for any kindness shown toward you.

Notable Quotations צִיטָטִים

אָנֹכִי הֹלֵךְ   I am going

בְּדֶרֶךְ כָּל־הָאָרֶץ.   the way of all the earth.

I Kings 2:2

וְחָזַקְתָּ וְהָיִיתָ   Be strong and show yourself

לְאִישׁ.   to be a man.

I Kings 2:2

שְׁמוֹת

Shemot (Exodus 1:1–6:1)

Summary הַסְכּוּם

1. A new Pharaoh comes to power who orders all the Israelite male children drowned.

2. Baby Moses is put into a basket and set afloat on the Nile River.

3. Moses is saved by Pharaoh's daughter.

4. Moses kills an Egyptian who was fighting with an Israelite and flees for his life to Midian.

5. God speaks to Moses out of a burning bush and tells him that he and his brother Aaron will liberate the Israelites from Egyptian slavery.

6. Pharaoh imposes hard labor upon the Israelites.

Key Concepts and Values מוּשָׂגִים

1. Justified civil disobedience. When Pharaoh commands that every male child born to an Israelite woman is to be drowned, the Hebrew midwives Shifra and Puah refuse to carry out his command. They refuse to follow Pharaoh's command out of "fear of God." It is obvious that they believe in the sanctity of life and act out of conviction that there is a Higher Power than Pharaoh who makes moral demands on human beings. This is history's first recorded case of civil disobedience in defense of a moral cause.

2. God is conceived by each generation in a different way. When God reveals Himself to Moses at the burning bush, God

73

calls himself אֶהְיֶה אֲשֶׁר אֶהְיֶה—"I will be what I will be." The medieval commentator Rashi suggests that this teaches that no tongue can ever express all that God will be to those who truly believe in Him (Midrash, Shemot Rabbah 3:6 ff.). To put it another way, every generation conceives of God in a different manner, and in every age God is likely to reveal Himself in new ways. Perhaps that is why in the Amidah prayer God is called the God of Abraham, the God of Isaac, and the God of Jacob, for each of the patriarchs saw God in a different manner.

3. The importance of humility עֲנִיוּת**.** In Judaism, humility is a virtue to be admired. When Moses is called by God to return to Egypt to lead the Jewish people to freedom, his first response is a question: "Who am I that I should go to Pharaoh and free the Israelites from Egypt?" Some commentators have argued that Moses was showing true humility when he asked this question, perhaps even fearing that he did not possess the political skills to liberate his people from Egypt. As Rabbi Eleazar ben Yehudah once said, "No crown carries such royalty as that of humility." The prophet Micah said that what God requires of us is to do right, love goodness, and walk humbly with God (Micah:6:8).

4. Sinnat chinam: gratuitous hatred שִׂנְאַת חִנָּם**.** By and large, Jewish law denounces hatred. "What is hateful to you, do not do to others," state the rabbis (Talmud Shabbat 31a). Gratuitous hatred, or hatred without any real cause, was considered to be especially vicious. In the opening of this Torah portion, Pharaoh expresses his disdain for the Israelites. He condemns them for increasing in numbers (Exodus 1:9). For this "crime" he has decided to obliterate all of the Israelites.

Notable Mitzvot מִצְווֹת

None

Notable Quotations צִיטָטִים

I brought him out of the water.   כִּי מִן־הַמַּיִם מְשִׁיתִהוּ.

Exodus 2:10

I have been a stranger   גֵּר הָיִיתִי

in a strange land.   בְּאֶרֶץ נָכְרִיָּה.

Exodus 2:22

The bush was burning with fire,   וְהִנֵּה הַסְּנֶה בֹּעֵר בָּאֵשׁ,

but the bush   וְהַסְּנֶה

was not consumed.   אֵינֶנּוּ אֻכָּל.

Exodus 3:2

. . . a land flowing with milk   . . . אֶרֶץ זָבַת חָלָב

and honey . . .   . . . וּדְבָשׁ

Exodus 3:8

הַפְטָרַת שְׁמוֹת

The Haftarah (Isaiah 27:6–28:13, 29:22–23)

Summary הַסְכּוּם

The prophet Isaiah's ministry extended for close to forty years, from 740 to 701 B.C.E. During this time, Assyria grew into a world power. The kingdoms of Syria and Israel fell before the Assyrians in 721 B.C.E. The kingdom of Judah became the sole representative of the true religion.

In the first part of the Haftarah, Isaiah comforts the Israelites, telling them that there will be a better future in store for them if they change their ways. Next, Isaiah criticizes the people of the Northern Kingdom for leading lives of dishonesty. They will be punished for their folly and unethical behavior. The Haftarah concludes with soothing words of comfort. Isaiah tells the people that God will remember His covenant and the promises made centuries ago to Abraham, Isaac, and Jacob.

The Haftarah Connection הַקֶּשֶׁר

The connecting link between the Torah portion and the Haftarah is the suffering in Egypt and the suffering of the Israelites in the time of Isaiah. Israel in Egypt is tired of the leadership of Moses and Aaron. The Israelites in the age of Isaiah found his teachings to be highly monotonous. Especially noteworthy is the Haftarah's use (Isaiah 28:10) of one-syllable rhyming words as a way of conveying the idea of the childish instruction that the people felt that they were receiving from Isaiah (in Hebrew, *tzav latzav, kav lakav*—"precept by precept, line by line").

76

Key Concepts and Values מוּשָׂגִים

Teaching that is monotonous and dull will often go unheeded.

Notable Quotations צִיטָטִים

Trodden underfoot	בְּרַגְלַיִם תֵּרָמַסְנָה
shall be the proud crown	עֲטֶרֶת גֵּאוּת
of the drunkards of Ephraim.	שִׁכּוֹרֵי אֶפְרָיִם.

Isaiah 28:3

It is precept by precept,	כִּי צַו לָצָו,
precept by precept,	צַו לָצָו,
line by line, line by line,	קַו לָקָו קַו לָקָו,
here a little, there a little.	זְעֵיר שָׁם זְעֵיר שָׁם.

Isaiah 28:10

They shall sanctify	וְהִקְדִּישׁוּ
the Holy One of Jacob	אֶת־קְדוֹשׁ יַעֲקֹב
and before the God of Israel	וְאֶת־אֱלֹהֵי יִשְׂרָאֵל
they will be awestruck.	יַעֲרִיצוּ.

Isaiah 29:23

וָאֵרָא

Va'era (Exodus 6:2–9:35)

Summary הַסְכּוּם

1. God tells Moses to go before Pharaoh and ask him to let the Israelites leave Egypt.

2. Moses responds that Pharaoh will not listen and apologetically explains that, because of a speech impediment, he is not the right person to represent the Jewish people.

3. God answers that Moses' brother Aaron will accompany him as spokesman.

4. Aaron and Moses appear before Pharaoh to request freedom for the Israelites.

5. Pharaoh refuses, and seven of the ten plagues are set upon Egypt.

6. Pharaoh remains stubborn and will not let the Israelites go.

Key Concepts and Values מוּשָׂגִים

1. **Go'el: redeemer** גּוֹאֵל. This is the Hebrew term for the kinsman whose duty it was in ancient times to provide ransom or to exact vengeance for the lives or property of members of his family. In this Torah portion (Exodus 6:6), God promises to act as the redeemer of the children of Israel, intervening to free them from Egyptian slavery.

2. **Morashah: heritage** מוֹרָשָׁה. God promises to give the land of Canaan to the children of Israel as their heritage (Exodus 6:8). A "heritage" may be spiritual, remaining in the recipient's possession regardless of his actions. The outstanding example of

78

such a heritage in Judaism is the Torah, which belongs to the people of Israel forever. The land of Canaan is a material heritage, conditional on the conduct of the children of Israel.

3. Hardening of the heart. The rabbis point out that the phrase "hardening of the heart" occurs nineteen times in the story of Pharaoh and the Israelites. It is recorded ten times that Pharaoh hardened his heart, and nine times that God caused Pharaoh's stubbornness. Several questions have often been asked: In the name of fair play, how could a just God harden Pharaoh's heart and then, every time he changed his mind, punish him with a new plague? How can God make it impossible for a person to obey and then punish him for disobeying? The sages explain that at first Pharaoh's stubbornness caused his vacillation. Eventually, however, Pharaoh was so conditioned by his stubbornness that it seemed as if God Himself had caused it. Judaism affirms the principle of free will. We are all the masters of our own spirits. "One evil deed leads to another" (Pirkei Avot 4:2). If we choose to do evil, it will, like Pharaoh, ultimately enslave us. Conversely, one good deed leads to another, and we are that much more liberated from slavery.

Notable Mitzvot מִצְווֹת

None

Notable Quotations צִיטָטִים

I shall free you	וְהוֹצֵאתִי אֶתְכֶם
from the burdens of Egypt,	מִתַּחַת סִבְלֹת מִצְרַיִם,
and I shall save you	וְהִצַּלְתִּי אֶתְכֶם
from their slavery.	מֵעֲבֹדָתָם

Exodus 6:6

Let My people go,	שַׁלַּח אֶת־עַמִּי,
so they may worship Me	וְיַעַבְדֻנִי
in the wilderness.	בַּמִּדְבָּר.

Exodus 7:16

Pharaoh's heart was stubborn,	וַיֶּחֱזַק לֵב־פַּרְעֹה,
and he did not listen to them.	וְלֹא־שָׁמַע אֲלֵהֶם.

Exodus 7:22

הַפְטָרַת וָאֵרָא

The Haftarah (Ezekiel 28:25–29:21)

Summary הַסְכּוּם

The Haftarah, from the Book of Ezekiel, warns the Israelites not to depend on the Egyptians, with whom they had made an alliance. Egypt, says Ezekiel, is not a dependable ally, and ought not to be relied upon. The Haftarah predicts that King Nebuchadnezzar of Babylon will conquer Egypt.

The Haftarah Connection הַקֶּשֶׁר

The connection between the message of this Haftarah and that of the Torah portion is Egypt, a country that Israel could not depend on either in the time of Moses or in the time of Ezekiel. Egypt, the house of bondage and oppression for Israel in the days of its youth, was again the enemy during the last years of the Jewish state.

Key Concepts and Values מוּשָׂגִים

Countries must always be careful to choose reliable allies when making alliances.

81

Notable Quotations צִיטָטִים

I will put hooks	וְנָתַתִּי חַחִיים
through your jaws,	בִּלְחָיֶיךָ,
and I will adhere	וְהִדְבַּקְתִּי
the fish of your rivers	דְגַת־יְאֹרֶיךָ
to your scales.	בְּקַשְׂקְשֹׂתֶיךָ

Ezekiel 29:4

On that day I send forth	בַּיּוֹם הַהוּא אַצְמִיחַ
a horn for the House of Israel,	קֶרֶן לְבֵית יִשְׂרָאֵל,
and I will give you	וּלְךָ אֶתֵּן
the opening of the mouth	פִּתְחוֹן־פֶּה
in the midst of it.	בְּתוֹכָם.

Ezekiel 29:21

בֹּא

Bo (Exodus 10:1–13:16)

Summary הַסְכּוּם

1. Moses and Aaron continue to plead with Pharaoh to let the Israelites go free.

2. Pharaoh continues to refuse, and the Egyptians are punished with the last three of the Ten Plagues—locusts, darkness, and the death of their firstborn.

3. Pharaoh lets the Israelites go.

4. The Israelites proclaim that each year, on the evening of the fourteenth day of the first month, a festival lasting seven days will be observed to recall their freedom from Egyptian bondage. Matzah (unleavened bread) will be eaten for seven days.

Key Concepts and Values מוּשָׂגִים

1. Rosh Chodesh: the new month רֹאשׁ חוֹדֶשׁ. According to God's command (Exodus 12:2), the month of the Exodus was to be the first month of the Jewish year. The proclamation of a new Jewish calendar to replace the Egyptian method of counting time marked Israel's final break with Egypt. In biblical times, Rosh Chodesh, the beginning of a new month was a minor festival on which special offerings were presented to God. Today Rosh Chodesh is marked in the synagogue with a special Torah reading recalling the sacrificial offerings and with the recitation of the Hallel psalms of praise. For many Jews, Rosh Chodesh serves as a day of renewal and reflection. It provides an opportunity to look at the month past and suggest ways of improving on it in the new month ahead.

2. Removing leaven and observing the festival of Passover בְּדִיקַת חָמֵץ. The Torah states that a seven-day feast shall be observed and all leaven must be removed from one's household (Exodus 12:15). Today the custom is to eat unleavened bread (matzah) throughout the festival of Passover. The holiday is an eternal reminder of one of the greatest miracles in all history, the exodus of the Jewish people from Egypt.

3. Sanctification of the firstborn פִּדְיוֹן־הַבֵּן/הַבַּת. In chapter 13:2, God tells Moses that all firstborns, both human and animal, shall be sanctified and belong to God. Just as the annual celebration of the Passover served to remind the Israelites of the great redemption, so too the sanctification of every male firstborn would keep the memory fresh in every home blessed with a firstborn son. The rite is remembered today in the lifecycle event known as pidyon haben—redemption of the firstborn son—which is solemnized any time after the thirtieth day of a child's birth. This ceremony symbolically relieves the firstborn child from service in the priesthood because those of priestly descent, the descendants of Aaron, were given the responsibility in his stead. Today, congregations have expanded the celebration to include first-born girls.

4. Telling your child the story of the exodus from Egypt וְהִגַּדְתָּ. In Exodus 13:8, it says that you shall tell your son the story of the exodus from Egypt. The rabbis derived from this verse the law that every parent should, on the evening of Passover, relate the story of the exodus from Egypt. Today, the story is found in the Haggadah, and the Haggadah is used by Jewish families around the world to tell the story at their Passover seder.

5. Tefillin: phylacteries תְּפִלִּין. God says that the Passover story shall be a sign on your hand and a memorial between your eyes (Exodus 13:9). Today the reminder on the arm and forehead are called tefillin (phylacteries); these are prayerboxes strapped to the head and arm, worn during daily morning services but not on holidays or Shabbat. They are a sign of the covenant between God and the Jewish people. Inside the tefillin are four passages from the Torah (Exodus 13:1–10 and 11–16, Deuteronomy 6:4–9 and 11:13–21) written on parchment. Tefillin are traditionally worn by all males (over the age of thirteen). Some Jewish females today have also chosen to wear tefillin.

Notable Quotations צִיטָטִים

They shall eat meat	וְאָכְלוּ אֶת־הַבָּשָׂר
that night,	בַּלַּיְלָה הַזֶּה,
roasted over fire;	צְלִי־אֵשׁ;
and unleavened bread	וּמַצּוֹת
together with bitter herbs	עַל־מְרֹרִים
shall they eat it.	יֹאכְלֻהוּ.

Exodus 12:8

Unleavened bread shall be eaten	מַצּוֹת יֵאָכֵל
for seven days;	אֵת שִׁבְעַת הַיָּמִים;
never shall be seen with you	וְלֹא־יֵרָאֶה לְךָ
yeast nor leavened bread	חָמֵץ וְלֹא־יֵרָאֶה לְךָ שְׂאֹר
in all your borders.	בְּכָל־גְּבֻלֶךָ.

Exodus 13:7

It shall be to you as a sign	וְהָיָה לְאוֹת
on your hand,	עַל־יָדְכָה,
and for frontlets	וּלְטוֹטָפֹת
between your eyes.	בֵּין עֵינֶיךָ.

Exodus 13:16

Sanctify to me all firstborn.	קַדֶּשׁ־לִי כָל־בְּכוֹר.

Exodus 13:1

הַפְטָרַת בֹּא

The Haftarah (Jeremiah 46:13–28)

Summary הַסְכּוּם

    Similar in theme to the Haftarah of Va'era, this Haftarah is also a prophecy against Egypt. Jeremiah, the author of the Haftarah, was an older contemporary of Ezekiel. During the last days of the Jewish state, both of them, Jeremiah in Jerusalem and Ezekiel in Babylon, denounced the sin and folly of seeking help from Egypt. This Haftarah, one of Jeremiah's last messages, tells of Egypt's defeat by Babylon. It concludes with words of hope for Israel, reminding the people not to fear, because God will always be with them.

The Haftarah Connection הַקֶּשֶׁר

    The theme link between the Haftarah and the Torah portion is Egypt, a land which could not be depended on either in Moses' time or in Jeremiah's.

Important Concepts מוּשָׂגִים

    Israel ought to always be filled with hope, for God is a saving God, and in times of trouble will eventually redeem her.

Notable Quotations צִיטָטִים

Pharaoh, king of Egypt,   פַּרְעֹה מֶלֶךְ־מִצְרַיִם

is but a noise.   שָׁאוֹן.

Jeremiah 46:17

Do not be afraid,   אַתָּה אַל־תִּירָא,

O Jacob My servant,   עַבְדִּי יַעֲקֹב,

says God.   נְאֻם־יְהֹוָה.

Jeremiah 46:28

בְּשַׁלַּח

Beshallach (Exodus 13:17–17:16)

Summary הַסְכּוּם

1. The Israelites depart Egypt, but Pharaoh changes his mind and decides to pursue them.

2. The Red Sea splits open, and the Israelites cross safely. The Egyptians drown in the Red Sea.

3. In celebration, the Israelites sing a song of victory to God.

4. The Israelites begin their trek through the wilderness with complaints to Moses about the lack of food and drink.

5. God grants the Israelites water and heavenly manna.

6. The Israelites are attacked by the Amalekites, and Joshua, an appointee of Moses, successfully destroys their forces.

Key Concepts and Values מוּשָׂגִים

1. **Miracles** נִסִּים. The splitting of the Red Sea is considered the greatest miracle in the Five Books of Moses. Scientific speculation related to this incident includes a strong east wind which, blowing all night, ebbed the tide. The modern philosopher Martin Buber argued that the details of the splitting of the Red Sea are not important. What is important is that the children of Israel understood the parting of the Red Sea as an act of their God, as a "miracle." The Song of the Sea (Exodus 15) which was chanted by Moses and the children of Israel is today a part of both the daily and festival morning services. Chanting it is a constant reminder of God's dependability in time of grave crisis.

2. The Sabbath הַשַׁבָּת. Even before the Israelites received the Ten Commandments at Mount Sinai, they were commanded to refrain from collecting the heavenly manna on the day Moses refers to as "a solemn rest, a holy Sabbath unto God" (Exodus 16:22–23). The Sabbath is thus a memorial not only of the creation of the world but also of the exodus from Egypt. Note that in the Kiddush over the wine it states that "the Sabbath is the first among our days of sacred assembly which recall the exodus from Egypt."

3. There are no shortcuts in life. In Exodus 23:17, we are told that God did not take the Israelites by the way of the land of the Philistines, which was nearby. Look at a map of the ancient Near East, and you will readily see that Moses followed a long and circuitous route to the Promised Land. He chose not to go north by the most direct route, a journey that would have taken only a few days. Perhaps Moses knew that if he took the short way, the unprepared Israelites would have become disheartened the first time they were challenged by an enemy, and would have turned in flight, only to return to Egypt. The message appears to be clear: there are no shortcuts to the Promised Land. Much time and effort must be invested in doing anything worthwhile in life.

4. The joy and beautification of a mitzvah הִדּוּר מִצְוָה. In Exodus 15:2 it states, "This is my God, and I will glorify Him." Some rabbis have interpreted the words "and I will glorify" to mean that Jews must revere God with beautiful ceremonials. For example, if one were building a sukkah to fulfill the mitzvah on the festival of Sukkot, the way to "glorify" God would be to decorate it as attractively as possible.

The rabbis used the Hebrew phrase *simchah shel mitzvah* שִׂמְחָה שֶׁל מִצְוָה to express the joy one feels every time one performs a mitzvah. They used the term *hiddur mitzvah* הִדּוּר מִצְוָה to refer to the beautification of a mitzvah. Essentially this means that one ought to do more than is required in order to fulfill every mitzvah in a special way.

5. Action is important, not only prayer. In Exodus 14:14 God says to Moses, "Why do you cry to Me?" With the sea before him and the Egyptians in the rear, Moses prayed to God. The Midrash tells us that God admonished Moses, saying, "There is a time to pray and a time for action. Now is the time to act. Speak to the children of Israel so that they will go forward" (Yalkut I, 233).

In Judaism, prayer is important, but prayer must inspire us to go forward in partnership to God. We must search for God, even as God searches for us.

Notable Mitzvot מִצְווֹת

Not to go beyond permitted limits on the Sabbath. There is one negative commandment in this Torah portion, which is that according to Jewish law one is restricted from walking on the Sabbath beyond the known bounds, as it is stated, "Let no person go out of his place on the seventh day" (Exodus 16:29). According to some commentators, at the root of this commandment lies the aim that we should not go on any lengthy journey on Shabbat but only walk for strolling and pleasure. This works to keep Shabbat truly holy and a day of peace, rest, and relaxation.

Let no man go out   אַל יֵצֵא אִישׁ

of his place   מִמְּקֹמוֹ

on the seventh day.   בַּיּוֹם הַשְּׁבִיעִי.

Exodus 16:29

Notable Quotations צִיטָטִים

The pillar of clouds did not move	לֹא־יָמִישׁ עַמּוּד הֶעָנָן
away by day	יוֹמָם
nor the pillar of fire	וְעַמּוּד הָאֵשׁ
by night.	לָיְלָה.

Exodus 13:22

Thus sang Moses	אָז יָשִׁיר־מֹשֶׁה
and the children of Israel,	וּבְנֵי יִשְׂרָאֵל,
this song	אֶת־הַשִּׁירָה הַזֹּאת
to God.	לַיהֹוָה.

Exodus 15:1

This is my God	זֶה אֵלִי
and I will glorify Him.	וְאַנְוֵהוּ.

Exodus 15:2

I will totally wipe out	כִּי־מָחֹה אֶמְחֶה
the memory of Amalek	אֶת־זֵכֶר עֲמָלֵק
from under heaven.	מִתַּחַת הַשָּׁמָיִם.

Exodus 17:14

הַפְטָרַת בְּשַׁלַּח

The Haftarah (Judges 4:4–5:31)

Summary הַסְכּוּם

The Haftarah features Deborah, considered both a prophet of God and a judge. The Israelites have been in the Promised Land for about seventy years. The Haftarah describes a battle between the Canaanites and the Israelites at Mount Tabor near the Kishon River. Deborah leads the Israelite army to victory. The song of victory forms the second part of the Haftarah.

The Haftarah Connection הַקֶּשֶׁר

The theme link between the Torah portion and the Haftarah portion is that of songs of thanksgiving. In both Moses' song and Deborah's song, God is praised for delivering the Israelites from the enemy. Note that the Sabbath upon which the Torah portion and the Haftarah are chanted is called Shabbat Shirah—the Sabbath of the Song, referring to the songs of Moses and Deborah.

Important Concepts מוּשָׂגִים

Women can be successful military leaders.

Notable Quotations צִיטָטִים

I will sing to God, אָזַמֵּר לַיהוָה,

the God of Israel. אֱלֹהֵי יִשְׂרָאֵל.

Judges 5:3

They that love Him וְאֹהֲבָיו

are like the sun rising כְּצֵאת הַשֶּׁמֶשׁ

in its glory. בִּגְבֻרָתוֹ

Judges 5:31

יִתְרוֹ

Yitro (Exodus 18:1–20:23)

Summary הַסְכּוּם

1. Jethro brings Zipporah, the wife of Moses, and their children to the Israelite camp.

2. Jethro suggests to Moses that the burden of leadership is too much for one man to bear. He advises Moses to choose people with whom to share the leadership. Moses heeds the advice.

3. Moses and the Israelites camp at Mount Sinai.

4. Moses ascends the mountain and God speaks to him, giving him the Ten Commandments.

Key Concepts and Values מוּשָׂגִים

1. Sharing leadership. One way of learning about a society's values is by analyzing its leaders. A leader ought to embody all the values and ideals that his or her group holds dear. In this Torah portion Moses decides, after his discussion with his father-in-law, Jethro, that the burden of leadership is too great for one person to handle. He appoints trustworthy people to help him. Leadership is an important value in Judaism. Caring for a community is a complex task. Jethro appreciated the need to share the burden of responsibility, an important Jewish value.

2. Revelation הִתְגַּלוּת. One of the greatest events in the entire Bible occurs in this Torah portion, the revelation of God at Mount Sinai, in which God communicates with the people of Israel. The nature of revelation and its meaning for the Jewish people have been understood in various ways by the different branches of

95

Judaism. Some believe that God communicated with us in actual words. Others believe that the revelation consisted of a mysterious human encounter with God.

3. The chosen people עַם סְגוּלָה. The Torah portion states in Exodus 19:5 that the children of Israel will be God's treasured people. This promise of special election or chosenness has been a core factor of Jewish life for thousands of years. God has singled out the Jewish people and made special demands upon them. They will have to conform to a standard set for no other people. Israel, of course, entered this covenant with God of their own free will by saying, "All that God has spoken, we will do."

4. A kingdom of priests מַמְלֶכֶת כּוֹהֲנִים. God tells the Israelites that He wants them to be a kingdom of priests and a holy nation (Exodus 19:6). This means that just as it is the duty of every priest (*kohen*) to bring other Jews near to God, so the Israelites have been called to play the part of a priest to other nations, bringing them closer to God and righteousness. Israel was also told by God to be a holy nation. Holy here means separated from the false beliefs and idolatry of the other nations. Israel becomes holy by cleaving to God and obeying God's commandments.

Notable Mitzvot מִצְווֹת

Ten of the most notable mitzvot are those of the Ten Commandments עֲשֶׂרֶת הַדִּבְּרוֹת:

1. Recognition that there is only one God.

2. Prohibition of making a graven image (i.e., one must not worship God through images).

3. Prohibition of taking God's name in vain (i.e., we are not allowed to dishonor God by invoking God's name to attest to what is untrue).

4. Keeping the Sabbath holy.

5. Honoring one's parents. (Note that longevity of days is stated to be the reward for performing this mitzvah [Exodus 22:12]).

6. Not committing murder.

7. Not committing adultery.

8. Prohibition of stealing.

9. Prohibition against bearing false witness against one's neighbor.

10. Prohibition against being envious of another's possessions (one of a number of commandments in the Torah related to a person's feelings).

Notable Quotations צִיטָטִים

You shall select from all the people	וְאַתָּה תֶחֱזֶה מִכָּל־הָעָם
brave men,	אַנְשֵׁי־חַיִל
who fear God,	יִרְאֵי אֱלֹהִים,
people of truth hating crooked gain.	אַנְשֵׁי אֱמֶת שֹׂנְאֵי בָצַע.

Exodus 18:21

I carried you	וָאֶשָּׂא אֶתְכֶם
on the wings of eagles.	עַל־כַּנְפֵי נְשָׁרִים.

Exodus 19:4

You shall be My own treasure	וִהְיִיתֶם לִי סְגֻלָּה
from among all peoples.	מִכָּל־הָעַמִּים.

Exodus 19:5

You shall be to Me	וְאַתֶּם תִּהְיוּ־לִי
a kingdom of priests	מַמְלֶכֶת כֹּהֲנִים
and a holy nation.	וְגוֹי קָדוֹשׁ

Exodus 19:6

הַפְטָרַת יִתְרוֹ

The Haftarah (Isaiah 6:1–7:6 and 9:5–6)

Summary הַסְכּוּם

The Haftarah records the revelation that came to the prophet Isaiah in his early manhood. One day in the Temple, he heard the fiery angels (seraphim) singing, "Holy, holy, holy, is Adonai Tzeva'ot, the whole earth is filled with God's Presence." Isaiah tells God that he is unworthy to assume the mantle of prophecy. God then sends a seraph angel with a glowing stone in its hands to Isaiah's mouth. When the stone touches it, Isaiah is purged and tells God that he is ready to be a leader.

In the second part of the Haftarah, Isaiah urges King Ahaz of Judea to keep his faith in God and not fear the enemy.

The Haftarah concludes when Isaiah makes known that the son of King Ahaz (i.e., Hezekiah) will be an outstanding ruler, and that during his reign as king, peace and justice will permeate the land.

The Haftarah Connection הַקֶּשֶׁר

The thematic link between the Torah portion and the Haftarah is that of revelation. In the Torah portion, God reveals His Will to the people at Mount Sinai. Centuries later, Isaiah learns by means of an angel that God has chosen him to serve the Israelites.

Key Concepts and Values מוּשָׂגִים

1. Most prophets are reluctant when asked to serve by God as a prophet. This is because they usually are called during a time of

social and political crisis, and are expected to tell people things that they would prefer not to hear.

2. Ultimately, when God chooses a person for prophecy, there is no escaping.

Notable Quotations צִיטָטִים

Holy holy holy	קָדוֹשׁ קָדוֹשׁ קָדוֹשׁ
is the Lord of Hosts,	יְהוָה צְבָאוֹת,
the whole world is filled	מְלֹא כָל־הָאָרֶץ
with His glory.	כְּבוֹדוֹ.

Isaiah 6:3

Then I said:	וָאֹמַר:
Here am I, send me.	„הִנְנִי, שְׁלָחֵנִי.‟

Isaiah 6:8

For a child is born to us . . .	. . . כִּי־יֶלֶד יֻלַּד־לָנוּ
and the government	וַתְּהִי הַמִּשְׂרָה
is on his shoulder,	עַל־שִׁכְמוֹ,
and his name is called	וַיִּקְרָא שְׁמוֹ
Pele Joetz El Gibbor	פֶּלֶא יוֹעֵץ אֵל גִּבּוֹר
Avi-Ad Sar-Shalom.	אֲבִי־עַד שַׂר־שָׁלוֹם.

Isaiah 9:5

מִשְׁפָּטִים

Mishpatim (Exodus 21:1–24:18)

Summary הַסְכּוּם

1. A variety of civil and criminal laws are presented, including treatment of slaves, crimes of murder and kidnapping, personal injuries, damages through neglect or stealing, offenses against others through lying, witchcraft, idolatry, oppression, unfair business practices, and unjust conduct of judges.

2. Israelites are reminded to be sensitive to the needs of strangers.

3. Rules are presented for the Sabbath, the Sabbatical Year, Passover, Shavuot, and Sukkot.

4. Commandment not to cook a kid in its mother's milk.

5. Ratification of the covenant.

Key Concepts and Values מוּשָׂגִים

1. Importance of civil law. The preceding Torah portion recorded the Ten Commandments, clearly the foundation stones of Judaism. But the words "these are the ordinances" which introduce this Torah portion are the preamble to our "constitution." The civil, property, and ethical laws are ordinances which concretize and establish in practice the spirit of the Ten Commandments.

2. Caring for the stranger גֵּר וְתוֹשָׁב. Twice in this Torah portion we find a commandment dealing with concern for the *ger*, or stranger (Exodus 22:20, 23:9). Commandments calling for sensitivity and justice for the stranger are found in thirty-six different places in the Torah, mentioned more often than any other mitzvah.

Early rabbinic interpreters often understood the Hebrew word *ger* to also mean "convert." The treatment of converts is a sensitive matter. Entering a new religious group can be very frightening, and the welcome given by a family or group to a newcomer can make the difference between feeling accepted or feeling rejected.

Notable Mitzvot מִצְווֹת

1. Lending a poor person money (Exodus 22:24). A loan to prevent a poor person from falling into poverty is considered one of the most meritorious of deeds, and among the greatest acts of lovingkindness that can be shown to a living person. Because of this feeling for the poor, free loan societies are found in every well-organized Jewish community. Such societies loan money to the poor without charging interest.

You shall not charge him	לֹא תְשִׂמוּן עָלָיו
any interest.	נֶשֶׁךְ.

Exodus 22:24

2. Protection of the weak. Widows, orphans, and strangers were to be protected and given every consideration. These are all people with whom fate had dealt harshly and who were likely to need special protection in order to survive. All Israel had suffered the fate of strangers in Egypt, and thereafter stranger, widow, and orphan together became the touchstone of biblical justice.

A widom or an orphan	כָּל אַלְמָנָה וְיָתוֹם
you shall not mistreat.	לֹא תְעַנּוּן

Exodus 22:21

Notable Quotations צִיטָטִים

An eye for an eye,   עַיִן תַּחַת עַיִן,

a tooth for a tooth . . .   . . . שֵׁן תַּחַת שֵׁן

Exodus 21:24

A stranger you shall neither abuse   וְגֵר לֹא־תוֹנֶה

nor oppress,   וְלֹא תִלְחָצֶנּוּ,

for you were strangers   כִּי־גֵרִים הֱיִיתֶם

in the land of Egypt.   בְּאֶרֶץ מִצְרָיִם.

Exodus 22:20

Do not follow a majority   לֹא־תִהְיֶה אַחֲרֵי־רַבִּים

to do evil.   לְרָעֹת

Exodus 23:2

All that God has spoken,   כֹּל אֲשֶׁר־דִּבֶּר יְהוָה,

we shall do   נַעֲשֶׂה

and obey.   וְנִשְׁמָע.

Exodus 24:7

הַפְטָרַת מִשְׁפָּטִים

The Haftarah (Jeremiah 34:8–22, 33:25–26)

Summary   הַסִכּוּם

The Torah portion opens with the enactment to free a Hebrew slave after six years of service. The Haftarah records a breach of this regulation at a critical hour of Israel's history. In the face of the disaster threatening Israel at the hands of the Babylonians, the last king of Judah, Zedekiah, had induced the ruling classes to bind themselves by oath to release their slaves, so that no Jew would any longer be a slave to a fellow Jew. They did so, but when all danger had passed, they broke their oaths and forced those who had been freed back into slavery. Jeremiah in this Haftarah is outraged at such horrendous conduct, and announces that the enemy will soon return.

The Haftarah concludes with a message of hope. Though the Babylonians will again conquer Israel, the Israelites in the future will once again be redeemed and returned to the land of their ancestors.

The Haftarah Connection   הַקֶּשֶׁר

The theme link between the Torah portion and Haftarah is that concerning the freeing of slaves. The Torah portion opens with the enactment to free a Hebrew slave after six years of bondage. The Haftarah describes a breach of this argument and the subsequent punishment of the Israelites.

103

Key Concepts and Values מוּשָׂגִים

1. One of the earliest occurrences of the word "Jew" in all of the Bible occurs in verse 9.

2. Oaths are to be taken seriously, and breaking them will result in dire consequences.

Notable Quotations צִיטָטִים

Every man should release	לְשַׁלַּח אִישׁ
his slave	אֶת־עַבְדּוֹ
and his Hebrew servant,	וְאִישׁ אֶת־שִׁפְחָתוֹ,
whether male or female,	הָעִבְרִי וְהָעִבְרִיָּה
to go free.	חָפְשִׁים.

Jeremiah 34:9

I will make the cities of Judah	וְאֶת־עָרֵי יְהוּדָה אֶתֵּן
a desolation,	שְׁמָמָה
without inhabitants.	מֵאֵין יֹשֵׁב.

Jeremiah 34:22

I will cause their captivity to return,	כִּי־אָשִׁיב אֶת־שְׁבוּתָם
but will have compassion on them.	וְרִחַמְתִּים.

Jeremiah 33:26

תְּרוּמָה

Terumah (Exodus 25:1–27:19)

Summary הַסְכּוּם

1. Moses instructs the Israelites to bring a *terumah* (donation) for the building of the sanctuary.

2. Concerning the tabernacle, God says to Moses, "And let them make Me a sanctuary, that I may dwell among them" (Exodus 25:8).

3. Instructions for the construction of the tabernacle are enumerated, including the ark and the poles for carrying it, made of acacia wood overlaid with gold, two gold cherubim facing each other, and so forth.

4. Moses is instructed to build a *menorah* (lampstand) to hold seven lamps.

Key Concepts and Values מוּשָׂגִים

1. Where does God dwell? Rabbinic commentators often ask: If God is everywhere, then why does God command the Israelites to build Him a sanctuary? The rabbis explain that God does not confine His presence to any one place in particular. Rather, God dwells among people everywhere, in all places. The sanctuary is only a symbol of the faith of the Israelites in the one and only God Who dwells in the hearts of the people.

The Kotzker Rebbe once asked: "Where does God dwell?" He answered: "Wherever you let Him in."

105

2. The mizbe'ach: altar מִזְבֵּחַ. The altar was used for the sacrificial offerings, whose intended purpose it was to bring the people closer to God. The rabbis pointed out that each of the consonants in the word for "altar" in Hebrew is the initial of a virtue or divine favor that can be attained through worship in the proper spirit:

מ: Mechilah	מְחִילָה	*forgiveness*
ז: Zechut	זְכוּת	*merit*
ב: Berachah	בְּרָכָה	*blessing*
ח: Chayim	חַיִּים	*life*

3. Terumah תְּרוּמָה. The Torah portion states: "Speak to the children of Israel, that they take for Me an offering" (Exodus 25:2). Here we see the importance of lending a helping hand in order that the construction of the tabernacle can take place. Today, in synagogues around the world, Jewish people continue to make offerings, both monetary ones as well as volunteering their time. Tzedakah in the highest sense is the giving of ourselves to others.

Notable Mitzvot מִצְווֹת

Building a house of God. During their journey through the desert, the Israelites prepared a mobile sanctuary from wood and cloth which could be set up and dismantled as they proceeded on their way. After entering the Promised Land, they erected a tabernacle in Gilgal which was in operation for fourteen years. The next sanctuary was the one at Shiloh, which remained in operation for close to four hundred years. From Shiloh the ark was moved first to Nob and then to Gibeon. After fifty-seven years of this temporary arrangement, the Israelites erected a permanent Temple on Mount Zion in Jerusalem. Today the synagogue or temple is the house of assembly and the spiritual home of the Jewish people. It is not only a place for prayer, but a center for study, charity, and social work.

Notable Quotations ציטטים

From every person	כָּל־אִישׁ
whose heart makes him willing,	אֲשֶׁר יִדְּבֶנּוּ לִבּוֹ,
shall you take My offering.	תִּקְחוּ אֶת־תְּרוּמָתִי.

Exodus 25:2

And they shall make Me	וְעָשׂוּ לִי
a sanctuary,	מִקְדָּשׁ,
that I may dwell	וְשָׁכַנְתִּי
in their midst.	בְּתוֹכָם.

Exodus 25:8

107

הַפְטָרַת תְּרוּמָה

The Haftarah (I Kings 5:26–6:13)

Summary הַסְכּוּם

It was King David's strong desire to build a Temple for God. He was not destined to see his life-dream realized, but his son Solomon made its fulfillment almost the first task of his reign. The Haftarah contains a number of details related to the building of the Temple. For instance, 30,000 construction workers were required, and their work may have taken upward of twenty years. The Temple building itself stood within a large court in which the worshippers could assemble. The Temple proper was a rectangular hall 60 by 20 by 30 cubits.

The Haftarah Connection הַקֶּשֶׁר

The Torah portion describes the construction of the tabernacle in the wilderness. This is paralleled in the Haftarah by the description of the Temple of Solomon in Jerusalem.

Important Concepts מוּשָׂגִים

1. The building of a house of worship takes an enormous amount of material goods and people-power.

2. The erection of the Temple was only an external sign of the allegiance of Solomon to God. To truly win God's favor, one must submit one's life and conduct to the guidance of divine law.

Notable Quotations צִיטָטִים

And God gave wisdom	וַיהֹוָה נָתַן חָכְמָה
to Solomon,	לִשְׁלֹמֹה,
as God had promised him.	כַּאֲשֶׁר דִּבֶּר־לוֹ.

I Kings 5:26

If you will walk in My statutes	אִם־תֵּלֵךְ בְּחֻקֹּתַי
and execute My ordinances,	וְאֶת־מִשְׁפָּטַי תַּעֲשֶׂה,
and keep all My commandments	וְשָׁמַרְתָּ אֶת־כָּל־מִצְוֹתַי
to walk in them,	לָלֶכֶת בָּהֶם,
then I will establish My word	וַהֲקִמֹתִי אֶת־דְּבָרִי
with you.	אִתָּךְ.

I Kings 6:12

תְּצַוֶּה

Tetzaveh (Exodus 27:20–30:10)

Summary הַסְכּוּם

1. The portion continues the description of the tabernacle begun in the preceding portion. It includes commandments to create a *ner tamid* (eternal lamp) above the sanctuary ark.

2. Aaron and his sons are appointed priests to manage the sacrifices offered in the sanctuary.

3. A description of the priestly clothing, including the ephod, breastplate, robe, fringed tunic, headdress, and sash.

4. Aaron's ceremony of ordination as a priest, along with instructions for the slaughtering of offerings.

5. The portion concludes with directions for building an altar for burning incense before the ark.

Key Concepts and Values מוּשָׂגִים

1. Ner tamid: eternal light נֵר תָּמִיד. Many commentators believe that the origin of the eternal light found in every synagogue is in the opening lines of the Torah portion: "You shall command the Israelites to bring you pure olive oil beaten for the light, to cause a lamp to burn continually" (Exodus 27:20). The sages saw the light that burned perpetually in the tabernacle as a symbol of Israel, which was to be a "light unto the nations" (Isaiah 42:7). Today the *ner tamid* continues to hang in synagogues before the holy ark, symbolizing the permanence of the Torah and the radiance of the Jewish faith, which like the *ner tamid* is eternal.

2. Priestly dress of Aaron and his sons. According to our Torah portion, the priests were to dress in uniquely designed and decorated clothing. Aaron himself is commanded to wear eight different garments: the ephod, breastplate of judgment, Urim and Thummim, blue robe, fringed tunic, embroidered sash, linen headdress, and gold plate over the headdress. Since the priests were set apart from the rest of the Israelites by special duties, it seems logical that their clothing should call attention to their unique work and holy role. Throughout human history, uniforms have been used to signify status or special skills.

In an earlier portion God designated the Jewish people as a kingdom of priests. Therefore all Jews must look upon themselves as priests in the House of God. They should always be fittingly attired, both in order to symbolize this special role and to present themselves as being fashioned in God's image.

Notable Mitzvot מִצְווֹת

1. Kindling the menorah הַדְלָקַת הַמְּנוֹרָה. The priests were obligated to tend to the lights of the seven-branched menorah every morning and evening. One of the purposes of the menorah was to symbolize the radiance that enters the life of those who commit themselves to God and the Torah. Still found in many synagogues today, the menorah enhances the beauty of God's sanctuary.

2. Ktoret: incense קְטֹרֶת. Incense was used in the ancient tabernacle (Exodus 30:1). The fragrant smoke of burning incense at dawn and sunset was a natural symbol of prayer ascending to heaven. The Book of Psalms says: "Let my prayer be set forth as incense before You" (Psalms 141:2). The sages point out that each of the consonants of the Hebrew word for "incense" (*ktoret*) is the initial of a quality associated with sincere prayer:

111

ק: Kedushah   קְדוּשָׁה   *holiness*

ט: Taharah   טָהֳרָה   *purity*

ר: Rachamim   רַחֲמִים   *compassion*

ת: Tikvah   תִּקְוָה   *hope*

Notable Quotations   צִיטָטִים

They shall bring you pure oil
crushed from olives for lighting.

וְיִקְחוּ אֵלֶיךָ שֶׁמֶן זַיִת זָךְ
כָּתִית לַמָּאוֹר.

Exodus 27:20

You shall speak to all
who are wise of heart,
whom I have filled
with the spirit of wisdom,
that they make Aaron's garments
to consecrate him,
that he may serve Me.

וְאַתָּה תְּדַבֵּר
אֶל־כָּל־חַכְמֵי־לֵב
אֲשֶׁר מִלֵּאתִיו
רוּחַ חָכְמָה,
וְעָשׂוּ אֶת־בִּגְדֵי אַהֲרֹן
לְקַדְּשׁוֹ
לְכַהֲנוֹ־לִי.

Exodus 28:3

112

הַפְטָרַת תְּצַוֶּה

The Haftarah (Ezekiel 43:10–27)

Summary הַסִכּוּם

The Haftarah describes the altar of burnt offering in the restored Temple of Ezekiel's vision, and its consecration. Ezekiel in this Haftarah is preaching to the Israelites who have been exiled to Babylon. He is so certain that one day they will return to the Holy Land that he describes in graphic detail God's return to the Temple and God's directions as to the construction and dedication of the altar of burnt offering. He lays great stress on performing the Temple ritual and service correctly.

The Haftarah Connection הַקֶשֶׁר

The theme link between the Torah portion and the Haftarah is clearly the building of the portable sanctuary in the wilderness after the exodus from Egypt and the rebuilding of the Jerusalem Temple after the Israelites return from Babylonian captivity.

Key Concepts and Values מוּשָׂגִים

It is important that the Temple ritual and service be performed correctly.

113

Notable Quotations צִיטָטִים

You, son of man,	אַתָּה בֶן־אָדָם,
describe to the people of Israel	הַגֵּד אֶת־בֵּית יִשְׂרָאֵל
the temple	אֶת־הַבַּיִת
so that they will be ashamed	וְיִכָּלְמוּ
of their sins.	מֵעֲוֹנוֹתֵיהֶם.

Ezekiel 43:10

On the eighth day,	וְהָיָה בַיּוֹם הַשְּׁמִינִי
and each day thereafter	וָהָלְאָה
the priests shall make	יַעֲשׂוּ הַכֹּהֲנִים
on the altar	עַל־הַמִּזְבֵּחַ
your burnt offerings	אֶת־עוֹלוֹתֵיכֶם
and your peace offerings,	וְאֶת־שַׁלְמֵיכֶם
and I will look kindly upon them,	וְרָצִאתִי אֶתְכֶם
says God.	נְאֻם אֲדֹנָי יְהֹוִה:

Ezekiel 43:27

כִּי תִשָּׂא

Ki Tissa (Exodus 30:11–34:35)

Summary הַסְכּוּם

1. God instructs Moses to collect a half-shekel from every person over the age of twenty when he takes a census of the community.

2. Moses is told that the sanctuary's furnishings are to be fashioned by the skilled artisan Bezalel.

3. Moses reminds the people that in observing the Sabbath they celebrate the covenant between themselves and God.

4. Moses is given the two tablets on Mount Sinai. Forty days have passed, and the Israelites have asked Aaron to make a golden calf. Aaron agrees.

5. When Moses sees the golden calf, he shatters the tablets.

6. God directs Moses to carve two new tablets and return to Mount Sinai.

7. After the second forty days, Moses returns to the people, radiant from speaking to God. He covers his face with a veil.

Key Concepts and Values מוּשָׂגִים

1. Sin of the golden calf עֵגֶל הַזָּהָב. Many commentators write that the Israelites were in a state of panic. Thinking that Moses had vanished atop Mount Sinai, they decided to take matters into their own hands. They hoped that the power of God would somehow enter the image they had fashioned and offer them proper guidance.

115

The Bible commentator Nechama Leibowitz sees in the story of the golden calf not just Aaron's failure as a leader or the sin of the Israelites, but a deliberate warning that human beings are capable of acting nobly one moment and badly at the next.

2. Moses protests on behalf of his people. God tells Moses of His plan to destroy the Israelites because of the sin of the golden calf. Moses protests, trying to defend his people. Rabbinic interpreters suggest several reasons that may have moved Moses to protest to God. Perhaps he was motivated by sensitivity to the Israelites' past and to the habits and customs they had learned through centuries of living in corruption and slavery. Perhaps he felt pity for the Israelites, sensing that they were frightened and unsure about where God was leading them. He may also have concluded that destroying the Israelites was a bad strategy for God. It would ruin God's reputation, for no one would have faith in a God who freed a people in order to destroy them.

3. God's thirteen attributes שָׁלוֹשׁ עֶשְׂרֵה עֲקָרִים. Although it is impossible to describe God's essence, the rabbis listed thirteen moral qualities by which God may be known to human beings. They derived these divine qualities from two verses in this Torah portion by analyzing the implications of each phrase: "The Lord! a God compassionate and gracious, slow to anger, rich in kindness and truth, extending kindness to the thousandth generation, forgiving iniquity, transgression, and sin; yet God will by no means clear the guilty" (Exodus 34:6–7). The verses comprising the thirteen attributes are recited before the open ark on all Jewish holidays except when the holiday falls on the Sabbath.

Notable Mitzvot מִצְוֹת

Donation of the half-shekel מַחֲצִית הַשֶּׁקֶל. Every year, during the month of Adar, every Jew was required to donate half a shekel to pay for the daily sacrifices brought by the priests on behalf of the entire people of Israel. The same amount had to be contributed by rich and poor alike, so that no one would experience feelings of moral superiority or inferiority because of the size of his contribution.

Notable Quotations צִיטָטִים

Whoever is for God, come to me.   מִי לַיהֹוָה אֵלָי
Exodus 32:26

a stubborn and stiff-necked people   עַם־קְשֵׁה־עֹרֶף
Exodus 34:9

Three times a year   שָׁלֹשׁ פְּעָמִים בַּשָּׁנָה
all your males shall appear   יֵרָאֶה כָּל־זְכוּרְךָ
before the Lord   אֶת־פְּנֵי הָאָדֹן יְהֹוָה
God of Israel.   אֱלֹהֵי יִשְׂרָאֵל.
Exodus 34:23

The Lord, the Lord—a merciful god   יְהֹוָה יְהֹוָה אֵל רַחוּם
and gracious, long-suffering   וְחַנּוּן אֶרֶךְ אַפַּיִם
filled with goodness and truth,   וְרַב־חֶסֶד וֶאֱמֶת,
merciful to many thousands,   נֹצֵר חֶסֶד לָאֲלָפִים,
forgiving evil, misdeeds, and sin   נֹשֵׂא עָוֹן וָפֶשַׁע וְחַטָּאָה
—He will not clear the guilty,   וְנַקֵּה לֹא יְנַקֶּה,
conferring the sins of the fathers   פֹּקֵד עֲוֹן אָבוֹת
upon the children   עַל־בָּנִים
and upon the children's children,   וְעַל־בְּנֵי בָנִים,
even to the third   עַל־שִׁלֵּשִׁים
and fourth generations.   וְעַל־רִבֵּעִים.
Exodus 34:6–7

הַפְטָרַת כִּי תִשָּׂא

The Haftarah (I Kings 18:1–39)

Summary הַסְכּוּם

In the Haftarah, the Israelites are wavering between God and Baal. King Ahab was a generous ruler, but weak-willed and dominated by his Phoenician wife, Jezebel, who pursued the prophets with murderous cruelty. It was high treason to proclaim the God of Israel. Against this dark figure, Elijah stands out in all his greatness. He meets and confronts the king and queen, and fearlessly pronounces the doom that will follow upon their apostasy and their outrage of justice.

Two altars are constructed on Mount Carmel. When the false priests offer sacrifices to Baal, nothing happens. When Elijah brings his sacrifice to God, however, it is miraculously burnt. It is then that the people proclaim God to be the one and only God. These famous words form the conclusion of the Yom Kippur service and are the last words uttered by dying Israelites.

The Haftarah Connection הַקֶּשֶׁר

The connection between the Torah portion and Haftarah is the worshipping of the golden calf in the time of Moses and the wavering of the Israelites between Baal and God centuries later in the time of Elijah the prophet.

118

Key Concepts and Values מוּשָׂגִים

1. God's actions can convince people to believe in Him.

2. The words "The Lord He is God, the Lord He is God" are the clearest recognition of one's belief in God's sovereign power.

Notable Quotations צִיטָטִים

Call on the name of your gods,	וּקְרָאתֶם בְּשֵׁם אֱלֹהֵיכֶם,
and I will call	וַאֲנִי אֶקְרָא
on the name of the Lord.	בְשֵׁם־יְהֹוָה.
And the God	וְהָיָה הָאֱלֹהִים
that answers by fire—	אֲשֶׁר־יַעֲנֶה בָאֵשׁ
he is the true God.	הוּא הָאֱלֹהִים.

I Kings 18:24

The Lord, He is God,	יְהֹוָה הוּא הָאֱלֹהִים
the Lord He is God.	יְהֹוָה הוּא הָאֱלֹהִים

I Kings 18:39

וַיַּקְהֵל

Vayakhel (Exodus 35:1–38:20)

Summary הַסִכּוּם

1. The commandment to observe the Sabbath is repeated.

2. Moses asks the Israelites to donate gifts of gold, silver, copper, precious stones, and the like, to be used for building the tabernacle.

3. Moses appoints Bezalel and Oholiab to oversee the sanctuary construction. They report that the people are giving more gifts than are needed.

4. Moses tells the people to stop bringing their donations.

5. Under the direction of Bezalel and Oholiab, skilled craftsmen work to construct the tabernacle.

Key Concepts and Values מוּשָׂגִים

1. Sanctity of the Sabbath קְדוּשַׁת הַשַּׁבָּת. The sanctity of the Sabbath is stressed again in the account of the construction of the tabernacle. The Sabbath was not to be violated even for so sacred a cause as the building of the House of God.

The Talmud tells us that a Roman emperor once asked a rabbi: "What is the secret of your happiness?" The rabbi replied: "We have a delicacy called the Sabbath, and its delicious aroma fills our lives with fragrance and joy" (Shabbat 119a).

2. Chochmah, binah, and da'at: wisdom, understanding, and knowledge חָכְמָה, בִּינָה וְדַעַת. These three qualities are bestowed by God on Bezalel, the chief architect of the tabernacle

120

(Exodus 35:31). *Chochmah* denotes intuitive wisdom, *binah* is the practical application of *chochmah*; *da'at* is obtained through study and education.

3. Fundraising. In Jewish history, Moses was the first building-fund campaign chairman. He had a truly successful campaign, since it was oversubscribed and the people had to be admonished not to bring additional contributions.

Why was the first fundraising campaign so successful? The Torah answers: "They brought free will offerings, everyone whose heart stirred him up" (Exodus 35:21). Thus the original concept of tzedakah was a free will offering of the heart. It was Hillel who once said: "The more charity, the more peace" (Pirkei Avot 2:7).

Notable Mitzvot מִצְווֹת

1. Prohibition of fire on the Sabbath. Exodus 35:3 states that "you shall not kindle fire throughout your habitations on the Sabbath." Fire was prominently used in work by the Israelites, and thus its prohibition on the Sabbath. This command was understood by certain Jewish sects to prohibit even the enjoyment of light or fire on the Sabbath. The rabbis, however, applied it only to cooking and baking. The Sabbath was meant to be a day of rest, holiness, and tranquility.

You shall not light a fire	לֹא תְבַעֲרוּ אֵשׁ
in any of your homes	בְּכָל מֹשְׁבֹתֵיכֶם
on Shabbat.	בְּיוֹם הַשַּׁבָּת.

Exodus 35:3

2. You shall not cook a kid in its mother's milk. Upon these words, found in Exodus 34:26, the rabbis based the prohibition against eating milk and meat together in any way or form whatsoever. Many explanations have been offered for this injunction, which is repeated in several other places in the Torah. Some explain the

121

commandment as leveled against idolatry. Others state that it is a humanitarian command intended to discourage a practice that would tend to harden the heart.

You shall not cook a goat	לֹא תְבַשֵּׁל גְּדִי
in its mother's milk.	בַּחֲלֵב אִמּוֹ

Exodus 34:26

Notable Quotations צִיטָטִים

He was filled	וַיְמַלֵּא אֹתוֹ
with the spirit of God,	רוּחַ אֱלֹהִים
with wisdom, with understanding,	בְּחָכְמָה בִּתְבוּנָה
and with knowledge.	וּבְדַעַת

Exodus 35:31

The people brought much more	מַרְבִּים הָעָם לְהָבִיא
than enough for the work	מִדֵּי הָעֲבֹדָה
to be done	לַמְּלָאכָה
which God commanded	אֲשֶׁר־צִוָּה יְהוָה
them to do.	לַעֲשֹׂת אֹתָהּ:

Exodus 36:5

For six days you shall do	שֵׁשֶׁת יָמִים תֵּעָשֶׂה
work,	מְלָאכָה,
and on the seventh day	וּבַיּוֹם הַשְּׁבִיעִי
there shall be for you	יִהְיֶה לָכֶם
a holy day,	קֹדֶשׁ
a solemn day of rest for the Lord	שַׁבַּת שַׁבָּתוֹן לַיהוָה

Exodus 35:2

הַפְטָרַת וַיַּקְהֵל

The Haftarah (I Kings 7:40–50)

Summary הַסִּכּוּם

The Haftarah describes in detail some of the artistic work that went into the building of the Jerusalem Temple. Many of the materials for the Temple were supplied by King Hiram of Phoenicia. Solomon had made strong economic and political alliances with Hiram, and thus there was a good working relationship between the two.

The Haftarah Connection הַקֶּשֶׁר

The theme link between the Torah portion and the Haftarah is the building of the sanctuary in the wilderness in the time of Moses and the building of the first Temple in Jerusalem.

Important Concepts מוּשָׂגִים

As a House of God, it was important that the ancient Temple be completed with attention to even the smallest detail. Similarly, when a synagogue is built today, there are rules regarding its architecture.

Notable Quotations צִיטָטִים

Hiram made	וַיַּעַשׂ חִירוֹם
the pots and the shovels	אֶת־הַכִּירוֹת וְאֶת־הַיָּעִים
and the basins.	וְאֶת־הַמִּזְרָקוֹת
I Kings 7:40	
Solomon made	וַיַּעַשׂ שְׁלֹמֹה
all the vessels	אֶת כָּל־הַכֵּלִים
that were in the house of the Lord.	אֲשֶׁר בֵּית יְהֹוָה
I Kings 7:48	

123

פְּקוּדֵי

Pekuday (Exodus 38:21–40:38)

Summary הַסְכּוּם

1. A description of the records kept of all the work and materials used in the construction of the tabernacle, as well as all of the donations by the Israelites.

2. Moses and the Israelites celebrate the completion of the tabernacle by anointing it.

3. God's Presence fills the tabernacle and leads the people throughout their journeys.

Key Concepts and Values מוּשָׂגִים

1. **Accountability of public officials.** The Torah portion's attention to the accounts of the contributions and donations to the Temple clearly points to the moral responsibility of leaders. Today too many public leaders have been found to violate the trust of the public. Jewish tradition maintains that public officials must be above suspicion. Handling the people's funds demands careful scrutiny. All public officials are accountable to the people and must be held to high ethical standards.

2. **Kevod Adonai: glory of God כְּבוֹד ה׳.** In this Torah portion we read that the glory of God filled the tabernacle (Exodus 40:34.) At the same time, Judaism has always taught that God's presence fills the entire universe and that God may be worshipped wherever good people dwell.

124

Notable Mitzvot מִצְווֹת

None.

Notable Quotations צִיטָטִים

Then the cloud covered	וַיְכַס הֶעָנָן
the tent of meeting,	אֶת־אֹהֶל מוֹעֵד,
and the glory of God	וּכְבוֹד יְהֹוָה
filled the Tabernacle.	מָלֵא אֶת־הַמִּשְׁכָּן.

Exodus 40:34

And Moses saw	וַיַּרְא מֹשֶׁה
all the work, and behold,	אֶת־כָּל־הַמְּלָאכָה. וְהִנֵּה
they did it	עָשׂוּ אֹתָהּ
—exactly as God commanded	כַּאֲשֶׁר צִוָּה יְהֹוָה
they did it—	כֵּן עָשׂוּ
and Moses blessed them.	וַיְבָרֶךְ אֹתָם מֹשֶׁה:

Exodus 39:43

YOU HAVE NOW FINISHED THE BOOK OF SHEMOT

חֲזַק חֲזַק וְנִתְחַזֵּק

Masoretic Notes:

The Book of Shemot contains:

	1209 verses
	40 chapters
	11 Sidrot

הַפְטָרַת פְּקוּדֵי

The Haftarah (I Kings 7:51–8:21)

Summary הַסְכּוּם

The Haftarah describes the dedication of King Solomon's Temple on Mount Zion in Jerusalem. The Temple took seven years to complete. The service took place during the festival of Sukkot. During the service, the Ten Commandments in the ark were brought into the Temple. Solomon blesses the people and expresses the hope that one day all nations of the earth will come to realize that there is One God.

The Haftarah Connection הַקֶּשֶׁר

The connection between the Torah portion and the Haftarah is the building of the tabernacle in the wilderness and the completion of the Jerusalem Temple centuries later.

Key Concepts and Values מוּשָׂגִים

It is important to dedicate houses of worship and prayer to God upon completion. This is the Jewish way of consecrating space as holy space and as a holy place for God.

Notable Quotations צִיטָטִים

Solomon assembled	אָז יַקְהֵל שְׁלֹמֹה
the elders of Israel	אֶת־זִקְנֵי יִשְׂרָאֵל
all the heads of the tribes,	אֶת־כָּל־רָאשֵׁי הַמַּטּוֹת
the princes of the father's houses	נְשִׂיאֵי הָאָבוֹת
of the children of Israel.	לִבְנֵי יִשְׂרָאֵל

I Kings 8:1

It was in the heart	וַיְהִי עִם־לְבַב
of my father David	דָּוִד אָבִי
to build a house for the sake	לִבְנוֹת בַּיִת לְשֵׁם
of the Lord, God of Israel.	יְהֹוָה אֱלֹהֵי יִשְׂרָאֵל:

I Kings 8:17

127

וַיִּקְרָא

Vayikra (Leviticus 1:1–5:26)

Summary הַסְכּוּם

1. Description of five different kinds of sacrifices to be offered in the sanctuary: the *olah*, or burnt offering; the *minchah,* or meal offering; the *zevach shelamim*, or sacrifice of well-being; the *chattat*, or sin offering; and the *asham*, or guilt offering.

Key Concepts and Values מוּשָׂגִים

1. Korbanot: sacrifices קָרְבָּנוֹת. In biblical times, sacrifices to God were considered an expression of faith. The word *korban* (sacrifice) literally means "to draw closer," and reveals the purpose of the offerings. They were meant to unite the worshipper with God. By offering sacrifices, a person said thanks to God or sought forgiveness for sins. In presenting a sacrifice, one was giving something important of oneself to God. For the ancients, the smoke of a burning sacrifice was proof of a person's love and reverence for God.

The *olah* עֹלָה symbolized a complete surrender to the will of God. The *shelamim* שְׁלָמִים was intended as a demonstration of gratitude to God for His bounties; the *chattat* חַטָּאת was symbolic of regret and sorrow at having strayed from the way of God. Unlike heathen cults, which permitted individuals to offer their sacrifices wherever they chose, the Jews were allowed to make their offerings only in the tabernacle (and later in the Temple). This was to teach them that each member of the community was responsible for the

128

acts of all the others, and that no one could live and act for himself alone without consideration for others.

Notable Mitzvot מִצְווֹת

The duty of giving testimony. The Torah in this portion states: "If anyone sins, if he hears a curse, he becomes a witness, if he has seen or known, if he does not testify, then he must bear his guilt." (Leviticus 5:1). Since justice is the foundation of society, anyone who deliberately impedes justice is thereby guilty of perpetrating an act of injustice. A person who could give testimony that would help a court of justice come to a decision, but fails to do so, has committed a sin. As a rule, courts of justice under Jewish law require the testimony of two witnesses to establish a fact.

If anyone sins, if he hears	וְנֶפֶשׁ כִּי־תֶחֱטָא, וְשָׁמְעָה
a curse, he becomes a witness,	קוֹל אָלָה, וְהוּא עֵד,
if he has seen or known,	אוֹ רָאָה אוֹ יָדָע,
if he does not testify,	אִם־לוֹא יַגִּיד,
then he must bear his guilt.	וְנָשָׂא עֲוֹנוֹ.

Leviticus 5:1

Notable Quotations צִיטָטִים

When anyone of you brings	אָדָם כִּי־יַקְרִיב מִכֶּם
a sacrifice to God	קָרְבָּן לַיהוָֹה
of cattle, of the herd	מִן־הַבְּהֵמָה, מִן־הַבָּקָר
or of the flock.	וּמִן־הַצֹּאן
you shall sacrifice your offering.	תַּקְרִיבוּ אֶת־קָרְבַּנְכֶם.

Leviticus 1:2

הַפְטָרַת וַיִּקְרָא

The Haftarah (Isaiah 43:21–44:23)

Summary הַסִכּוּם

The Haftarah deplores Israel's neglect of all worship. It is addressed by the prophet Isaiah to the Jews exiled to Babylon after the first destruction of Jerusalem. Israel has been punished because of its failure to live up to God's expectations. Isaiah reminds the people that there is only one God in whom to believe. As for the idols that the other nations worship, they are mere blocks of wood, and it would be foolish to worship them because they are of no use. Israel must return to God, the ultimate Redeemer.

The Haftarah Connection הַקֶּשֶׁר

The shared theme of the Torah portion and the Haftarah is the authentic worship of God by Israel in early biblical times at the sanctuary and their falling away from God in the time of Isaiah, a stark contrast to earlier practice.

Key Concepts and Values מוּשָׂגִים

1. Israel is God's chosen people.
2. God wants more than ritual; God wants our hearts and minds.
3. Belief in idols is vanity.

Notable Quotations   צִיטָטִים

Now listen, O Jacob My servant,	וְעַתָּה שְׁמַע יַעֲקֹב עַבְדִּי,
and Israel, whom I have chosen.	וְיִשְׂרָאֵל בָּחַרְתִּי בוֹ.

Isaiah 44:1

So says the Lord,	כֹּה־אָמַר יְהוָֹה,
the Ruler of Israel:	מֶלֶךְ־יִשְׂרָאֵל:
"I am the first,	"אֲנִי רִאשׁוֹן,
and I am the last,	וַאֲנִי אַחֲרוֹן,
and beside Me there is no God."	וּמִבַּלְעָדַי אֵין אֱלֹהִים."

Isaiah 44:6

Those that make idols are nothing	יֹצְרֵי־פֶסֶל כֻּלָּם תֹּהוּ
and their treasures are worthless.	וַחֲמוּדֵיהֶם בַּל־יוֹעִילוּ

Isaiah 44:9

צַו

Tzav (Leviticus 6:1–8:36)

Summary הַסְכּוּם

1. A continuation of the preceding Torah portion, enlarging upon the description of the sacrificial offerings.

2. The ordination of Aaron and his sons as priests and the dedication of the first sanctuary.

Key Concepts and Values מוּשָׂגִים

1. Mishmarot: watches מִשְׁמָרוֹת. The concept of watches is based on, "and you shall abide at the door of the tent of meeting day and night seven days, and keep the charge of God" (Leviticus 8:35). The adult males of the Jewish people were divided into twenty-four watches of priests, Levites, and ordinary Israelites for duty at the Temple, with every watch performing Temple services for one week at a time. The ordinary Israelites in the watch assisted the priests and Levites. Some of them were in the Temple, standing near the priests and reciting prayers during the sacrificial rites, while others read to the congregation the portions of the Torah relating to the sacrifices then being offered in Jerusalem. In this manner all Jewish men, regardless of wealth or status, had an opportunity to participate, both directly and indirectly, in the sacrificial rites.

2. The holiness of blood. Jewish law forbids the eating of blood. The Torah portion states: "You must not consume any blood, either of bird or of animal" (Leviticus 7:26). Most commentators

132

agree that there are several reasons for this prohibition. The first is related to the use of blood in pagan cult rituals. In these ceremonies, animal blood was eaten in the belief that it would provide strength from sickness. Nachmanides, a medieval commentator, made the point that blood is sacred because it contains the soul given by God and therefore ought not to be eaten. Others saw the refusal to eat blood as a way of sensitizing us toward reverence for life, since blood was often a sign of human cruelty.

Notable Mitzvot מִצְווֹת

Kashering of meat using salt to drain the blood. According to Jewish law, before meat can be eaten, all its blood must be removed. This is usually done by soaking and salting, but liver contains so much blood that it must be broiled over an open flame.

Notable Quotations צִיטָטִים

You shall eat no kind of blood,	וְכָל־דָּם לֹא תֹאכְלוּ . . .
whether from fowl or beast . . .	לָעוֹף וְלַבְּהֵמָה . . .
Anyone who eats	כָּל־נֶפֶשׁ אֲשֶׁר־תֹּאכַל
any blood	כָּל־דָּם
will be ejected	וְנִכְרְתָה הַנֶּפֶשׁ הַהִוא
from his people.	מֵעַמֶּיהָ.

Leviticus 7:26–27

הַפְטָרַת צַו

The Haftarah (Jeremiah 7:21–8:3, 9:22–23)

Summary   הַסְכּוּם

The Haftarah reveals the true purpose of sacrifice and of all outward worship, namely, to stimulate us toward living a life of holiness. In the Haftarah, spoken by the prophet Jeremiah, mere mechanical ritual divorced from morality and ethics is condemned. Jeremiah points out to the people that they have forgotten who the true God is, having become worshippers of idols. For this wrongdoing, the people of Judah will have to suffer punishment. The Haftarah concludes by stating that God delights in those who practice the important ideals of truth, justice, and righteousness.

The Haftarah Connection   הַקֶּשֶׁר

The link between the Torah portion and the Haftarah is that of sacrifices during the time when the Israelites were wandering in the desert and the Temple sacrifices many centuries later.

Important Concepts   מוּשָׂגִים

1. God does not want mere mechanical performance of acts of worship.

2. If you must glory, do not glory in ephemeral things, but in things that are of eternal worth, such as justice and righteousness.

134

Notable Quotations   צִיטָטִים

Let not the wise man take pride	אַל־יִתְהַלֵּל חָכָם
in his wisdom	בְּחָכְמָתוֹ
neither let the mighty person glory	וְאַל־יִתְהַלֵּל הַגִּבּוֹר
in his might.	בִּגְבוּרָתוֹ

Jeremiah 9:22

I am the Lord	כִּי אֲנִי יְהֹוָה
who rules with mercy, justice,	עֹשֶׂה חֶסֶד מִשְׁפָּט
and righteousness on Earth.	וּצְדָקָה בָּאָרֶץ
In these things I take pleasure.	כִּי־בְאֵלֶּה חָפַצְתִּי

Jeremiah 9:23

שְׁמִינִי

Shemini (Leviticus 9:1–11:47)

Summary הַסְכּוּם

1. Moses instructs Aaron and his sons Nadav and Avihu concerning offerings for atonement of sins.

2. Nadav and Avihu bring unauthorized fire offerings of their own, and God punishes them with death.

3. God tells Moses and Aaron which foods are permitted and forbidden to be eaten.

Key Concepts and Values מוּשָׂגִים

The attainment of holiness. The rules of conduct of the priests were designed to keep foremost in their minds the task of distinguishing between good and evil. In addition, one of the purposes of the Jewish dietary laws is to help the individual strive after holiness. God says, "Sanctify yourselves, and be holy" (Leviticus 11:44). Mordecai Kaplan, founder of the Reconstructionist branch of Judaism, explained that the purpose of the dietary laws was to make the people of Israel aware of their dedication to God as a priestly and a holy people. The laws regulate what a Jew may and may not eat, and are a means of preserving Jewish identity and Jewish loyalty.

Notable Mitzvot מִצְווֹת

Laws of kashrut: keeping kosher דִּינֵי כַּשְׁרוּת. The dietary laws are one of the fundamentals of Judaism. The rabbinic sages taught that keeping kosher is conducive to holiness. As the popular saying goes, "we are what we eat." The observance of the dietary laws has, in large measure, enabled the Jewish people to survive through the ages in the midst of a hostile world.

This Torah portion carefully enumerates the animals that are permissible to be eaten and those forbidden to be eaten. Fish must have fins and scales, animals must have split hooves and chew their cuds.

Many reasons for the rules of kashrut have been offered by commentators over the ages. The physician and commentator Moses Maimonides believed that the foods forbidden by the laws of the Torah are unfit for human consumption. Others, such as Abarbanel, wrote that the laws of kashrut protect the Jew's spiritual health. Still others explain that the dietary laws teach human beings to control their bodily appetites. Since eating is a continuing activity, observing the laws of kashrut becomes a constant reminder of the values, traditions, and special obligations of Jewish living.

Notable Quotations צִיטָטִים

To those close to Me	בִּקְרֹבַי
I will show my holiness,	אֶקָּדֵשׁ,
and before all the people	וְעַל־פְּנֵי כָל־הָעָם
I will be praised.	אֶכָּבֵד.

Leviticus 10:3

To distinguish
the holy from the ordinary,
the impure from the pure.

וּלְהַבְדִּיל
בֵּין הַקֹּדֶשׁ וּבֵין הַחֹל
וּבֵין הַטָּמֵא וּבֵין הַטָּהוֹר:

Leviticus 10:10

Animals that part the hoof,
and are fully cloven-footed
and chews its cud,

those you may eat.

כֹּל מַפְרֶסֶת פַּרְסָה
וְשֹׁסַעַת שֶׁסַע
פְּרָסֹת מַעֲלַת גֵּרָה
בַּבְּהֵמָה
אֹתָהּ תֹּאכֵלוּ:

Leviticus 11:3

הַפְטָרַת שְׁמִינִי

The Haftarah (II Samuel 6:1–7:17)

Summary הַסִּכּוּם

Kind David captured the city of Jerusalem from the Jebusites in the year 1000 B.C.E. He brought the Ark of the Covenant to Jerusalem. When Uzzah puts forth his hand to the ark to take hold of it, God is displeased and kills him (apparently because Uzzah did not treat the Ark with proper reverence).

It is now the hope of King David that a Temple will be built in Jerusalem which will permanently house the Ark of the Covenant. He discusses his idea with the prophet Nathan, who informs King David that God does not want him to build the Temple. Indeed, it will remain for Solomon, the successor of David, to build Jerusalem's first Temple.

The Haftarah Connection הַקֶּשֶׁר

The Torah portion describes the consecration of the tabernacle in the wilderness, while the Haftarah tells of the transportation of the Ark of the Covenant to the holy city of Jerusalem. Tragic incidents mark both the Torah portion and the Haftarah. In the Torah portion, Nadav and Avihu are slain by God, and Uzzah is slain by God in the Haftarah when he touches the Ark. These incidents clearly show that no kind of caprice can be tolerated in the service of God.

139

Important Concepts מוּשָׂגִים

Irreverence to God is a crime that will not be tolerated.

Notable Quotations צִיטוּטִים

God was angry	וַיִּחַר־אַף יְהֹוָה
at Uzzah	בְּעֻזָּה
and God struck him on the spot	וַיַּכֵּהוּ שָׁם הָאֱלֹהִים
for his error.	עַל־הַשַּׁל.

II Samuel 6:7

He will build a house for My name,	הוּא יִבְנֶה־בַיִת לִשְׁמִי,
and I will secure the throne	וְכֹנַנְתִּי אֶת־כִּסֵּא
of his kingdom forever.	מַמְלַכְתּוֹ עַד־עוֹלָם:

II Samuel 7:13

140

תַזְרִיעַ

Tazria (Leviticus 12:1–13:59)

Summary הַסְכּוּם

1. Rituals of purification for a woman after childbirth.

2. Methods for diagnosing and treating a variety of skin diseases.

Key Concepts and Values מוּשָׂגִים

1. Priests as medical diagnosticians. In this Torah portion we see that the priest functions not only in his religious role but also as a kind of diagnostician. The priests were called upon to diagnose the various skin diseases and offer treatment.

2. Laws of leprosy. Leprosy was one of the most dreaded of all biblical diseases. Lepers, because of their physical impurity, were debarred from fulfilling their duties as Israelites to the sanctuary. After recovering from leprosy, a person needed to be formally rededicated as an Israelite to the service of God. The rabbis regarded leprosy as a divine affliction in punishment for slander or talebearing. They metaphorically understood the word *metzora* (leprosy) as *motzi shem ra* (bringing a bad name upon another person). According to the Talmud, slander is a hideous capital crime. A slanderer is like one who denies God. God says of the slanderer: "He and I cannot live together in the world" (Talmud Arachin 15b)

Listeners who encourage slander are also guilty. If there were not so many open ears, there would not be so many open mouths. God gave us two ears and one tongue. Therefore, we should listen twice as much as we talk.

141

Notable Mitzvot מִצְווֹת

1. Defilement due to discharges from the body. According to biblical law, any discharge from the sex organs renders a person unclean, and defiles any other person or object with whom the person having the discharge comes in contact. The biblical attitude toward discharges from sex organs does not readily lend itself to interpretation. Medical science has studied such discharges, but so far has found no conclusive evidence that they are toxic in character.

A woman who has given birth becomes unclean because of the afterbirth and other postnatal discharges. After childbirth, she has to count seven "clean" days for a boy (and fourteen "clean" days for a girl). She then immerses herself in a ritual bath (*mikveh*). In addition, since a woman is unclean during her normal menstrual period, she must, according to Jewish law, count seven clean days after menstruating and then go to the mikveh. From ancient times until the present, spiritual purity using a mikveh has played a most important part in maintaining Jewish family purity.

Notable Quotations צִיטָטִים

When a man or woman	וְאִישׁ אוֹ אִשָּׁה
has a sore	כִּי־יִהְיֶה בוֹ נָגַע
upon the head or upon the beard,	בְּרֹאשׁ אוֹ בְזָקָן,
then the priest shall examine	וְרָאָה הַכֹּהֵן
the sore.	אֶת־הַנָּגַע.

Leviticus 13:29–30

If a woman gives birth	אִשָּׁה כִּי תַזְרִיעַ
and bears a male child,	וְיָלְדָה זָכָר,
then she shall be unclean	וְטָמְאָה
for seven days.	שִׁבְעַת יָמִים

Leviticus 12:2

הַפְטָרַת תַזְרִיעַ

The Haftarah (II Kings 4:42–5:19)

Summary   הַסְכּוּם

In the Haftarah, Naaman, the commander of Syria's army, is ill with leprosy. An Israelite slave girl informs Naaman's wife of a prophet in Israel who is known as a healer. This person is none other than Elisha, known for his miraculous works and abilities. When Naaman consults Elisha, he is advised to go directly to the Jordan River and bathe in it seven times. A miracle occurs, and after bathing in the Jordan the seventh time, Naaman's skin becomes healthy. Naaman offers Elisha a reward, but Elisha refuses.

The Haftarah Connection   הַקֶּשֶׁר

The thematic link between the Torah portion and the Haftarah is that of leprosy. The Torah portion deals with the diagnosis and treatment of the dreaded disease, while the Haftarah recounts an incident in the life of the Syrian general Naaman, who was afflicted with leprosy.

Important Concepts   מוּשָׂגִים

1. Elisha is a proven healer of people.
2. Leprosy was a dreaded disease in ancient times.

143

Notable Quotations צִיטָטִים

Go and bathe	הָלוֹךְ וְרָחַצְתָּ
in the Jordan seven times,	שֶׁבַע־פְּעָמִים בַּיַּרְדֵּן
and your flesh shall be restored,	וְיָשֹׁב בְּשָׂרְךָ לְךָ
and you shall be clean.	וּטְהָר:

II Kings 5:10

And he said to him: "Go in peace."	וַיֹּאמֶר לוֹ לֵךְ לְשָׁלוֹם
So he departed from him	וַיֵּלֶךְ מֵאִתּוֹ
a short distance.	כִּבְרַת־אָרֶץ:

II Kings 5:19

144

מְצוֹרָע

Metzora (Leviticus 14:1–15:33)

Summary הַסְכּוּם

1. Methods for purification of the leper.

2. Appearance and treatment of fungus or mildew in the home. Ritual impurity resulting from contact with discharges from sex organs.

Key Concepts and Values מוּשָׂגִים

1. Asham: the guilt offering. This offering was the leper's symbolic act of purification, marking his return to the community after having been "outside the camp" of Israel. The meal-offering was made after the leper had become clean again. It was an expression of gratitude for regained purity and for the privilege of being permitted to return to the community.

2. Contributing according to one's means. "And if he be poor, and his means suffice not, then he shall take one he-lamb" (Leviticus 14:21). Jews are enjoined to contribute offerings according to their individual means. The wealthy bring more, the poor bring what they can. In the words of the Talmud: "But one and the same are the generous and the meager offering, provided that a person's intention and sincerity are directed to heaven" (Berachot 5b).

The small gift of a less rich person may be a far greater sacrifice than a large gift of a wealthy person. Contributing time and service to some worthy cause may be an even more valuable gift than money.

Notable Mitzvot מִצְווֹת

1. All of the mitzvot in this Torah portion relate to the purification of the leper and the leper's dwellings, or to purification from other sources of defilement. The ritual bath at the end of a period of defilement marked the onset of cleanliness. The laws of purity were greatly elaborated by the rabbinic teachers.

Notable Quotations צִיטְטִים

This shall be the law of the leper	זֹאת תִּהְיֶה תּוֹרַת הַמְצֹרָע
on the day of his purification:	בְּיוֹם טָהֳרָתוֹ:
he shall be taken to the priest.	וְהוּבָא אֶל־הַכֹּהֵן.

Leviticus 14:2

You shall warn the children of Israel	וְהִזַּרְתֶּם אֶת־בְּנֵי־יִשְׂרָאֵל
about the uncleanliness . . .	מִטֻּמְאָתָם . . .
if they disgrace My tabernacle	בְּטַמְּאָם אֶת־מִשְׁכָּנִי
that is in their midst.	אֲשֶׁר בְּתוֹכָם.

Leviticus 15:31

הַפְטָרַת מְצֹרָע

The Haftarah (II Kings 7:3–20)

Summary הַסִּכּוּם

The Haftarah recounts an incident that occurred during the siege of Samaria by the Syrians. Late one night God caused the Syrians to panic and flee. In the morning, four lepers who were living outside the city because of their disease discover that the Syrian camp is deserted. They snatch food to satisfy their hunger. Then, remembering that Samaria's people are starving, they go to the outskirts of the city and inform the guards that the Syrians have fled. The city's inhabitants are saved from starvation.

The Haftarah Connection הַקֶּשֶׁר

The theme link is the story of the lepers in the Haftarah and the details of leprosy in the Torah portion.

Important Concepts מוּשָׂגִים

1. Elisha the prophet makes it clear to the Israelites that God had saved them from the Arameans.

Notable Quotations צִיטָטִים

Now there were four men	וְאַרְבָּעָה אֲנָשִׁים
who were leprous	הָיוּ מְצֹרָעִים
at the entrance of the gate;	פֶּתַח הַשָּׁעַר;
and they said to one another:	וַיֹּאמְרוּ אִישׁ אֶל־רֵעֵהוּ:
"Why do we sit here	"מָה אֲנַחְנוּ יֹשְׁבִים פֹּה
until we die?"	עַד־מָתְנוּ?„

II Kings 7:3

147

אַחֲרֵי מוֹת

Achare Mot (Leviticus 16:1–18:30)

Summary   הַסְכּוּם

1. The portion begins by recalling the deaths of Aaron's sons, Nadav and Avihu.

2. Next it describes the rituals for the sin offerings that Aaron is to present in the sanctuary for himself and the people.

3. Laws regarding sexual relations are presented.

Key Concepts and Values   מוּשָׂגִים

1. Scapegoat עֲזָאזֵל. When Aaron enters the inner sanctuary, he is told to bring sin offerings for himself and his household, and for all the people of Israel. For himself, he is to bring a bull. For the people, two male goats. Standing at the entrance of the sanctuary, he is to mark one of the goats "for God" and the other "for Azazel" as the scapegoat for the mistakes and errors the people have committed. When the ritual is completed, the male goat marked "for Azazel" is brought to Aaron. Aaron places his hands upon it and confesses all the wrongdoings of the people. The goat is then sent off into the wilderness.

There are many different interpretations of the ritual of the scapegoat. Maimonides states that the scapegoat is an active allegory meant to make the sinner understand that his sins will inevitably lead him to a wasteland. Abarbanel sees the two goats as reminders of brothers Esau and Jacob. Esau was a hunter in the wilderness, while Jacob's life was marked "for God."

148

2. Sin פֶּשַׁע, עָוֹן וְחֵטְא. In Judaism, there are three categories of sin. *Chet* (usually translated as "sin") is to be understood as missing the mark or goal set by God. *Avon* ("transgression") implies a willful violation of the law. *Pesha* ("iniquity") is the most serious of the three violations. It usually implies outright revolt against God's ordinances.

3. Incestuous unions. The Torah portion enumerates all of the marriages prohibited by Jewish law. Offspring of incestuous unions are classified as *mamzerim*, children born of a couple who cannot be married under Jewish law.

Notable Mitzvot מִצְווֹת

Prohibitions regarding marital relations. The Torah portion enumerates a variety of forbidden marriages and sexual relationships, including those between mother and son, brother and sister, father and daughter (Leviticus 18:6–18). Offspring of such incestuous unions are classed as *mamzerim* (contrary to popular belief, this term does not refer exclusively to children born out of wedlock; it denotes children born to any couple, whether married or not, who are not permitted to marry under Jewish law; e.g., where one of the parties was previously married but has not been divorced with a *get*).

In addition, the Torah portion emphasizes the importance of sexual abstinence during a woman's menstrual cycle (Leviticus 18:19). All of these laws relate to the sanctity of the institution of marriage. Impurity in marriage and incestuous promiscuity among near relations were considered unpardonable sins. In Israel, marriage was clearly regarded as a divine institution under whose shadow alone there can be true reverence.

Notable Quotations צִיטָטִים

And the goat shall carry upon him	וְנָשָׂא הַשָּׂעִיר עָלָיו
all their sins	אֶת־כָּל־עֲוֹנֹתָם
to a land which is desolate,	אֶל־אֶרֶץ גְּזֵרָה
and he shall let the goat go free	וְשִׁלַּח אֶת־הַשָּׂעִיר
into the wilderness.	בַּמִּדְבָּר:

Leviticus 16:22

And you shall keep My statutes	וּשְׁמַרְתֶּם אֶת־חֻקֹּתַי
and My laws,	וְאֶת־מִשְׁפָּטַי
which man must observe	אֲשֶׁר יַעֲשֶׂה אֹתָם הָאָדָם
and live by them.	וָחַי בָּהֶם
I am the Lord.	אֲנִי יְהֹוָה:

Leviticus 18:5

הַפְטָרַת אַחֲרֵי מוֹת

The Haftarah (Ezekiel 22:1–19)

Summary הַסְכּוּם

The Haftarah, written by the prophet Ezekiel, is a terrible indictment of the holy city of Jerusalem for its callous violation of regulations and prohibitions. The Israelites had rejected the laws of family purity and were presenting sacrifices to pagan idols. For all of these transgressions the Israelites would suffer God's punishment, which would include being exiled from the land.

The Haftarah Connection הַקֶּשֶׁר

The Torah portion ordains strict regulations for assuring the religious and moral purity of Israel. The Haftarah strongly criticizes the Israelites for their rejection of family purity.

Important Concepts מוּשָׂגִים

Only when Israel sincerely repents for its apostasies can its redemption occur.

Notable Quotations צִיטָטִים

Now son of man, are you prepared	וְאַתָּה בֶן־אָדָם הֲתִשְׁפֹּט
to judge the murderous city	הֲתִשְׁפֹּט אֶת־עִיר הַדָּמִים
to make her confess to	וְהוֹדַעְתָּהּ
all of her crimes.	אֵת כָּל־תּוֹעֲבוֹתֶיהָ:

Ezekiel 22:2

You have scorned My holy things	קָדָשַׁי בָּזִית
and have violated My sabbaths.	וְאֶת־שַׁבְּתֹתַי חִלָּלְתְּ:

Ezekiel 22:8

Since you have all become	יַעַן הֱיוֹת כֻּלְּכֶם
loose fragments.	לְסִגִים.
therefore, I will gather you	לָכֵן הִנְנִי קֹבֵץ אֶתְכֶם
into the midst of Jerusalem.	אֶל־תּוֹךְ יְרוּשָׁלִָם

Ezekiel 22:19

קְדוֹשִׁים

Kedoshim (Leviticus 19:1–20:27)

Summary הַסְכּוּם

1. Ceremonial and moral laws are listed in detail.

2. Injunctions against Moloch worship.

3. Punishments for unlawful marriages and immoral practices.

Key Concepts and Values מוּשָׂגִים

1. Holiness to God and as Jews. This Torah portion is part of what has become to be known as the "Holiness Code." It contains the ritual and ethical practices that one must carry out to live a sacred or holy Jewish life. Leviticus 19:2 states: "You shall be holy, for I the Lord your God am holy." Echoing the laws given to Mount Sinai, the Israelites are told to honor their parents, observe the Sabbath and holy days, refrain from worshipping idols, and leave corners of their fields for the poor. All of these laws are meant to set the Jewish people apart from (the literal meaning of "holiness") the other peoples. Just as God is a holy God (i.e., unique and set apart in His greatness), so too Israel is called upon in this portion to imitate God's ways.

1. Genevat da'at: stealing of one's mind גְּנֵבַת דַּעַת. In Leviticus 19:11 the Torah states that we must not steal, deal falsely, or lie to one another. This prohibition includes creating a false impression (*genevat da'at*, the stealing of another person's mind). Thus it is forbidden to cheat people in trade or to deceive them. This prohibition does not only apply to business dealings. A deceitful person may be honest in his commercial transactions and yet "steal the heart" of his neighbor. Thus, someone who urges his neighbor to be his guest when in his heart he does not mean to invite him is guilty of deception.

3. Love your neighbor as yourself וְאָהַבְתָּ לְרֵעֲךָ כָּמוֹךְ. Dr. Erich Fromm explains this law to mean that one must love one's neighbor because he is *kamocha*—"like us"! We must first respect ourselves as unique human beings. Only then can we come to have the same regard for our fellow human beings. Not selfishness, but love and respect for the real self make it possible for us to obey this principle of faith.

Hillel paraphrased this precept as follows: "Whatever is harmful to you, you shall not do to your fellow human being" (Talmud Shabbat 31a). The rabbis taught that each individual is a miniature universe in his own right, and that saving one person is like saving an entire world.

Finally, Maimonides declares that what is meant by this precept is that one should love one's neighbor with all the qualities and modes of love with which one loves oneself. Loving your neighbor as yourself, for Maimonides, includes visiting the sick, comforting the mourners, joining a funeral procession, celebrating the marriage ceremony with bride and groom, offering hospitality to others, and caring for the dead.

4. Prohibition of talebearing רְכִילוּת. Leviticus 19:16 states that "you should not go up and down as a talebearer among your people." The Hebrew word *rechilut* (talebearing) is derived from *rachal* (merchant). A talebearer, retailing his gossip, goes from one person to another with his "stories." Malicious gossip has always been portrayed in Jewish tradition as a way of severely damaging the reputation of a person. It is thus a grave mistake which is to be severely punished.

5. Respect for the elderly מִפְּנֵי שֵׂיבָה תָּקוּם. Leviticus 19:32 states that "you shall rise before the hoary head." The affection that Jews are taught to feel for the aged is an example of intelligent respect for the experience of our elders. The Bratslaver Rebbe once wrote that "the prosperity of the nation is directly related to its treatment of the elderly."

Notable Mitzvot מִצְווֹת

This Torah portion contains approximately fifty mitzvot. Here is a cross-section of some of the more important ones:

1. Reverence for one's mother and father (Leviticus 19:3).

2. Leaving an edge of one's field unreaped, for the poor (Leviticus 19:10).

3. Not stealing or dealing falsely (Leviticus 19:11).

4. Paying for day labor on the same day (Leviticus 19:13).

5. Not putting a stumbling block before the blind (Leviticus 19:14).

6. Not doing unrighteousness in judgment (Leviticus 19:15).

7. Not standing idly by the blood of one's neighbor (Leviticus 19:16).

8. Not hating one's brother in one's heart (Leviticus 19:17).

9. Not taking vengeance or bearing a grudge (Leviticus 19:18).

10. Loving one's neighbor (Leviticus 19:18).

11. Not practicing divination (Leviticus 19:26).

Notable Quotations צִיטָטִים

Be holy,	קְדשִׁים תִּהְיוּ,
for holy am I,	כִּי קָדוֹשׁ אֲנִי,
the Lord your God.	יְהוָֹה אֱלֹהֵיכֶם.

Leviticus 19:2

One must	אִישׁ
respect his mother and father.	אִמּוֹ וְאָבִיו תִּירָאוּ.

Leviticus 19:3

You shall not exploit your neighbor	לֹא־תַעֲשֹׁק אֶת־רֵעֲךָ
or rob him;	וְלֹא תִגְזֹל
nor shall you hold	לֹא־תָלִין אִתְּךָ
the wages of a hired servant	פְּעֻלַּת שָׂכִיר
until the morning.	עַד־בֹּקֶר:

Leviticus 19:13

You shall not curse the deaf	לֹא־תְקַלֵּל חֵרֵשׁ
and before the blind	וְלִפְנֵי עִוֵּר
you shall not place an obstacle.	לֹא תִתֵּן מִכְשֹׁל

Leviticus 19:14

You shall not circulate as a talebearer.	לֹא־תֵלֵךְ רָכִיל

Leviticus 19:16

You shall not take revenge	לֹא־תִקֹּם
and bear a grudge	וְלֹא־תִטֹּר
against your people,	אֶת־בְּנֵי עַמֶּךָ,
but love your neighbor as yourself.	וְאָהַבְתָּ לְרֵעֲךָ כָּמוֹךָ.

Leviticus 19:18

156

הַפְטָרַת קְדֹשִׁים

The Haftarah (Amos 9:7–15)

Summary הַסִּכּוּם

The Haftarah is taken from the Book of Amos, a shepherd who lived in the days of King Jeroboam II (750 B.C.E.). For this prophet, the masterword of existence was righteousness. Amos was extremely troubled by the inhumanity of the people to one other, and especially criticized the rich for ignoring the plight of the poor, alien, widow, and orphan. Pagan forms of worship also corrupted the land. In God's dealing with people and nations, God has but one single test—their loyalty to the laws of righteousness. God judges people according to their devotion to justice and ethics.

The Haftarah concludes by stating that God's mercy will ultimately prevail, and that God will find a way of bringing back His banished people to a state of prosperity and purity.

The Haftarah Connection הַקֶּשֶׁר

The opening of the Torah portion ("you shall be holy to God") strikes the note of consecration in the individual life. Similarly, this Haftarah, in its earlier verses, is an oracle against those who have rejected that high Jewish ideal and bring about the downfall of the Israelites. But Israel will yet be true to its high and holy ideal, and will one day in the future again be worthy of the blessings that follow in the way of such loyalty.

Important Concepts מוּשָׂגִים

1. God's most important test for humanity is to test their loyalty to the laws of righteousness.

2. All nations are equally dear to God.

Notable Quotations צִיטָטִים

Are you not	הֲלוֹא
like the children of the Cushites	כִּבְנֵי כֻשִׁיִּים
to me?	אַתֶּם לִי

Amos 9:7

By the sword shall perish	בַּחֶרֶב יָמוּתוּ
all the wrongdoers of my people.	כֹּל חַטָּאֵי עַמִּי

Amos 9:10

And I will return	וְשַׁבְתִּי
from captivity My people Israel;	אֶת־שְׁבוּת עַמִּי יִשְׂרָאֵל;
they shall rebuild the ruined cities	וּבָנוּ עָרִים נְשַׁמּוֹת
and live in them.	וְיָשָׁבוּ

Amos 9:14

אֱמֹר

Emor (Leviticus 21:1–24:23)

Summary הַסְכּוּם

1. Laws regulating the lives of the priests.

2. Donations and offerings that are acceptable for the sanctuary.

3. Qualifications for sacrificial animals.

4. The major festivals.

5. The lamps and the show-bread of the tabernacle.

6. Laws dealing with profanity, murder, and the maiming of others.

Key Concepts and Values מוּשָׂגִים

1. Kiddush HaShem: sanctification of the name of God קִדּוּשׁ הַשֵּׁם. In Leviticus 22:23 it states: "You shall not profane My holy Name, but I will be hallowed among the children of Israel." All Jews are duty bound to sanctify God's Name through their way of life, and if need be, by martyrdom for the sake of the way of life taught by God in the Torah. The Jewish people must be on their guard to do nothing that would disgrace the honor of Jews or of Judaism. Improper conduct on the part of any Jew may bring shame upon the entire Jewish people and dishonor to the Name of God.

2. Equality before the law. Leviticus 24:22 states that "you shall have one manner of law for the stranger as for the homeborn, for I am the Lord your God." Jewish law does not allow for a double standard. Every individual—stranger and citizen alike—is

159

equal before the law. This precept is another classic example of democratic thought found in the Bible.

3. *Lex talionis*: **an eye for an eye** עַיִן תַּחַת עַיִן. This statement, found in Leviticus 24:19–20, deals with compensation for physical harm inflicted by one person upon another. It has often been misunderstood to mean that the Bible was in favor of crude vengeance. The rabbis of the Talmud (Baba Kamma 84a), however, reinterpreted this law to refer to monetary compensation.

Nechama Leibowitz states that the body is sacred because it is the house of the human soul and a gift from God. Thus, we have no right to inflict harm on anyone else's body or even on our own body. When justice demands compensation for damages to another's body, only financial compensation will do.

Notable Mitzvot מִצְוֹת

1. Sanctification of the priest. Leviticus 21:8, in referring to the *kohen*, states that "you shall therefore sanctify him." A priest must be respectfully elevated to a higher status than that of a Jewish layperson. The dignity of the *kohen* and image of superiority demands that we accord the priest great honor and respect. In an open forum, the priest should be given the right to speak first. When the Torah is read in the synagogue, the priest is the first one called to the bimah.

And you shall sanctify him   וְקִדַּשְׁתּוֹ
Leviticus 21:8

2. Prohibition against profaning God's Name. One of the strongest behavioral guidelines for Jews is the requirement to sanctify God's Name and the strict prohibition against profaning it (Leviticus 22:32). In our daily routines, we must continually ask whether our deeds will bring honor and add luster to the Name of God. This pertains not only to prayers or worship, but to our everyday activities.

160

Maimonides states that if a highly moral person of impeccable character commits a wrong, that person is profaning God's Name. For example, if someone famous for wisdom and piety buys something and puts off paying for it, even if he can afford it and intends to pay later on, this profanes God's Name.

You shall not desecrate   וְלֹא תְחַלְּלוּ

My holy Name.   אֶת שֵׁם קָדְשִׁי.

Leviticus 22:32

3. Counting of the omer סְפִירַת הָעוֹמֶר. In order to appreciate a momentous experience to the fullest extent, we must prepare our mood and direct our perspective in order to receive its full impact. Seven weeks after Passover the revelation at Mount Sinai took place, when God gave the Jewish people His commandments. The Israelites were commanded to count forty-nine days after the first day of Passover, in order to heighten their anticipation of this monumental event. Jews today continue to fulfill this mitzvah, referred to as the counting of the omer. The word *omer* referred to a sheaf of new barley that customarily was brought to the ancient Temple on the second day of Passover. Only after the sheaf had been offered in the Temple was the produce of the new harvest permitted for general use. After the Temple was destroyed, the omer could no longer be brought to the priest, but the tradition of counting the days between Passover and Shavuot continued to be observed throughout the centuries.

Notable Quotations ציטטים

Do not pervert	וְלֹא תְחַלְּלוּ
My holy Name,	אֶת־שֵׁם קָדְשִׁי,
but I shall be sanctified	וְנִקְדַּשְׁתִּי
among the children of Israel.	בְּתוֹךְ בְּנֵי יִשְׂרָאֵל.

Leviticus 22:32

Six days shall you do	שֵׁשֶׁת יָמִים תֵּעָשֶׂה
work, but	מְלָאכָה,
on the seventh day there shall be	וּבַיּוֹם הַשְּׁבִיעִי
a Sabbath of solemn rest,	שַׁבַּת שַׁבָּתוֹן,
a holy assembly;	מִקְרָא־קֹדֶשׁ;
you shall do no kind of work.	כָּל־מְלָאכָה לֹא תַעֲשׂוּ.

Leviticus 23:3

You shall count	וּסְפַרְתֶּם לָכֶם
from the morrow after the Sabbath,	מִמָּחֳרַת הַשַּׁבָּת,
from the day that you brought	מִיּוֹם הֲבִיאֲכֶם
the *omer* as an offering	אֶת־עֹמֶר הַתְּנוּפָה
seven weeks	שֶׁבַע שַׁבָּתוֹת
shall be counted.	תְּמִימֹת תִּהְיֶינָה.

Leviticus 23:15

You shall take for yourselves	וּלְקַחְתֶּם לָכֶם
on the first day	בַּיּוֹם הָרִאשׁוֹן
the fruit of a citron tree,	פְּרִי עֵץ הָדָר,
branches of palm trees,	כַּפֹּת תְּמָרִים,
boughs from thick trees,	וַעֲנַף עֵץ־עָבֹת
and willows of the brook;	וְעַרְבֵי־נָחַל;
and you shall rejoice before	וּשְׂמַחְתֶּם לִפְנֵי
the Lord your God	יְהֹוָה אֱלֹהֵיכֶם
for seven days.	שִׁבְעַת יָמִים.

Leviticus 23:40

162

הַפְטָרַת אֱמֹר

The Haftarah (Ezekiel 44:15–31)

Summary הַסִכּוּם

The Haftarah, taken from the last portion of the Book of Ezekiel, is a vision of the New Jerusalem and the New Temple that are to be built after the Babylonian captivity is over. If the Temple is to represent God's holiness, then its priests must not, as in the past, permit any violations. Therefore, only descendants of the loyal family of Zadok shall be the Jewish priests of the future. Such priests will be honorable, always working to teach the people the difference between right and wrong. In this Haftarah, Ezekiel undertakes to define their duties.

The Haftarah Connection הַקֶּשֶׁר

The theme relationship between the Torah portion and the Haftarah is that of the priestly duties. The Torah portion presents the many duties of the priests, such as keeping the sanctuary lamp burning at all times and placing twelve challot on the sanctuary table, freshly baked each Sabbath. Ezekiel, in the Haftarah, reviews the priestly duties for the exiled Babylonian Jews.

Important Concepts מוּשָׂגִים

1. Those who minister in the Temple must be free of violations.

2. One task of the priests is to teach people the difference between the holy and the profane.

163

Notable Quotations צִיטָטִים

The priests, the Levites,	וְהַכֹּהֲנִים, הַלְוִיִּם,
the sons of Zadok,	בְּנֵי צָדוֹק,
who were in charge of	אֲשֶׁר שָׁמְרוּ
My Sanctuary	אֶת־מִשְׁמֶרֶת מִקְדָּשִׁי
while the children of Israel strayed	בִּתְעוֹת בְּנֵי־יִשְׂרָאֵל
away from Me,	מֵעָלַי הֵמָּה
they may draw near to Me	יִקְרְבוּ אֵלַי
to serve Me.	לְשָׁרְתֵנִי.

Ezekiel 44:15

They shall teach My people	וְאֶת־עַמִּי יוֹרוּ
the difference between the holy	בֵּין קֹדֶשׁ
and the ordinary	לְחֹל
and between the unclean	וּבֵין־טָמֵא
and the clean.	לְטָהוֹר.

Ezekiel 44:23

Anything that dies a natural death	כָּל־נְבֵלָה
or that dies violently,	וּטְרֵפָה,
whether fowl or beast,	מִן־הָעוֹף וּמִן־הַבְּהֵמָה
shall not be eaten by the priests.	לֹא יֹאכְלוּ הַכֹּהֲנִים:

Ezekiel 44:31

בְּהַר

Behar (Leviticus 25:1–26:2)

Summary הַסְכּוּם

1. Laws regulating the Sabbath and the Jubilee Year.
2. Caring for the poor.
3. God's rewards and punishments.

Key Concepts and Values מוּשָׂגִים

1. The Sabbatical and Jubilee Year יוֹבֵל. Just as the Torah calls for a Sabbath day of rest for people after six days of work, it also commands a Sabbath year of rest for the land after every six years of cultivation. It also calls for a *Yovel*, or Jubilee, every fiftieth year, completing a cycle of seven Sabbatical years.

The Sabbatical year was meant to teach us that the land is not owned by us but by God, who has given it to us to hold in trust and manage in keeping with God's purposes. Every fiftieth year, Hebrew slaves and their families were given their freedom, and all tangible goods, except for houses within a walled city, reverted to their original owners. This law was likely intended as a safeguard against poverty. Economically, the Jubilee was designed to maintain an even distribution of wealth. Ethically speaking, the Jubilee reminded people that "the earth belongs to God" and that human beings must control their natural acquisitive instincts.

2. Free loans to the poor. In keeping with the biblical prohibition against usury (Leviticus 25:36–37), Jewish communities the world over have free loan societies which advance loans free of interest to Jews in need of such assistance. These organizations are often known as gemilut chasadim societies (i.e., societies for practicing acts of kindness).

Notable Mitzvot מִצְוֹת

1. Wronging one's neighbor (extortion). Leviticus 25:14 states that "if you sell ought to your neighbor . . . you shall not wrong one another." The Torah regards an exorbitant profit, whether on the part of the buyer or the seller, as extortion, and lays down one-sixth of the market value of the article as the maximum profit that may be made. Any greater profit renders the sale legally invalid, and the buyer or seller affected is permitted to annul the transaction.

> You shall not deceive　　אַל תּוֹנוּ
> one another.　　אִישׁ אֶת אָחִיו.
> *Leviticus 25:14*

2. Caring for the poor. Several examples of this mitzvah are mentioned in the Torah portion. The Israelites are told that when a kinsman must sell his property, another should raise funds for its repurchase. If a kinsman falls into debt, it is forbidden to charge interest on any money or food given to him. If his situation of poverty continues, and becoming enslaved is his only solution, he is to be treated as a hired laborer, not as a slave. If a poor Israelite is purchased by a resident alien (a non-Israelite), it is the obligation of his family to raise funds for his release. If he is fortunate and prospers while enslaved, he may purchase his own release (Leviticus 25:25, 35, 39, 47).

> They shall not be sold　　לֹא יִמָּכְרוּ
> as slaves are sold.　　מִמְכֶּרֶת עָבֶד.
> *Leviticus 25:42*

The Talmud sums up the art of doing tzedakah when it states that "the greatest charity is to enable the needy to earn a living" (Shabbat 63a).

Notable Quotations צִיטָטִים

In the seventh year there shall be a	וּבַשָּׁנָה הַשְּׁבִיעִת
Sabbath of solemn rest for the land,	שַׁבַּת שַׁבָּתוֹן יִהְיֶה לָאָרֶץ,
a Sabbath unto the Lord.	שַׁבָּת לַיהוָה.

Leviticus 25:4

And you shall proclaim liberty	וּקְרָאתֶם דְּרוֹר
throughout the land to	בָּאָרֶץ
all its inhabitants.	לְכָל־יֹשְׁבֶיהָ

Leviticus 25:10

This verse, in a somewhat different translation, is inscribed on the Liberty Bell.

The land shall not be sold	וְהָאָרֶץ לֹא תִמָּכֵר
in perpetuity,	לִצְמִתֻת,
for the land is Mine	כִּי־לִי הָאָרֶץ
because strangers and settlers	כִּי־גֵרִים וְתוֹשָׁבִים
are you to Me.	אַתֶּם עִמָּדִי:

Leviticus 25:23

הַפְטָרַת בְּהַר

The Haftarah (Jeremiah 32:6–27)

Summary הַסְכּוּם

It was in the year 587 B.C.E., during the siege of Jerusalem, when Jeremiah was in prison because of his outspoken foretelling of the inevitable capture of the city by the Babylonians. At that dark hour, Jeremiah redeemed a piece of land, so that it would not pass out of his family.

Jeremiah now looks beyond the storm of judgment to the hope for brighter times. In the offer of redemption that is made to him by a kinsman, he sees a God-sent opportunity to show forth to his people a divine pledge that the night of captivity will be followed by the morning of return, when houses will once again be freely bought and sold.

The Haftarah Connection הַקֶּשֶׁר

Jeremiah's act of redeeming land is the link with the Jubilee redemption in the Torah portion, where the land was to be returned to its original owners so that a new beginning could be made.

Important Concepts מוּשָׂגִים

1. There is nothing too difficult for God.
2. Ownership of land and family plots was a serious enterprise.

Notable Quotations צִיטָטִים

Buy my field	קְנֵה לְךָ אֶת־שָׂדִי
that is in Anatoth,	אֲשֶׁר בַּעֲנָתוֹת,
for the right of redemption is yours	כִּי לְךָ מִשְׁפַּט הַגְּאֻלָּה
to buy it.	לִקְנוֹת.

Jeremiah 32:7

Behold, I am the Lord,	הִנֵּה אֲנִי יְהוָֹה,
the God of all humankind;	אֱלֹהֵי כָּל־בָּשָׂר;
is there anything impossible for Me?	הֲמִמֶּנִּי יִפָּלֵא כָּל־דָּבָר?

Jeremiah 32:27

בְּחֻקֹּתַי

Bechukkotai (Leviticus 26:3–27:34)

Summary הַסִּכּוּם

1. Ban on idolatry.

2. Sabbath observance.

3. Reverence for the tabernacle.

4. Rewards for obedience to God's law and punishments for disobedience.

5. Tithes and valuations of offerings.

6. Vows.

Key Concepts and Values מוּשָׂגִים

1. Rewards and punishments: the consequences of our choices and actions. Many ancient Near Eastern nations developed legal systems that promised great rewards for those who observed the laws and punishments for those who did not. This Torah portion offers a list of the blessings and curses facing the Israelites. They are promised prosperity, peace, and victory over their enemies if they follow God's laws. On the other hand, if they do not choose to follow God's laws, they will be punished with diseases, crop failures, and the death of their flocks and children (Leviticus 26:3–38).

The Hebrew name for the chapter of admonitions is *tochechah* תּוֹכֵחָה (lit. "warning"). Many commentaries on the Torah discuss God's relationship to human beings, and whether God rewards and punishes us according to our deeds. The only consensus seems to be that everything we do has consequences, and therefore that we ought always to think about the consequences of our acts. There is no necessary relationship between a person's merits and fortunes. A person of noble character may be lucky or miserable. The same holds true for the less noble. However, an honest and dependable

170

person is almost always respected and trusted. Kindness to others often evokes a similar response from them.

2. Keeping promises. Leviticus 27:2 speaks of vows. Keeping promises and meeting one's obligations are basic principles of Jewish faith. "It is better not to vow than to vow and not fulfill" (Ecclesiastes 5:4).

Notable Mitzvot מִצְוֹת

None.

Notable Quotations צִיטָטִים

You shall eat your bread	וַאֲכַלְתֶּם לַחְמְכֶם
until you are full	לָשׂבַע
and dwell in your land securely.	וִישַׁבְתֶּם לָבֶטַח בְּאַרְצְכֶם.

Leviticus 26:5

I will give peace to the land,	וְנָתַתִּי שָׁלוֹם בָּאָרֶץ,
you shall sleep	וּשְׁכַבְתֶּם
and no one shall frighten you.	וְאֵין מַחֲרִיד.

Leviticus 26:6

You shall eat last year's harvest;	וַאֲכַלְתֶּם יָשָׁן נוֹשָׁן;
and the old from before the new	וְיָשָׁן מִפְּנֵי חָדָשׁ
shall be thrown out.	תּוֹצִיאוּ.

Leviticus 26:10

YOU HAVE NOW FINISHED THE BOOK OF VAYIKRA

חֲזַק חֲזַק וְנִתְחַזֵּק

Masoretic Notes:

The Book of Vayikra contains: 859 verses

27 chapters

10 Sidrot

הַפְטָרַת בְּחֻקֹּתַי

The Haftarah (Jeremiah 16:19—17:14)

Summary הַסִכּוּם

Jeremiah in the Haftarah is troubled by all of the wrongdoing of the people of Israel. He warns them about the difficult times ahead, but the people are inattentive. Jeremiah does, however, hold out a message of great hope. God will in the future redeem the Israelites from Babylonian captivity.

The Haftarah Connection הַקֶּשֶׁר

The theme that links the Torah portion and the Haftarah is reward and punishment. The Torah portion deals with the blessings and curses that will befall the Israelites, depending upon whether or not they heed the word of God. In the Haftarah, Jeremiah reaffirms the same theme. Blessed will be the person who trusts in God, but cursed, says Jeremiah, will be the person whose heart departs from God.

Important Concepts מוּשָׂגִים

1. People who trust in God will be blessed by God.
2. Human nature is such that people are prone to sin.

Notable Quotations צִיטָטִים

A curse on the man · אָרוּר הַגֶּבֶר

that trusts people, · אֲשֶׁר יִבְטַח בָּאָדָם

and relies on things of flesh. · וְשָׂם בָּשָׂר זְרֹעוֹ.

Jeremiah 17:5

Blessed is the man · בָּרוּךְ הַגֶּבֶר

that relies on God, · אֲשֶׁר יִבְטַח בַּיהוָה,

for whom God is a refuge. · וְהָיָה יְהוָה מִבְטַחוֹ.

Jeremiah 17:7

Heal me, God, and I shall be healed, · רְפָאֵנִי יְהוָה וְאֵרָפֵא,

Save me, and I shall be saved, · הוֹשִׁיעֵנִי וְאִוָּשֵׁעָה,

for You are my hope. · כִּי תְהִלָּתִי אָתָּה.

Jeremiah 17:14

בְּמִדְבַּר

Bemidbar (Numbers 1:1–4:20)

Summary הַסְכּוּם

1. God commands Moses to take a census of the entire Israelite community.

2. Arrangement of the Israelite camp and order of march.

3. The Levites and their duties.

Key Concepts and Values מוּשָׂגִים

1. Taking a census. God commands Moses to take a census of the Israelites. The numbering of the people will assist in organizing those who are eligible for army duty. Several censuses are conducted in the Torah, and the ancient sages often asked why this was so. Numbers Rabbah 2:19 says that it was to demonstrate God's love for the Jewish people. God, it explained, is like a king who possesses an amazing treasure. Adoring it, He takes it into His hands each day to caress it and count it, making sure that nothing is lost. So too, said the rabbis, with the Jewish people. God loves to count them, and with each counting declares, "I have created the magnificent stars of the universe, yet it is Israel who will do My Will."

2. Pidyon haben: redemption of the firstborn פִּדְיוֹן הַבֵּן**.** At the age of thirty days, all male Jewish infants except those of Aaronide or levitical descent pass through a ritual known as pidyon haben (redemption of the firstborn). Originally, all firstborn sons of the children of Israel were required to perform priestly services, because the firstborn of Israel had been spared when the firstborn of Egypt were slain. In Numbers 3:12 we are told that the Levites were assigned to perform these services instead of the firstborn sons. All other firstborns must be redeemed. In ancient times this was done by a special offering. Since the destruction of the Temple, a donation to tzedakah has taken the place of a sacrifice.

Notable Mitzvot מִצְווֹת

Redemption of the firstborn son. See above for explanation.

Notable Quotations צִיטָטִים

<table>
<tr><td>From twenty years old</td><td>מִבֶּן עֶשְׂרִים שָׁנָה</td></tr>
<tr><td>and upward, all those who go war</td><td>וָמַעְלָה כָּל־יֹצֵא צָבָא</td></tr>
<tr><td>in Israel,</td><td>בְּיִשְׂרָאֵל,</td></tr>
<tr><td>you shall number them</td><td>תִּפְקְדוּ אֹתָם</td></tr>
<tr><td>by their divisions,</td><td>לְצִבְאֹתָם</td></tr>
<tr><td>you and Aaron.</td><td>אַתָּה וְאַהֲרֹן.</td></tr>
</table>

Numbers 1:3

<table>
<tr><td>Behold, I have separated</td><td>וַאֲנִי הִנֵּה לָקַחְתִּי</td></tr>
<tr><td>the Levites</td><td>אֶת־הַלְוִיִּם</td></tr>
<tr><td>from among the children of Israel</td><td>מִתּוֹךְ בְּנֵי יִשְׂרָאֵל</td></tr>
<tr><td>instead of all the firstborn</td><td>תַּחַת כָּל־בְּכוֹר פֶּטֶר רֶחֶם</td></tr>
<tr><td>children of Israel,</td><td>מִבְּנֵי יִשְׂרָאֵל,</td></tr>
<tr><td>and the Levites shall be Mine.</td><td>וְהָיוּ לִי הַלְוִיִּם.</td></tr>
</table>

Numbers 3:12

<table>
<tr><td>They shall not be allowed to see</td><td>וְלֹא־יָבֹאוּ לִרְאוֹת</td></tr>
<tr><td>the holy things as they are packed,</td><td>כְּבַלַּע אֶת־הַקֹּדֶשׁ,</td></tr>
<tr><td>lest they die.</td><td>וָמֵתוּ.</td></tr>
</table>

Numbers 4:20

הַפְטָרַת בְּמִדְבַּר

The Haftarah (Hosea 2:1–22)

Summary הַסְכּוּם

The Haftarah tells the story of the unhappy marriage of Hosea. Although he loved his wife, Gomer, she was unfaithful to him. He would often plead with her to return home. Hosea uses the story of his own personal life as a parallel to that of the life of the Israelites vis-à-vis God. God had betrothed the children of Israel, and they had now forsaken Him by following idolatrous ways. As a result, Israel would have to pay the penalty. However, in the end, there would be a reunion between the Israelites and God, and God would again shine his blessings down upon His people.

The Haftarah Connection הַקֶּשֶׁר

The theme link between the Torah portion and the Haftarah is that of infidelity. Hosea's marital difficulties symbolized the story of the nation of Israel. God had chosen the poor, downtrodden Israelites to be His love, showering blessings upon them and giving them a national home. Instead of serving God in truth, the Israelites turned to idolatrous practices. Similarly, Hosea loved Gomer, but she forsook him.

Important Concepts מוּשָׂגִים

1. Repentance must be deep and lasting.
2. God will endow Israel, His bride, with righteousness, lovingkindness, and faithfulness.

Notable Quotations צִיטָטִים

I will uncover her shame
before her lovers,
and none shall rescue her
from My hand.

וְעַתָּה אֲגַלֶּה אֶת־נַבְלֻתָהּ
לְעֵינֵי מְאַהֲבֶיהָ,
וְאִישׁ לֹא־יַצִּילֶנָּה
מִיָּדִי.

Hosea 2:12

I will betroth you to Me
with faithfulness,
and you shall know the Lord.

וְאֵרַשְׂתִּיךְ לִי
בֶּאֱמוּנָה,
וְיָדַעַתְּ אֶת־יְהֹוָה.

Hosea 2:22

This verse is recited when putting tefillin on one's hand.

נָשֹׂא

Naso (Numbers 4:21–7:89)

Summary הַסְכּוּם

1. Enumeration of Levite families and their duties.
2. Removal of unclean persons from the Israelite camp.
3. Law of jealousy.
4. The Nazirite Code.
5. The Priestly Blessing.
6. Offerings of the tribal chieftains.

Key Concepts and Values מוּשָׂגִים

1. Ma'al: trespass מַעַל. "When a man or woman shall commit any sin that men commit, to commit a trespass against the Lord . . . then they shall confess their sin . . . and he shall make restitution for his guilt in full" (Numbers 5:6–7). Bachya Ibn Pakuda taught that someone who has committed a wrong against another person has thereby sinned against God, since God requires of us that we deal justly with everyone else. Accordingly, we can expect forgiveness from God only if we have made amends for whatever wrong we may have done to others.

2. Nazirite נָזִיר. The Nazirite was a person who vowed to abstain from various pleasures and to dedicate himself to God for a specific period of time not less than thirty days. Jewish tradition, however, has always discouraged austerity and frowns on hermits or recluses who permanently isolate themselves from the rest of the Jewish community.

178

3. Birkat Kohanim: the Priestly Blessing בִּרְכַּת כּוֹהֲנִים.
The Priestly Blessing (Numbers 6:24–27) was an impressive feature of the ancient Temple service. It appears in the daily morning service. On the major festivals in traditional synagogues, it is pronounced by the kohanim from the bimah. On the eve of the Sabbath, parents often invoke God's blessing on their children with the words of the Priestly Blessing. It is also frequently recited at the conclusion of a service, at Bar and Bat Mitzvahs, and at weddings.

Notable Mitzvot מִצְווֹת

1. Confession of sins וִדּוּי. "They shall confess their sin which they have committed" (Numbers 5:7). Through confession of one's mistakes, one recognizes and pinpoints one's transgressions and resolves to avoid repeating the same mistake. Without this opportunity to confess, there would be less hope for atonement. The criterion of sincere repentance is the true change of heart that one has, when faced with the same temptation to commit a sin to which one had previously succumbed.

They shall confess their sins	וְהִתְוַדּוּ אֶת חַטָּאתָם
which they have committed.	אֲשֶׁר עָשׂוּ.

Numbers 5:7

2. The Priestly Blessing בִּרְכַּת כּוֹהֲנִים. The priest was delegated to offer God's blessings. The blessing consists of three parts: "The Lord bless you and keep you; the Lord make His face to shine upon you and be gracious to you; the Lord lift up His countenance unto you and give you peace." Many families bless their children before sitting down to the Sabbath evening meal. The blessing for boys invokes the shining examples of Jacob's grandchildren Ephraim and Manasseh, who, although raised in Egypt, did not lose their identity as Jews. The blessing for girls refers to

179

the four matriarchs, Sarah, Rebekah, Rachel, and Leah, all of whom were known for their concern and compassion for others.

Notable Quotations צִיטָטִים

When either a man or woman	אִישׁ אוֹ־אִשָּׁה
wishes to make a vow,	כִּי יַפְלִא לִנְדֹּר,
the vow of a Nazirite,	נֶדֶר נָזִיר,
to consecrate himself to the Lord,	לְהַזִּיר לַיהוָה,
from wine and strong drink	מִיַּיִן וְשֵׁכָר
he shall abstain.	יַזִּיר.

Numbers 6:2–3

May God bless you	יְבָרֶכְךָ יְהוָה
and keep you	וְיִשְׁמְרֶךָ.
May God shine His face upon you	יָאֵר יְהוָה פָּנָיו אֵלֶיךָ
and be gracious to you.	וִיחֻנֶּךָּ.
May God lift up His face to you	יִשָּׂא יְהוָה פָּנָיו אֵלֶיךָ
and grant you peace.	וְיָשֵׂם לְךָ שָׁלוֹם.

Numbers 6:24–26

הַפְטָרַת נָשֹׁא

The Haftarah (Judges 13:2–25)

Summary הַסְכּוּם

The Haftarah describes the beginnings of Samson's life. Samson was a judge, a military and political leader of the Israelites. Judges were the leaders of Israel in the period immediately following the conquest of the land under Joshua until the anointing of Saul as Israel's first king.

Samson's mother is childless, but an angel of God appears to her and announces that she will become pregnant. He instructs her not to drink alcoholic beverages because her son is to be a Nazirite, consecrated to God. Nazirites were not permitted to cut their hair, use alcoholic beverages, or have contact with the dead. The angel further informs Samson's mother that her son will save Israel from the Philistines.

The Haftarah Connection הַקֶּשֶׁר

The theme link between the Torah portion and the Haftarah is that of the Nazirite and his devotion to God. The Torah portion describes the details of the Nazirite, while the Haftarah tells of the birth of Samson who is destined to be a Nazirite.

Important Concepts מוּשָׂגִים

Nazirites in ancient times totally gave their lives to God.

181

Notable Quotations צִיטָטִים

You shall conceive	כִּי הִנָּךְ הָרָה
and bear a son,	וְיָלַדְתְּ בֵּן,
and no razor shall touch	וּמוֹרָה לֹא־יַעֲלֶה
his head,	עַל־רֹאשׁוֹ,
for a Nazirite to God	כִּי־נְזִיר אֱלֹהִים
shall the boy be	יִהְיֶה הַנַּעַר
at birth.	מִן־הַבָּטֶן.

Judges 13:5

And the woman bore a son,	וַתֵּלֶד הָאִשָּׁה בֵּן,
and called his name Samson.	וַתִּקְרָא אֶת־שְׁמוֹ שִׁמְשׁוֹן.
The child grew up,	וַיִּגְדַּל הַנַּעַר,
and the Lord blessed him.	וַיְבָרְכֵהוּ יְהֹוָה.

Judges 13:24

בְּהַעֲלֹתְךָ

Beha'alotecha (Numbers 8:1–12:16)

Summary הַסְכּוּם

1. Description of the seven-branched candelabrum (menorah).
2. The dedication of the Levites.
3. The second Passover.
4. Journey from Sinai to Moab.
5. Murmurings of the children of Israel.
6. Appointment of seventy elders to assist Moses.
7. Miriam and Aaron speak against Moses.

Key Concepts and Values מוּשָׂגִים

1. Responding to complaints. Two years after receiving the commandments at Mount Sinai and building the sanctuary, the Israelites raise their voices with bitter complaints. The people wax nostalgic, deceiving themselves about the conditions under which they lived in Egypt. "If only we had meat to eat. Remember the cucumbers, the melons, the leeks, the onions, and the garlic" (Numbers 11:4–7).

Bible commentators ask two questions about the grievances and grumbling of the people: What caused them? What might have been an appropriate response by Moses? Rashi suggested that the Israelites were exhausted from their journey, and, not having enough time to rest, raise their voices in protest. Rabbi Samson Raphael Hirsch argued that the Israelites are suffering from boredom, since almost all of their needs have been met. Each day they are given

183

heavenly manna and fresh water. Frustrated at having no goal, they complain to Moses.

Hearing their complaints, Moses voices a few of his own. Feeling isolated and besieged, he asks God: "Why have you dealt ill with Your servant, and why have I not enjoyed Your favor?" According to the Torah, God responds by telling him to appoint seventy elders and officers, men of experience, to share the burden of leadership with him. Here we see the Torah's suggested model for leadership—not to grumble or complain but rather to gather experienced people around you to share the burden.

2. No monopoly on spiritual leadership. Rather than being consumed with jealousy when he hears that Eldad and Medad are prophesying in the camp, Moses encourages all of the Israelites to join the ranks of the prophets by bearing witness to God. Rabbi Samson Raphael Hirsch commented that there is no monopoly on spiritual leadership, which is granted by God to all people. In Judaism, the synagogue and its other institutions encourage active participation by all, and ought not to be the exclusive privilege of the wealthy.

Notable Mitzvot מִצְוֹת

1. Sounding the shofar תְּקִיעַת שׁוֹפָר. In this Torah portion we learn of the obligation to sound the shofar as an alarm in time of war. The shofar was also to be sounded on holidays. Today all Jews have the obligation to listen to the sounds of the shofar as they are sounded on Rosh Hashanah. The shofar's shrill sounds are designed to awaken us to contemplate our mistakes and make amends. In addition, the shofar was sounded on Rosh Chodesh, the new month. Many congregations today continue to sound the shofar to usher in every new month.

If you go to war,	‏. . . וְכִי תָבֹאוּ מִלְחָמָה
you will blow *teruot* with trumpets	‏. . . וַהֲרֵעֹתֶם בַּחֲצֹצְרֹת
You will blow *tekiot* with trumpets	‏וּתְקַעְתֶּם בַּחֲצֹצְרֹת עַל
over your burnt offerings and over	‏עֹלֹתֵיכֶם וְעַל
your sacrifices of peace.	‏זִבְחֵי שַׁלְמֵיכֶם.

Numbers 10:9–10

2. Observance of the so-called Second Passover ‏פֶּסַח שֵׁנִי.
The Torah specifies that persons on a long journey are privileged
to observe the Passover a month later. Among the rituals
accompanying this Passover were the eating of unleavened bread
and bitter herbs as well as the negative precept not to break any
bones of the Second Passover offering (Numbers 9:12).

Notable Quotations ‏צִיטָטִים

When you light the lamps,	‏בְּהַעֲלֹתְךָ אֶת־הַנֵּרֹת,
by the front of the candlestick	‏אֶל־מוּל פְּנֵי הַמְּנוֹרָה
the seven lamps shall cast light.	‏יָאִירוּ שִׁבְעַת הַנֵּרוֹת.

Numbers 8:2

And it came to pass	‏וַיְהִי
when the ark travelled forward,	‏בִּנְסֹעַ הָאָרֹן,
that Moses said:	‏וַיֹּאמֶר מֹשֶׁה
"Rise up, O God!	‏"קוּמָה יְהֹוָה!
May Your enemies be scattered	‏וְיָפֻצוּ אֹיְבֶיךָ
and let them flee	‏וְיָנֻסוּ מְשַׂנְאֶיךָ
from in front of You	‏מִפָּנֶיךָ."
and when it stopped, he said:	‏וּבְנֻחֹה יֹאמַר:
"Return, God, to the ten thousands	‏"שׁוּבָה יְהֹוָה רִבְבוֹת
of the families of Israel."	‏אַלְפֵי יִשְׂרָאֵל."

Numbers 10:35–36

**This verse forms the opening paragraph of the service for
taking out the Torah scroll on Sabbaths and festivals.**

If you go to war, . . . וְכִי תָבֹאוּ מִלְחָמָה . . .

you will blow *teruot* with trumpets . . . וַהֲרֵעֹתֶם בַּחֲצֹצְרֹת . . .

You will blow *tekiot* with trumpets וּתְקַעְתֶּם בַּחֲצֹצְרֹת עַל

over your burnt offerings and over עֹלֹתֵיכֶם וְעַל

your sacrifices of peace. זִבְחֵי שַׁלְמֵיכֶם.

Numbers 10:9–10

If only the Lord's people וּמִי יִתֵּן כָּל־עַם יְהוָה

were all prophets. נְבִיאִים.

Numbers 11:29

הַפְטָרַת בְּהַעֲלֹתְךָ

The Haftarah (Zechariah 2:14–4:7)

Summary הַסִּכּוּם

Zechariah was one of the exiles who returned from Babylon when Cyrus promulgated his decree of restoration in the year 537. In this Haftarah, Zechariah assures the exiled people of the divine assistance in their work of rebuilding the Temple and of national rehabilitation. The Haftarah concludes with the famous words "Not by might, nor by power, but by My spirit, says the Lord of Hosts." These words proclaim the lesson of all of Jewish history. It is certainly the prophetic teaching of the Maccabean festival of Hanukkah, with which Zechariah's name is linked in the synagogue service.

The Haftarah Connection הַקֶּשֶׁר

Toward the end of the Haftarah Zechariah has a vision of a seven-branched candleholder, the kind that stood in the Second Temple. The candleholder provides the theme link between the Haftarah and the Torah portion, which begins with the lighting of the seven-branched menorah by Aaron.

Important Concepts מוּשָׂגִים

1. It is not through might but by means of God's spirit that great things have been achieved by the Jewish people.

2. The first condition of the priesthood is that a priest shall observe the divine requirements of conduct.

187

Notable Quotations צִיטָטִים

Sing and rejoice, Daughter of Zion,	רָנִּי וְשִׂמְחִי בַּת־צִיּוֹן,
for I am coming,	כִּי הִנְנִי־בָא,
and I will dwell in your midst,	וְשָׁכַנְתִּי בְתוֹכֵךְ,
says the Lord.	נְאֻם־יְהֹוָה.

Zechariah 2:14

Thus says the Lord of Hosts:	כֹּה־אָמַר יְהֹוָה צְבָאוֹת:
If you will walk in My ways,	אִם־בִּדְרָכַי תֵּלֵךְ
and if you will observe	וְאִם אֶת־מִשְׁמַרְתִּי
my requirements	תִּשְׁמֹר
you govern My house,	וְגַם־אַתָּה תָּדִין אֶת־בֵּיתִי
and preside over My courts,	וְגַם תִּשְׁמֹר חֲצֵרָי
then I will give you free access	וְנָתַתִּי לְךָ מַהְלְכִים
among these that stand by.	בֵּין הָעֹמְדִים הָאֵלֶּה.

Zechariah 3:7

Not by might, nor by power,	לֹא בְחַיִל וְלֹא בְכֹחַ,
but by My spirit,	כִּי אִם־בְּרוּחִי,
says the Lord of Hosts.	אָמַר יְהֹוָה צְבָאוֹת.

Zechariah 4:6

שְׁלַח־לְךָ

Shelach Lecha (Numbers 13:1–15:41)

Summary הַסְכּוּם

1. The ten spies and their reports.
2. The children of Israel rebel.
3. The punishment of the children of Israel.
4. Rules pertaining to various sacrificial offerings.
5. Tzitzit—the fringes of the prayer shawl.

Key Concepts and Values מוּשָׂגִים

1. The sin of the spies: looking on oneself as insignificant.
The twelve spies reported back to Moses that the Canaanites who
inhabited the land were so large and powerful that they felt, in
comparison, like grasshoppers. It is not clear whether their report
was credible or only a figment of their imagination. In any event,
the Torah appears to be warning that if we look upon ourselves as
small and insignificant, others will take us precisely at our own
self-evaluation.

2. The tallit טַלִּית. Moses instructs the Israelites in this Torah
portion to wear tzitzit (fringes) on the corners of their garments
throughout their generations. He explains that the fringe is to recall
all of God's commandments. Today the prayershawl has become
the four-cornered garment of responsibility, worn by adult males
who become Bar Mitzvah and by many adult females as well.
Commenting on the Hebrew word צִיצִית, the commentator Rashi
notes that its numerical value is 600 (צ = 90, י = 10, צ = 90, י =

10, ת = 400) and that the fringe is tied with eight threads and five knots. Together the full numerical equivalent comes to 613, which is the total number of commandments in the Torah.

Notable Mitzvot מִצְוֹת

   1. Challah חַלָּה. This mitzvah relates to the precept of challah, a portion of dough set aside for the kohen (Numbers 15:20). At the root of this precept lies the reason that our sustenance is by food, and that most of the world lives on bread. God wishes to make us meritorious by a means of a constant mitzvah with bread, so that blessing will dwell on it through the religious good deed. Today, when they bake challah, traditional Jews often remove a token amount of dough and throw it into the oven while reciting a specific blessing. This custom reflects the ancient custom of giving challah to the priests.

As the first of your doughs	רֵאשִׁית
you shall set aside a cake	עֲרִסֹתֵכֶם חַלָּה
for a heave-offering.	תָּרִימוּ תְרוּמָה.

Numbers 15:20

   2. Tzitzit צִיצִית. The mitzvah of the tzitzit is considered one of the most important of all mitzvot. The rabbis often equated this one mitzvah with the rest of the 613. First, the Torah hints at its importance when it says, "When you see it, you shall remember all the mitzvot" (Numbers 15:39). Today the tzitzit of the prayershawl are constant reminders to us of our duties to God and of the special relationship in which we stand to God. The blue thread in the tzitzit, say the rabbis, resembles the sea, the sea resembles the heavens, and the heavens resemble the Throne of Glory. Thus, the outward act of looking upon the tzitzit was to the Israelite an inward act of spiritual conformity with the precepts of God.

Notable Quotations צִיטָטִים

Go up in the south,	עֲלוּ זֶה בַּנֶּגֶב,
and go up into the mountains	וַעֲלִיתֶם אֶת־הָהָר
and see the land,	וּרְאִיתֶם אֶת־הָאָרֶץ,
for what it is.	מַה־הִוא.
And the people that dwell in it,	וְאֶת־הָעָם הַיּשֵׁב עָלֶיהָ,
whether they are strong or weak,	הֶחָזָק הוּא הֲרָפֶה,
few or many.	הַמְעַט הוּא אִם־רָב.

Numbers 13:17–18

And they cut from there a branch	וַיִּכְרְתוּ מִשָּׁם זְמוֹרָה
with one cluster of grapes,	וְאֶשְׁכּוֹל עֲנָבִים אֶחָד,
and they carried it on a pole	וַיִּשָּׂאֻהוּ בַמּוֹט
between the two.	בִּשְׁנָיִם.

Numbers 13:23

And we were in our own eyes	וַנְּהִי בְעֵינֵינוּ
as grasshoppers	כַּחֲגָבִים
and so we were in their eyes.	וְכֵן הָיִינוּ בְּעֵינֵיהֶם.

Numbers 13:33

Speak to the children of Israel,	דַּבֵּר אֶל־בְּנֵי יִשְׂרָאֵל,
and say to them	וְאָמַרְתָּ אֲלֵהֶם
that they shall make fringes	וְעָשׂוּ לָהֶם צִיצִת
on the corners of their garments	עַל־כַּנְפֵי בִגְדֵיהֶם
throughout their generations.	לְדֹרֹתָם.

Numbers 15:38

הַפְטָרַת שְׁלַח־לְךָ

The Haftarah (Joshua 2:1–24)

Summary הַסְכּוּם

The Haftarah tells the story of two men sent by Joshua to Jericho. The purpose of this venture was to determine the morale of the Canaanites. The two spies are eventually sheltered in the home of Rachab, a prostitute, who assures them that the Israelites will be able to conquer the country. She asks the spies to save her and her family when Israel is victorious, and they agree to do so. On their return to the camp of the Israelites, the two men assure Joshua that victory is indeed close at hand.

The Haftarah Connection הַקֶּשֶׁר

The Torah portion and the Haftarah are linked by the theme of spies in the time of Moses and in the time of Joshua.

Important Concepts מוּשָׂגִים

1. God is both in the heavens and on earth.
2. An act of kindness often begets another.

Notable Quotations   צִיטָטִים

Now,	וְעַתָּה
swear to me by the Lord,	הִשָּׁבְעוּ־נָא לִי בַּיהוָה
since I have shown kindess to you,	כִּי־עָשִׂיתִי עִמָּכֶם חָסֶד
that you will also show kindness	וַעֲשִׂיתֶם גַּם־אַתֶּם
to my father's house.	עִם־בֵּית אָבִי חֶסֶד

Joshua 2:12

Our life for yours, to death	נַפְשֵׁנוּ תַחְתֵּיכֶם לָמוּת
if you do not betray	אִם לֹא תַגִּידוּ
our mission.	אֶת־דְּבָרֵנוּ זֶה.
Then, when the Lord gives	וְהָיָה בְּתֵת־יְהוָה
the land to us, then we will deal	לָנוּ אֶת־הָאָרֶץ
kindly and faithfully with you.	וְעָשִׂינוּ עִמָּךְ חֶסֶד וֶאֱמֶת.

Joshua 2:14

Truly the Lord has delivered	כִּי־נָתַן יְהוָה
into our hands	בְּיָדֵנוּ
all of the land.	אֶת־כָּל־הָאָרֶץ

Joshua 2:24

קֹרַח

Korach (Numbers 16:1–18:32)

Summary הַסְכּוּם

1. The rebellion of Korach, Dathan, Abiram, and On.
2. The destruction of the rebels.
3. The vindication of Aaron.
4. Additional rules pertaining to the Levites.
5. The priestly tithes and tithes for the support of the Levites.

Key Concepts and Values מוּשָׂגִים

1. Challenging authority. Korach's uprising came immediately following the frightening report brought by the twelve scouts. Korach exploited the people's despair, sensing that this would be an opportune time to spur a revolt. Challenging the authority of Moses, Korach's clear intent was to undercut Moses and gain the priesthood for himself. Woven into this battle was a second protest against Moses led by Dathan, Abiram, and On. They accused him of promising the people a land flowing with milk and honey, but instead exposing them to death in the desert. Like Korach, they too were intent on stirring up a revolt against Moses' leadership. Ultimately, the rebellion of all of these men was thwarted by God, who "drowned" them in a massive earthquake.

This story comes to warn us to exercise caution in time of national and domestic crisis. There will always be contemporary Korachs who will attempt to collapse the prevailing leadership. We must do all that we can to thwart their efforts.

2. Ma'aser: Tithe מַעֲשֵׂר. In the days of the Temple, the Levites were supported by tithes (a tax in the amount of ten percent of total income) from every Israelite. The Levites in turn donated a tithe for the support of the kohanim.

3. Miracles in the Bible נִפְלָאוֹת. Some commentators consider the earthquake which swallows Korach and his followers to have been one of God's many miracles. Later in the Torah portion, Moses commands each of the twelve tribal chieftains to bring a staff to be placed in the sanctuary. The next day he discovered that Aaron's staff had miraculously sprouted, producing blossoms and almonds. Miraculous events are reported throughout the Bible: Balaam's talking donkey, the splitting of the Red Sea, manna from heaven, just to mention a few.

Early Jewish commentators suggested that all these miracles were planned by God at the very beginning of creation.

Notable Mitzvot מִצְווֹת

1. Pidyon Haben: redemption of the firstborn son פִּדְיוֹן הַבֵּן. It is a religious duty incumbent on every member of the Jewish people to redeem from the kohen his son who is the firstborn of his Jewish mother (Numbers 18:15). In earliest Jewish history, the firstborn males were dedicated to God's service, acting as servants in the Temple. This practice must have proven a hardship in many families. When the tribe of Levi was appointed to act as servants in the Temple, the requirements of service for the firstborn were eliminated. Every firstborn Israelite had to be redeemed by a payment of five shekels to a member of the tribe of Levi.

You shall redeem   פָּדֹה תִפְדֶּה

the first-born of man.   אֶת בְּכוֹר הָאָדָם.

Numbers 18:15

2. Levitical service at the sanctuary. The Levites were required to serve in the sanctuary, to be gatekeepers and singers over the offerings every day (Numbers 18:23). For the maintenance of the Levites, the people set aside a tenth of all of their yearly produce. The Levites in turn were to contribute to the priests a tenth part of that which they received from the people. Today, those of levitical heritage are entitled to receive the second aliyah to the Torah. In addition, in traditional synagogues, Levites wash the hands of the kohanim before they bless the congregation during the Musaf additional service on Sabbaths and festivals.

The Levi shall perform	וְעָבַד הַלֵּוִי הוּא
the service of the Tent of Meeting.	אֶת עֲבֹדַת אֹהֶל מוֹעֵד.

Numbers 18:23

Notable Quotations צִיטָטִים

It is too much for you;	רַב־לָכֶם כִּי
for this entire congregation is holy	כָל־הָעֵדָה כֻּלָּם קְדֹשִׁים
and God is in their midst.	וּבְתוֹכָם יְהֹוָה.
Why, then, do you place yourselves	וּמַדּוּעַ תִּתְנַשְּׂאוּ
above the assembly of God?	עַל־קְהַל יְהֹוָה?

Numbers 16:3

You must redeem	אַךְ פָּדֹה תִפְדֶּה
the firstborn of man,	אֵת בְּכוֹר הָאָדָם,
and the firstborn of unclean animals	וְאֵת בְּכוֹר־הַבְּהֵמָה
you must redeem.	הַטְּמֵאָה תִּפְדֶּה.

Numbers 18:15

הַפְטָרַת קֹרַח

The Haftarah (I Samuel 11:14–12:22)

Summary הַסְכּוּם

Samuel was the last and greatest of the judges. Samuel's task was to recreate the disintegrated Jewish nation and rebuild it out of ruins. He proved to be an outstanding judge and was able to reunite the Israelite tribes during the years of his leadership. The Haftarah tells of Saul's coming to the throne. Samuel's address bidding farewell to the people is also in this Haftarah.

When Samuel grew old, the Israelite leaders asked him to appoint a king over them. Samuel asked for God's help, and God told Samuel that Saul was the one who would be anointed the first king of Israel.

The Haftarah Connection הַקֶּשֶׁר

The theme link between the Haftarah and the Torah portion is that of the ingratitude of Israel toward its leaders. In the Torah portion, Korach and his followers try to wrest the leadership from the hands of Moses. In the time of Samuel, the Israelites call for a king to lead them in place of Samuel the judge.

Important Concepts מוּשָׂגִים

1. Leaders must be prepared to experience protests among their constituents.

2. Even a great leader will call on God for assistance from time to time.

197

Notable Quotations   צִיטָטִים

And they cried to God and said:	וַיִּזְעֲקוּ אֶל־יְהֹוָה וַיֹּאמְרוּ:
"We have sinned,	״חָטָאנוּ,
because we have deserted God,	כִּי עָזַבְנוּ אֶת־יְהֹוָה,
and have worshipped the Baalim	וַנַּעֲבֹד אֶת־הַבְּעָלִים
and the Ashtarot	וְאֶת־הָעַשְׁתָּרוֹת
now save us	וְעַתָּה הַצִּילֵנוּ
from the hands of our enemies	מִיַּד אֹיְבֵינוּ
and we will serve You."	וְנַעַבְדֶךָ.״

I Samuel 12:10

Samuel said to the people:	וַיֹּאמֶר שְׁמוּאֵל אֶל־הָעָם
"Do not be afraid.	״אַל־תִּירָאוּ
You have indeed done	אַתֶּם עֲשִׂיתֶם
all of this evil,	אֵת כָּל־הָרָעָה הַזֹּאת,
but do not turn away	אַךְ אַל־תָּסוּרוּ
from God,	מֵאַחֲרֵי יְהֹוָה,
instead serve God	וַעֲבַדְתֶּם אֶת־יְהֹוָה
with all your heart."	בְּכָל־לְבַבְכֶם.״

I Samuel 12:20

חֻקַּת

Chukkat (Numbers 19:1–22:1)

Summary הַסְכּוּם

1. The law of the red heifer.

2. The death of Miriam.

3. The sin of Moses and Aaron, and its punishment.

4. The king of Edom refuses the children of Israel permission to pass through his land.

5. The death of Aaron.

6. Rebellion, the resulting plague and its cure.

7. War with the Canaanites and the defeat of Og, king of Bashan.

Key Concepts and Values מוּשָׂגִים

1. Red heifer פָּרָה אֲדֻמָּה. The red heifer provides for the removal of defilement resulting from contact with the dead. A red cow, free from blemish and not yet broken to the yoke, was to be slain outside the camp. It was then to be burned on a pyre with cedarwood, hyssop, and scarlet. The gathered ashes were dissolved in fresh water and sprinkled on those who had become contaminated through contact with a dead body. Ironically, those who prepared the ashes of purification were defiled in the act of preparation.

Many commentators discussed this seemingly irrational law. The Targum Yerushalmi and Midrash Numbers Rabbah (chap. 2) held that the red heifer was intended to atone for the idolatry of the golden calf. Obadiah Sforno, the Italian commentator, offered a symbolic explanation for the red heifer. He points out that each element in the preparation is symbolic: the cedarwood stands tall, representing pride; the hyssop, a low-growing bush, represents humility; and the scarlet thread represents sinfulness. Thus, the ashes of the heifer combine pride, humility, and sinfulness. The sinner, who has allowed pride to rule, is purified and reminded to pursue humility and more moderate paths of behavior.

2. Punishment of Moses and Aaron. The people of Israel complain to Moses and Aaron that there is a shortage of water. Moses raises his hand and strikes the rock twice with his rod. Water flows forth, allowing them to drink. Moses is then told that because he did not trust in God, he will not lead the congregation of Israel into the Promised Land. Several rabbinic commentators point out that both Moses and Aaron were guilty of arrogance. Their instruction from God was to speak to the rock. Instead, Moses publicly strikes the rock two times, implying that he lacked faith in God.

Moses Maimonides claims that God punished Moses because of his exasperation with the complaints and quarreling of the Israelites. (Shemonah Perakim 4).

Notable Mitzvot מִצְווֹת

Ritual uncleanliness of the dead. In biblical times, a person who touched a corpse became defiled for seven days (Numbers 19:14). Today, too, it is customary to wash your hands with water before entering your home after visiting a cemetery. The commentator known as the Chinnuch explains that a person's only claim to sanctity, while alive, is in the possession of a soul. Without the soul, the body is mere waste matter. At death, when the soul departs, the body sinks to a degree of impurity (*Sefer HaChinnuch*, mitzvah no. 398).

This is the law for the instance   זֹאת הַתּוֹרָה

of a person dying in a tent.   אָדָם כִּי־יָמוּת בְּאֹהֶל.

Numbers 19:14

Notable Quotations   צִיטָטִים

You shall speak to the rock   וְדִבַּרְתֶּם אֶל־הַסֶּלַע

before their eyes,   לְעֵינֵיהֶם,

and it will pour out its waters,   וְנָתַן מֵימָיו,

and you shall bring them water   וְהוֹצֵאתָ לָהֶם מַיִם

from the rock to quench the thirst of   מִן־הַסֶּלַע וְהִשְׁקִיתָ

the community and their livestock.   אֶת־הָעֵדָה וְאֶת־בְּעִירָם.

Numbers 20:8

"Listen, you rebels!   שִׁמְעוּ־נָא הַמֹּרִים!"

From this rock, shall we   הֲמִן־הַסֶּלַע הַזֶּה,

make water gush for you?"   נוֹצִיא לָכֶם מַיִם?„

And Moses raised his hand   וַיָּרֶם מֹשֶׁה אֶת־יָדוֹ

and smote the rock   וַיַּךְ אֶת־הַסֶּלַע

with his rod twice;   בְּמַטֵּהוּ פַּעֲמָיִם;

water came out abundantly,   וַיֵּצְאוּ מַיִם רַבִּים,

and the congregation drank   וַתֵּשְׁתְּ הָעֵדָה

along with their cattle.   וּבְעִירָם.

Numbers 20:10–11

201

God said to Moses
and to Aaron:
"Because you did not believe in Me,
to respect Me
in the eyes of the children of Israel,
you therefore shall not bring
this assembly
into the land
which I have given to them."

וַיֹּאמֶר יְהֹוָה אֶל־מֹשֶׁה
וְאֶל־אַהֲרֹן:
״יַעַן לֹא־הֶאֱמַנְתֶּם בִּי
לְהַקְדִּישֵׁנִי
לְעֵינֵי בְּנֵי יִשְׂרָאֵל,
לָכֵן לֹא תָבִיאוּ
אֶת־הַקָּהָל הַזֶּה
אֶל־הָאָרֶץ
אֲשֶׁר־נָתַתִּי לָהֶם.״

Numbers 20:12

הַפְטָרַת חֻקַּת

The Haftarah (Judges 11:1–33)

Summary הַסְכּוּם

The Haftarah describes the days of lawlessness in Israel, the immorality of the neighboring nations, and the new judge called Jephthah who saved Israel from slavery. The Israelites, harried and troubled by the Ammonites, turned for assistance to Jephthah, whom they had previously ostracized because of his questionable background. Jephthah tried to negotiate a peaceful settlement with the Ammonites. When they did not accept, he had no choice but to fight them, leading his people to victory.

Before the battle, Jephthah makes a vow, stating that if God helps him in battle, he will offer whatsoever comes forth from the doors of his house as a burnt offering. It turns out that Jephthah's own daughter is the first to come forth from the doors of his home.

The Haftarah Connection הַקֶּשֶׁר

The theme link between the Haftarah and the Torah portion is the struggle with the Amorite peoples in the Torah portion and the Ammonites in the Haftarah.

Important Concepts מוּשָׂגִים

1. Persons of infamous origins may yet be the destined instrument of deliverance of a people.

2. One must be careful when making a vow or a promise.

203

Notable Quotations צִיטָטִים

They said to Jephthah:	וַיֹּאמְרוּ לְיִפְתָּח:
"Come and be our commander,	"לְכָה וְהָיִיתָה לָּנוּ לְקָצִין,
that we may do battle	וְנִלָּחֲמָה
with the children of Ammon."	בִּבְנֵי עַמּוֹן."

Judges 11:6

Jephthah made a vow to God	וַיִּדַּר יִפְתָּח נֶדֶר לַיהֹוָה
and said:	וַיֹּאמַר:
"If you will deliver	"אִם־נָתוֹן תִּתֵּן
the children of Ammon	אֶת־בְּנֵי עַמּוֹן
into my hand, then	בְּיָדִי: וְהָיָה
whoever meets me at	הַיּוֹצֵא אֲשֶׁר יֵצֵא
the doors of my house	מִדַּלְתֵי בֵיתִי לִקְרָאתִי
when I return in peace	בְּשׁוּבִי בְשָׁלוֹם
from the children of Ammon,	מִבְּנֵי עַמּוֹן,
shall belong to God."	וְהָיָה לַיהֹוָה."

Judges 11:30–31

בָּלָק

Balak (Numbers 22:2–25:9)

Summary הַסְכּוּם

1. Balak, king of Moab, sends Balaam to put a curse on the Israelites.

2. Balaam's prophecies.

3. Balak's anger at Balaam.

4. Balaam blesses the children of Israel.

5. Israel practices the cult of the Baal of Peor.

Key Concepts and Values מוּשָׂגִים

1. Sinnat chinam: causeless hatred שִׂנְאַת חִנָּם. The plot of the Moabites against the children of Israel is but one more example of hatred for no just cause. Jewish tradition has always denounced hatred. "What is hateful to you, do not do to others," state the rabbis (Talmud Shabbat 31a). Hatred without any real cause was considered the most vicious form, and the rabbis denounced it in extreme terms. The Talmud states that causeless hatred is as wicked as idolatry, adultery, and murder combined (Yoma 9b).

2. Curses קְלָלוֹת. Among biblical peoples, a curse was more than an expressed wish for evil, it was also considered a method of translating such harmful efforts into reality. Curses were usually (though not always) pronounced in the name of a god or demon. Many ancient Near Eastern peoples relied on professional prophets or sorcerers to curse their enemies in battle. In our story, even God viewed the intent of Balaam with alarm.

Notable Mitzvot מִצְווֹת

None.

Notable Quotations צִיטָטִים

Even if Balak would give me	אִם־יִתֶּן־לִי בָלָק
his house full of silver and gold,	מְלֹא בֵיתוֹ כֶּסֶף וְזָהָב,
I cannot go against	לֹא אוּכַל לַעֲבֹר
the word of God,	אֶת־פִּי יְהוָה אֱלֹהָי,
to do anything, small or great.	לַעֲשׂוֹת קְטַנָּה אוֹ גְדוֹלָה:

Numbers 22:18

How good are your tents,	מַה־טֹבוּ אֹהָלֶיךָ
O Jacob,	יַעֲקֹב,
your dwelling-places,	מִשְׁכְּנֹתֶיךָ
O Israel.	יִשְׂרָאֵל.

Numbers 24:5

This text is part of the opening prayer of the daily morning service, for which it provides a wonderful psychological warmup.

הַפְטָרַת בָּלָק

The Haftarah (Micah 5:6–6:8)

Summary הַסְּכוּם

The prophet Micah, a minor prophet who revealed his message during the last part of the eighth century B.C.E., saw the oppression of the Hebrew peasants, who were being robbed and overly taxed by the greedy and wealthy. Micah spoke out against this unfair exploitation of the poor. In addition, having seen the conquest of the Northern Kingdom by Assyria, Micah predicts that the wrongdoing of the Israelites will bring on God's wrath and ultimate punishment. Eventually, though, they will arise to become a shining example to the world's other peoples. The Haftarah concludes with the following well-known statement: "It has been told, O man, what is good, and what God wants of you. Only to do justly, love mercy, and walk humbly with your God."

The Haftarah Connection הַקֶּשֶׁר

The theme link between the Haftarah and the Torah portion is the experience of the Israelites with Balak, king of the Moabites, one of Israel's archenemies. The direct reference to Balaam in Micah 6:5 provides the connection.

Important Concepts מוּשָׂגִים

God's requirements include humility, justice, and kindness. These are the cardinal virtues of life itself.

Notable Quotations צִיטָטִים

Will the Lord be pleased	הַיִּרְצֶה יְהֹוָה
by thousands of rams,	בְּאַלְפֵי אֵילִים,
with ten thousands of rivers of oil?	בְּרִבְבוֹת נַחֲלֵי־שָׁמֶן?

Micah 6:7

You have been told what is good,	הִגִּיד לְךָ אָדָם מַה־טּוֹב,
and what God wants you to do.	וּמָה־יְהֹוָה דּוֹרֵשׁ מִמְּךָ.
Only to act justly	כִּי אִם־עֲשׂוֹת מִשְׁפָּט
and love mercy	וְאַהֲבַת חֶסֶד
and walk humbly with your God.	וְהַצְנֵעַ לֶכֶת עִם־אֱלֹהֶיךָ.

Micah 6:8

פִּינְחָס

Pinchas (Numbers 25:10–30:1)

Summary הַסִכּוּם

1. Pinchas, Aaron's grandson, is rewarded for his zeal.
2. Another census of the Israelites is taken.
3. Apportionment of the land of Canaan among the tribes.
4. Census of the Levites.
5. Laws of inheritance—the case of the daughters of Zelophechad.
6. Daily and festival offerings.

Key Concepts and Values מוּשָׂגִים

1. Inheritance נַחֲלָה. In this Torah portion, Zelophechad, an Israelite of the tribe of Manasseh, dies, leaving five daughters and no sons. His daughters claimed his portion of the Promised Land. As a result, new laws were written permitting daughters to inherit (in the absence of sons), but only when married to a member of their father's tribe (Numbers 27:36).

2. Fanaticism. The incident of Pinchas' killing of Zimri raised serious moral questions. As the Torah states, the Israelites are lusting after Midianite women, who are also enticing them into the worship of their idol Ba'al Peor. God commands Moses to put to death all the ringleaders who have led the people into the wrongdoing. At that moment Zimri and Cozbi walk past Moses and enter a tent with the intention of having sexual relations. Pinchas is furious; he takes a spear, rushes into the tent, and stabs them both.

Early rabbinic opinion was divided on whether or not the act of Pinchas was justified. Certainly Pinchas does not consult Moses, and takes the law into his own hands.

Rav, the head of the Sura Academy, condemned Pinchas for his fanaticism. On the other hand, Samuel, head of the Nehardea Academy, in Babylonia, praised Pinchas for his zeal, claiming that this was a case where God's law was being publicly desecrated, and therefore, Pinchas was correct.

The diversity of opinions leaves modern readers of the Torah with the constant challenge of answering the question: Was Pinchas a dangerous fanatic or a genuine hero?

Notable Mitzvot מִצְווֹת

1. Laws of inheritance דִּינֵי יְרוּשָׁה. It is a religious duty for us to act and render judgment regarding inheritance.

The order of inheritance under Jewish law can be summarized as follows:

1. Sons of the deceased and their descendants.

2. Daughters of the deceased and their descendants.

3. Father of the deceased.

4. Brothers of the deceased and their descendants.

5. Sisters of the deceased and their descendants.

6. Paternal grandfather of the deceased.

7. Paternal uncles (father's brothers) of the deceased and their descendants.

8. Paternal aunts (father's sisters) of the deceased and their descendants.

9. According to rabbinic law, a husband can inherit his wife's property.

2. Musaf: the additional offering מוּסָף. On every Sabbath and festival an additional offering was brought to signify the uniqueness of the day. This sacrifice was called a *korban musaf*. Today, in the absence of the Temple and the sacrifices, we substitute the Musaf additional service in the prayer service on Sabbaths and festivals.

Notable Quotations צִיטָטִים

To the larger	לָרַב
you shall give more land,	תַּרְבֶּה נַחֲלָתוֹ,
and to the lesser	וְלַמְעַט
you shall give less land,	תַּמְעִיט נַחֲלָתוֹ,
in proportion to the number of	אִישׁ לְפִי פְקֻדָיו
names shall each one be given land.	יֻתַּן נַחֲלָתוֹ.

Numbers 26:54

Why must the name	לָמָּה
of our father be lost	יִגָּרַע שֵׁם־אָבִינוּ
to his family just because	מִתּוֹךְ מִשְׁפַּחְתּוֹ
he has no son?	כִּי אֵין לוֹ בֵּן?
Grant us a claim along with	תְּנָה־לָּנוּ אֲחֻזָּה
the relatives of our father.	בְּתוֹךְ אֲחֵי אָבִינוּ.

Numbers 27:4

הַפְטָרַת פִּינְחָס

The Haftarah (I Kings 18:46–19:21)

Summary הַסְכּוּם

Under the evil influence of Jezebel, the Phoenician wife of King Ahab, the people had been led astray to worship Baal. Ahab was weak-willed and dominated by Jezebel, who had pursued the prophets of God with murderous cruelty. It was high treason to proclaim the God of Israel. In this Haftarah, the prophet Elijah meets and confronts the king and queen, pronouncing the doom that will follow on their apostasy.

At the top of Mount Carmel two altars were built. The Baal priests brought sacrifices to their god, but nothing happened. Elijah brought a sacrifice on his altar to God, and it was consumed by fire. For a brief time the people proclaimed God to be the One and the only true Ruler, and abandoned Baal.

Queen Jezebel, angered by Elijah's victory, forced Elijah to flee for safety in the Judean desert. God appeared to Elijah and instructed him to return north to carry out his work against idolatry and evil.

The Haftarah Connection הַקֶּשֶׁר

The zeal of Pinchas in the Torah portion and of Elijah in the Haftarah is the connecting theme link. Both men are highly devoted to God's service.

212

Important Concepts מוּשָׂגִים

1. Elijah is a prophet of great zeal, who is not afraid to stand up for what he believes is the truth.

2. Wind, fire, and earthquake are often spoken of as heralds of God. They do not, however, disclose him so perfectly as the calm which follows the storm. People need to concentrate more and listen to God's still small voice (v. 12).

Notable Quotations צִיטָטִים

Behold, the Lord passed by,	וְהִנֵּה יְהוָֹה עֹבֵר,
and a great and strong wind	וְרוּחַ גְּדוֹלָה וְחָזָק
tore mountains	מְפָרֵק הָרִים
and shattered rocks	וּמְשַׁבֵּר סְלָעִים
before the Lord.	לִפְנֵי יְהוָֹה.
But the Lord was not in the wind;	לֹא בָרוּחַ יְהוָֹה;
After the wind an earthquake,	וְאַחַר הָרוּחַ רַעַשׁ,
but the Lord was not in it;	לֹא בָרַעַשׁ יְהוָֹה;
And after the earthquake a fire,	וְאַחַר הָרַעַשׁ אֵשׁ,
but the Lord was not in it;	לֹא בָאֵשׁ יְהוָֹה;
And after the fire	וְאַחַר הָאֵשׁ
came a gentle small voice.	קוֹל דְּמָמָה דַקָּה:

I Kings 19:11–12

I will spare in Israel	וְהִשְׁאַרְתִּי בְיִשְׂרָאֵל
seven thousand	שִׁבְעַת אֲלָפִים,
all the knees	כָּל־הַבִּרְכַּיִם
that did not bow to Baal	אֲשֶׁר לֹא־כָרְעוּ לַבַּעַל
and all the mouths	וְכָל־הַפֶּה
that have not kissed him.	אֲשֶׁר לֹא־נָשַׁק לוֹ.

I Kings 19:18

213

מַטּוֹת

Mattot (Numbers 30:2–32:42)

Summary הַסְכּוּם

1. The making of vows. Both men and women would take upon themselves special obligations beyond those required by the Law.

2. War against the Midianites.

3. Apportionment of spoils of battle.

4. Tribes that settled east of the Jordan River.

Key Concepts and Values מוּשָׂגִים

Vows. The few lines in the Torah portion related to vows form the core of a tractate of the Talmud called Nedarim ("Vows"). According to Jewish tradition, vowing and making promises are serious commitments. Ecclesiastes 5:4 states that "it is better that you should not vow, than that you should vow and fail to fulfill." We cannot be ethical members of society unless we honor our vows and promises.

Notable Mitzvot מִצְווֹת

Law of nullifying a vow הַתָּרַת נְדָרִים. The Torah, by implication, and the rabbis, in explicit terms, denounce those who resort to vows and oaths. A person should be able to act correctly without taking such extreme measures. Many people regret making a vow soon after uttering it. In that case, if the vow is formally cancelled, it becomes invalid retroactively. This is an annulment. The Torah allowed a way out through *hattarat nedarim* (release

214

from vows and oaths). In this process, a learned sage or three ordinary persons can absolve someone from his vow by asking him whether he would still have made it had he known beforehand what the consequences of the vow would be. Anyone who made a vow or took an oath and did not keep it was subject to the penalty of lashes.

If someone makes a vow . . .   אִישׁ כִּי יִדֹּר נֶדֶר

Numbers 3:30

Notable Quotations   צִיטָטִים

He shall not break his word;   לֹא יַחֵל דְּבָרוֹ;

everything all that he expresses   כְּכָל־הַיֹּצֵא

with his mouth he must do.   מִפִּיו יַעֲשֶׂה.

Numbers 30:3

If we have found favor   אִם־מָצָאנוּ חֵן

in your eyes,   בְּעֵינֶיךָ,

let this land be given   יֻתַּן אֶת־הָאָרֶץ הַזֹּאת

to your servants as property,   לַעֲבָדֶיךָ לַאֲחֻזָּה,

do not bring us across the Jordan.   אַל־תַּעֲבִרֵנוּ אֶת־הַיַּרְדֵּן.

Numbers 32:5

הַפְטָרַת מַטּוֹת

The Haftarah (Jeremiah 1:1–2:3)

Summary הַסְכּוּם

This Haftarah is one of the three so-called Haftarot of Rebuke that precede the Ninth of Av, the anniversary of the destruction of the Temple. Born of a priestly family, Jeremiah began prophesying as a young lad. He saw the dangers that threatened his country by the Babylonians. He criticized the many wrongdoings of his people and urged them to return to God's laws.

The Haftarah tells of God's call to Jeremiah. Like most of the other prophets, Jeremiah tries to absolve himself from the prophetic mantle by pleading that he is too young. God tells Jeremiah that he was already chosen for prophecy while in his mother's womb.

The Haftarah Connection הַקֶּשֶׁר

This Haftarah precedes the Fast of Av because it deals with the wrongdoing of the Israelites which ultimately led to their downfall.

Important Concepts מוּשָׂגִים

1. It is impossible for a prophet to shirk or escape his God-given mission.

2. Israel's loyalty to God is that of an affectionate bride who follows the chosen of her heart even into a wilderness.

216

Notable Quotations   צִיטָטִים

Before I formed you	בְּטֶרֶם אֶצׇּרְךָ
in the womb, I knew you;	בַּבֶּטֶן יְדַעְתִּיךָ;
before you came out of the womb,	וּבְטֶרֶם תֵּצֵא מֵרֶחֶם,
I made you holy.	הִקְדַּשְׁתִּיךָ.

Jeremiah 1:5

Then I said,	וָאֹמַר,
"O Lord God,	"אֲהָהּ אֲדֹנָי יֱהֹוִה
alas, I cannot speak,	הִנֵּה, לֹא־יָדַעְתִּי דַּבֵּר
for I am a child."	כִּי־נַעַר אָנֹכִי„.
But the Lord said to me:	וַיֹּאמֶר יְהֹוָה אֵלַי:
"Say not 'I am a child,'	"אַל־תֹּאמַר, 'נַעַר אָנֹכִי'
for wherever I shall send you,	כִּי עַל־כָּל־אֲשֶׁר אֶשְׁלָחֲךָ
you shall go."	תֵּלֵךְ„.

Jeremiah 1:6–7

I remember	זָכַרְתִּי לָךְ
the kindness of your youth	חֶסֶד נְעוּרַיִךְ
the love of your wedding day,	אַהֲבַת כְּלוּלֹתָיִךְ
how you followed Me	לֶכְתֵּךְ אַחֲרַי
in the wilderness,	בַּמִּדְבָּר
in an unplanted land.	בְּאֶרֶץ לֹא זְרוּעָה.

Jeremiah 2:1

217

מַסְעֵי

Massay (Numbers 33:1–36:13)

Summary הַסְכּוּם

1. Israel's route from Egypt to the Jordan River.
2. Commandments for Israel's entry into the Land of Canaan.
3. Boundaries of the Promised Land.
4. Cities assigned to the Levites.
5. Cities of Refuge.
6. Reiteration of laws pertaining to female heirs to property.

Key Concepts and Values מוּשָׂגִים

Cities of refuge. Six cities, three each on either side of the Jordan River, were set aside in biblical times as places of asylum for persons who committed manslaughter. This provision was made to avoid unnecessary bloodshed, since the Israelites at that time still practiced the primitive principle in which a kinsman of the murdered person (*go'el hadam*) took it upon himself to pursue and slay the murderer.

Notable Mitzvot מִצְווֹת

1. The requirement of two witnesses. In Numbers 35:30 we learn that the testimony of a single witness was not enough to make anyone liable to the death penalty. The reason for two witnesses is that it provides a safeguard, since one witness might have a bias in the case.

If two witnesses were related to each other, they were disqualified. In rabbinic times, among those excluded from giving testimony as witnesses in capital cases were women, minors, slaves, deaf mutes, professional gamblers, and everyone who knowingly transgressed the laws of the Torah or was ignorant of them.

Notable Quotations צִיטָטִים

The cities shall be	וְהָיוּ לָכֶם הֶעָרִים
safe haven from the avenger,	לְמִקְלָט מִגֹּאֵל,
so the slayer will not die,	וְלֹא יָמוּת הָרֹצֵחַ,
until he stands before	עַד־עָמְדוֹ לִפְנֵי
the community for judgment.	הָעֵדָה לַמִּשְׁפָּט.

Numbers 35:12

Whoever kills any person,	כָּל־מַכֵּה־נֶפֶשׁ,
by the testimony of witnesses	לְפִי עֵדִים
the murderer shall be slain.	יִרְצַח אֶת־הָרֹצֵחַ
A single witness cannot testify	וְעֵד אֶחָד לֹא־יַעֲנֶה
against any person for death.	בְנֶפֶשׁ לָמוּת:

Numbers 35:30

You shall not take a ransom	וְלֹא תִקְחוּ כֹפֶר
for the life of a murderer	לְנֶפֶשׁ רֹצֵחַ
who is liable for death.	אֲשֶׁר־הוּא רָשָׁע לָמוּת

Numbers 35:31

YOU HAVE NOW FINISHED THE BOOK OF BEMIDBAR

חֲזַק חֲזַק וְנִתְחַזֵּק

Masoretic Notes:

The Book of Bemidbar contains:

	1228 verses
	36 chapters
	10 Sidrot

הַפְטָרַת מַסְעֵי

The Haftarah (Jeremiah 2:4–28, 3:4, 4:1–2)

Summary הַסִּכּוּם

In this Haftarah Jeremiah brings his message to his Judean brethren, warning them of difficult times ahead. He pleads with his people to do away with idol worship and return to the worship and service of One God.

The Haftarah Connection הַקֶּשֶׁר

This Haftarah was chosen as one that precedes the commemoration of the Ninth of Av. It warns the Israelites of difficult times ahead.

Important Concepts מוּשָׂגִים

1. Israel will be punished for its unfaithfulness to God.

2. Idols are futile in time of trouble.

3. God accepts true repentance; and no matter how far we have strayed from Him, He will take us back in love and grace.

Notable Quotations צִיטָטִים

The priests have not said:	הַכֹּהֲנִים לֹא אָמְרוּ:
"Where is the Lord?"	„אַיֵּה יְהֹוָה‟
And they that dispense the law	וְתֹפְשֵׂי הַתּוֹרָה
do not know Me.	לֹא יְדָעוּנִי.

Jeremiah 2:8

220

I planted you as	וְאָנֹכִי נְטַעְתִּיךְ
an exalted vine,	שׂוֹרֵק כֻּלֹּה,
a true seed.	זֶרַע אֱמֶת.
How then have you transformed	וְאֵיךְ נֶהְפַּכְתְּ לִי
into the abnormal plant,	סוּרֵי הַגֶּפֶן
an alien vine?	נָכְרִיָּה?

Jeremiah 2:21

If you want to return	אִם־תָּשׁוּב
O Israel, says God,	יִשְׂרָאֵל, נְאֻם־יְהֹוָה,
then return to Me.	אֵלַי תָּשׁוּב.
But only if you will take	וְאִם־תָּסִיר
your hateful things	שִׁקּוּצֶיךָ
out of My presence,	מִפָּנַי,
and stop flickering like a candle.	וְלֹא תָנוּד.

Jeremiah 4:1– 2

YOU HAVE NOW FINISHED THE BOOK OF BEMIDBAR

חֲזַק חֲזַק וְנִתְחַזֵּק

Masoretic Notes:

The Book of Bemidbar contains:

	1228 verses
	36 chapters
	10 Sidrot

דְּבָרִים

Devarim (Deuteronomy 1:1-3:22)

Summary הַסְכּוּם

1. Introduction to farewell discourses of Moses.

2. First discourse—review of the journey from Sinai to the wilderness of Kadesh.

Key Concepts and Values מוּשָׂגִים

The art of making judgments. To aid him in his leadership of the Israelites, Moses appoints judges to decide justly and who will be impartial in their deliberations. In commenting on the difficult burden of making judgments, the ancient rabbis compared the responsibility of judging to dealing with fire. When one comes too close to fire, one is burnt. If one strays too far from it, one will be cold. The art of making judgments, they concluded, is to find the right distance.

In his presentation to the Israelites, Moses suggests three significant rules for making judgments: "hear out" those with conflicting views; do not show partiality to high or low, Israelite or stranger; and fear no one when you are ready to render your decision. Using these guidelines, Torah commentators elaborate on the art of achieving justice in human relationships (Mechilta on Yitro).

Notable Mitzvot מִצְווֹת

The appointment of judges. When Israel was an autonomous people dwelling in its own land, and all of its religious activities were centered around the Temple, judges were not elected but selected, and those who were commissioned to make the appointments were forbidden to show any favoritism whatsoever. The candidates had to meet certain qualifications of the highest level.

In rabbinic times, the highest court was the Great Sanhedrin, composed of seventy-one judges. The head of this body of jurists was called the *nasi*. In view of the fact that Moses was the first nasi, every succeeding one was to be considered in the same light as Moses in his day. A lower court called the Small Sanhedrin was composed of twenty-three sages. Such a court was appointed for every community that had more than 120 people.

Notable Quotations צִיטָטִים

How can I bear alone	אֵיכָה אֶשָּׂא לְבַדִּי
your weight,	טָרְחֲכֶם,
your burden,	וּמַשַּׂאֲכֶם,
and your quarrel?	וְרִיבְכֶם.

Deuteronomy 1:12

You shall not show partiality	לֹא־תַכִּירוּ פָנִים
in legal matters.	בַּמִּשְׁפָּט.
Hear out the small and great alike.	כַּקָּטֹן כַּגָּדֹל תִּשְׁמָעוּן.
Do not be influenced by anyone,	לֹא תָגוּרוּ מִפְּנֵי־אִישׁ,
for the judgment	כִּי הַמִּשְׁפָּט
belongs to God.	לֵאלֹהִים הוּא

Deuteronomy 1:17

הַפְטָרַת דְּבָרִים

The Haftarah (Isaiah 1:1–27)

Summary הַסְכּוּם

This Haftarah always precedes the Fast of Av, the anniversary of the fall of Jerusalem. Assyria had defeated the Northern Kingdom of Israel. In this Haftarah, the prophet Isaiah criticizes the Judeans for their weaknesses and wrongdoing. God does not simply want their animal sacrifices; but rather, what God asks of His people is that they do justly and act ethically. If the people do not learn to become righteous again, God will bring upon them a punishment that will purge their iniquities.

The Haftarah Connection הַקֶּשֶׁר

This Haftarah was chosen to be read preceding the Fast of Av in order to warn Israel in every generation about the moral transgressions that led to the downfall of the Jewish people.

Important Concepts מוּשָׂגִים

1. Ingratitude reduces Israel below the level of animals.

2. God does not want rituals that do not lead to ethical living.

3. There will always be a sanctified minority of people which will survive God's judgment of punishment by repenting and changing their ways (v. 27).

Notable Quotations צִיטָטִים

"What use to me	״לָמָּה־לִּי
are all of your sacrifices?"	רֹב־זִבְחֵיכֶם?״
says God.	יֹאמַר יְהֹוָה.
I am full of the burnt offerings of rams	״שָׂבַעְתִּי עֹלוֹת אֵילִים
and the fat of fed beasts.	וְחֵלֶב מְרִיאִים.״

Isaiah 1:11

Learn to do well.	לִמְדוּ הֵיטֵב.
Search for justice,	דִּרְשׁוּ מִשְׁפָּט,
aid the oppressed,	אַשְּׁרוּ חָמוֹץ,
be true to the orphan,	שִׁפְטוּ יָתוֹם,
plead for the widow.	רִיבוּ אַלְמָנָה.

Isaiah 1:17

Zion shall be redeemed in justice,	צִיּוֹן בְּמִשְׁפָּט תִּפָּדֶה,
and they that return to her	וְשָׁבֶיהָ
in righteousness.	בִּצְדָקָה.

Isaiah 1:27

225

וָאֶתְחַנַּן

Va'etchanan (Deuteronomy 3:23–7:11)

Summary הַסְכּוּם

1. First discourse of Moses continued:

    a. God rejects Moses' request to enter the Promised Land.

    b. Repeated warning against idolatry.

2. Moses assigns the first three cities of refuge.

3. Second discourse of Moses:

    a. Basis of the covenant between God and Israel.

    b. Reiteration of the Ten Commandments.

    c. The Shema.

    d. The exodus as an object lesson.

Key Concepts and Values מוּשָׂגִים

1. The Shema: Hear, O Israel שְׁמַע יִשְׂרָאֵל. Israel is commanded to hearken to God's law and take it to heart. Israel's duty is to love the One God and to study God's law. What does it mean to love God? Maimonides asserts that to love God means to dwell upon and think about God's commandments. Just as a lover tries to please and follow the desire of his beloved, so, too, we in our love of God, must try to understand God's will. We do this by studying God's Torah.

2. Prohibition of "trying" God. Deuteronomy 6:16 states that one must not try the Lord your God. According to the commentator known as the Chinnuch, we try God "by fulfilling a mitzvah as if we were putting God to the test, to see if God will reward us, instead of doing good out of love for God." Some people reject

226

God when their petitions are not granted or when they meet with suffering or distress in their lives. Receiving a reward ought not to be the expectation when performing a religious obligation. As Pirkei Avot states, "The reward of a mitzvah is a mitzvah." Indeed, it is a delight to serve God.

Notable Mitzvot מִצְווֹת

1. Duty of transmitting the Torah's teachings תַּלְמוּד תּוֹרָה. Deuteronomy 6:7 states that "you shall teach them diligently to your children." In Judaism, Torah education is a religious obligation imposed by biblical commandment. In Jewish eyes no human endeavor deserves greater respect than *talmud torah*, the study of Torah. Whereas almost every advanced society provides schools and some degree of compulsory education, the Torah places the onus of teaching on the parents.

Teach them to your children.　　　וְשִׁנַּנְתָּם לְבָנֶיךָ.
Deuteronomy 6:7

2. Tefillin: phylacteries תְּפִלִּין. Deuteronomy 6:8 states that "you shall bind them for a sign upon your hand, and they shall be for frontlets between your eyes." The reference here is to tefillin, leather capsules containing parchments on which are written four biblical passages (Exodus 13:1–10, 11–16; Deuteronomy 6:4–9, 11:13-21). These passages stress the duty of loving and serving God with our whole being, and demand that we give living expression to our love of God by the careful observance of mitzvot. By binding the tefillin on our arm and forehead, we subject our thoughts and actions to the service of God. This is intimated by wearing the tefillin on the head, symbolizing our mental faculties, and on the left arm next to the heart, the seat of emotions.

And you shall bind them as a sign   וּקְשַׁרְתֶּם לְאוֹת

upon your arm.   עַל יָדֶךָ.

Deuternomy 6:8

3. Mezuzah   מְזוּזָה. The Torah states that "you shall write them on the doorposts of your home and upon your gates" (Deuteronomy 6:9). The mezuzah serves as a distinctive mark of the Jewish home. It consists of a small roll of parchment on which is written the Shema prayer and two biblical passages concerning love for God and God's mitzvot (Deuteronomy 6:4–9, 11:13–21). Enclosed in a metal or wooden receptacle, it is fastened in a slanting position on the upper doorpost on the right side of the entrance of each room. Upon entering the house or leaving it, it is customary to touch the mezuzah with the fingers and then kiss them. This is symbolic of affectionately embracing God's commandments.

And you shall write them   וּכְתַבְתָּם

on the doorposts of your house   עַל מְזֻזוֹת בֵּיתֶךָ

and upon your gates.   וּבִשְׁעָרֶיךָ.

Deuteronomy 6:9

4. Prohibition against marrying out of the faith. The Torah states, "neither shall you make marriages with them" (Deuteronomy 7:3). Judaism has always discouraged intermarriage. There are, of course, many advantages to a Jewish marriage. A Jewish couple will be able to share the warmth and strength of Jewish customs and observances, without the need for constant interpretation. Also, the children of a Jewish couple will not be torn between two religious traditions. Finally in a Jewish marriage, the aspirations of the Jewish people as a whole become part of the shared goals of the two partners. The couple will also be helping to assure the continuity of Judaism and the Jewish people.

... nor shall you marry them.   וְלֹא תִתְחַתֵּן בָּם.

Deuteronomy 7:3

Notable Quotations צִיטָטִים

You shall not add   לֹא תֹסְפוּ

to the command   עַל־הַדָּבָר

that I issue you   אֲשֶׁר אָנֹכִי מְצַוֶּה אֶתְכֶם

and do not subtract from it.   וְלֹא תִגְרְעוּ מִמֶּנּוּ.

Deuteronomy 4:2

But you who are attached   וְאַתֶּם הַדְּבֵקִים

to the Lord your God   בַּיהוָה אֱלֹהֵיכֶם

are all alive this day.   חַיִּים כֻּלְּכֶם הַיּוֹם.

Deuteronomy 4:4

Hear, O Israel   שְׁמַע יִשְׂרָאֵל

the Lord is our God,   יְהוָה אֱלֹהֵינוּ,

the Lord is One.   יְהוָה אֶחָד.

Deuteronomy 6:4

When your son asks in the future,   כִּי־יִשְׁאָלְךָ בִנְךָ מָחָר,

saying: "What is the meaning   לֵאמֹר: "מָה

of the testimonies   הָעֵדֹת

and the laws and the ordinances   וְהַחֻקִּים וְהַמִּשְׁפָּטִים

commanded by God   אֲשֶׁר צִוָּה יְהוָה

our Lord to you?"   אֱלֹהֵינוּ אֶתְכֶם?„

Then you shall say to your son: וְאָמַרְתָּ לְבִנְךָ:

"We were Pharaoh's slaves   "עֲבָדִים הָיִינוּ לְפַרְעֹה

in Egypt."   בְּמִצְרָיִם.„

Deuteronomy 6:20–21

הַפְטָרַת וָאֶתְחַנַּן
The Haftarah (Isaiah 40:1–26)

Summary הַסְכּוּם

This Haftarah is the first of the seven so-called Haftarot of
Consolation that follow the Fast of Av. The Judeans have now
been living in exile in Babylonia for close to fifty years. The prophet
Isaiah assures the new generation of Israelites that God has forgiven
them for the wrongs committed in the past. Better times are clearly
ahead, and Zion will soon be restored to its former glory.

The Haftarah Connection הַקֶּשֶׁר

In this selection, chosen as the first Haftarah of Consolation
after the commemoration of the Fast of Av, the prophet Isaiah
offers comforting words of encouragement to the exiled Judeans.
The opening Hebrew word of the Haftarah, *nachamu* ("comfort"),
provided the name for the Sabbath on which the Haftarah is read,
Shabbat Nachamu—the Sabbath of Comfort.

Important Concepts מוּשָׂגִים

1. One of the tasks of a prophet is to act as a comforter to his
people. Comforting people, in particular mourners, is an important
Jewish religious obligation.

2. The word of God alone is forever certain of triumphant
fulfillment.

Notable Quotations צִיטָטִים

Comfort you My people,	"נַחֲמוּ נַחֲמוּ עַמִּי„
says your God.	יֹאמַר אֱלֹהֵיכֶם.

Isaiah 40:1

A voice says: "Cry!"	קוֹל אֹמֵר "קְרָא„
And he says: "What shall I cry?	וְאָמַר "מָה אֶקְרָא?
all flesh is grass,	כָּל־הַבָּשָׂר חָצִיר
and all the beauty thereof	וְכָל־חַסְדּוֹ
is like the flower of the field."	כְּצִיץ הַשָּׂדֶה„.

Isaiah 40:6

To whom will you liken God?	וְאֶל־מִי תְּדַמְּיוּן אֵל?
What image will you	וּמַה־דְּמוּת
compare God to?	תַּעַרְכוּ לוֹ?

Isaiah 40:18

231

עֵקֶב

Ekev (Deuteronomy 7:12–11:25)

Summary הַסְכּוּם

1. Second discourse of Moses continued:
   a. The rewards of obedience.
   b. The lessons of past history.
   c. Warning against arrogance.

Key Concepts and Values מוּשָׂגִים

1. Reverence and awe for God יִרְאַת ה׳. The Torah states that "you shall fear the Lord your God" (Deuteronomy 10:20). In Proverbs 1:7 we are told that "the fear of God is the beginning of wisdom." Reverence for God, an acknowledgment of God's infinite power and righteousness, is one of the keys to human wisdom.

2. Blessing God for one's food בִּרְכַּת הַמָּזוֹן. The Torah states "and you shall eat and be satisfied, and bless the Lord your God" (Deuteronomy 8:10). The rabbis of the Talmud (Berachot) admonish us, "It is forbidden to enjoy the fruits of this world without pronouncing a blessing, and whosoever derives such enjoyment without uttering a blessing has committed a trespass" (Berachot 35a). A pundit has pointed out that if we change the Hebrew letter *chaf* in *u'veirachta* ("and bless") to a *chet*, we change the meaning to "you shall eat and be satisfied, and run away [without saying the blessing after the meal]." How often people fail to express any appreciation for the blessings of life, including the blessing of eating a satisfying meal.

3. Warning against arrogance. Deuteronomy 8:17 states the following: "And you say in your heart: 'My power and the might of my hand have gotten me this wealth.'" When blessed with prosperity, people often attribute their good fortune solely to their own efforts. Deuteronomy comes to remind us that all things ultimately come from God, and it is God who gives people the power to accumulate riches and win victories.

Notable Mitzvot מִצְווֹת

1. Loving the stranger. Deuteronomy 10:19 states: "Love you, therefore, the stranger." The Jew is required to extend a warm hand of cordiality and friendship to the stranger. In later Hebrew, the Hebrew word for "stranger," *ger*, came to denote a convert, a man or woman who voluntarily joins the ranks of Judaism. Indeed, according to the Chinnuch, anyone who leaves his people, family, and friends in order to enter the Jewish faith deserves our wholehearted love and esteem.

Love you, therefore, the stranger.　וַאֲהַבְתֶּם אֶת הַגֵּר.
Deuteronomy 10:19

2. Serving God. From the earliest period of history, Jews have endeavored to serve God through prayer. The ancient rabbis understood Deuteronomy 10:20, "You shall fear the Lord your God, serve Him, and cleave to Him," as referring to prayer, since in praying a Jew serves God with his heart. The Torah does not specify that prayers must be recited at a certain time or with a certain text. It was only later, by rabbinic decree, that the texts and frequency of prayer were decided.

Him you shall serve.　אֹתוֹ תַעֲבֹד.
Deuteronomy 10:20

Notable Quotations צִיטָטִים

You shall eat and be satisfied,	וְאָכַלְתָּ וְשָׂבָעְתָּ
and bless the Lord your God	וּבֵרַכְתָּ אֶת־יְהֹוָה אֱלֹהֶיךָ
for the rich land	עַל־הָאָרֶץ הַטֹּבָה
which God has given you.	אֲשֶׁר נָתַן־לָךְ.

Deuteronomy 8:10

You say in your heart:	וְאָמַרְתָּ בִּלְבָבֶךָ
"The power and strength	"כֹּחִי וְעֹצֶם יָדִי
of my hand has won me	עָשָׂה לִי
this wealth."	אֶת־הַחַיִל הַזֶּה„.

Deuteronomy 8:17

Now, Israel,	וְעַתָּה, יִשְׂרָאֵל,
what does the Lord your God	מָה יְהֹוָה אֱלֹהֶיךָ
ask of you	שֹׁאֵל מֵעִמָּךְ
but to fear	כִּי אִם־לְיִרְאָה
the Lord your God,	אֶת־יְהֹוָה אֱלֹהֶיךָ,
to walk in all His ways,	לָלֶכֶת בְּכָל־דְּרָכָיו,
and to love Him,	וּלְאַהֲבָה אֹתוֹ,
and to serve the Lord your God	וְלַעֲבֹד אֶת־יְהֹוָה אֱלֹהֶיךָ
with all your heart	בְּכָל־לְבָבְךָ
and with all your soul?	וּבְכָל־נַפְשֶׁךָ?

Deuteronomy 10:12

You shall love the stranger,	וַאֲהַבְתֶּם אֶת־הַגֵּר,
for you have been strangers	כִּי־גֵרִים הֱיִיתֶם
in the land of Egypt.	בְּאֶרֶץ מִצְרָיִם.

Deuteronomy 10:19

234

הַפְטָרַת עֵקֶב

The Haftarah (Isaiah 49:14–51:3)

Summary הַסִכּוּם

This Haftarah is the second of the Haftarot of Consolation, recited after the commemoration of the Ninth of Av. These Haftarot are primarily chosen because of the message of comfort and hope that they bring during the weeks that follow the Fast of the Ninth of Av. This Haftarah, written by Isaiah, speaks to the exiled Babylonian Jews. It reassures the Jewish people that there is an unbreakable covenantal bond between God and Israel which continues to be binding, even in the land of exile. Just as God's promise to make Abraham a great nation to all the families of the earth has been fulfilled, so would the faith of the righteous remnant in Zion's restoration be rewarded.

The Haftarah Connection הַקֶּשֶׁר

The Torah portion speaks of Israel's relationship with the Canaanites and the need to keep the faith and God's laws in spite of living among idol worshippers. The Haftarah reassures the Israelites that the ancient covenant which God sealed with their ancestors will always be binding, in spite of the fact that the Israelites now find themselves in exile in Babylon.

Important Concepts מוּשָׂגִים

God will always restore Israel in time of difficulty because of the covenant He made with our ancestor Abraham.

Notable Quotations צִיטָטִים

Does a woman forget
her nursing child,
or showing compassion
for the son of her womb?

הֲתִשְׁכַּח אִשָּׁה
עוּלָהּ,
מֵרַחֵם
בֶּן־בִּטְנָהּ?

Isaiah 49:15

Look unto Abraham
your father,
and to Sarah that gave birth to you.
For when he was one I called him,
and I blessed him,
and increased his number.

הַבִּיטוּ אֶל־אַבְרָהָם
אֲבִיכֶם,
וְאֶל־שָׂרָה תְּחוֹלֶלְכֶם.
כִּי־אֶחָד קְרָאתִיו,
וַאֲבָרְכֵהוּ,
וְאַרְבֵּהוּ.

Isaiah 51:2

236

רְאֵה

Re'eh (Deuteronomy 11:26–16:17)

Summary הַסְכּוּם

1. Destruction of places of idolatry.
2. Prohibition of private altars.
3. Prohibition against eating blood.
4. Attitude to false prophets and seducers.
5. Prohibition of heathen abuses.
6. Clean and unclean animals.
7. Tithing.
8. The year of release.
9. The three pilgrimage festivals.

Key Concepts and Values מוּשָׂגִים

1. Freedom of choice בְּחִירָה חוֹפְשִׁית. Deuteronomy 11:26 states: "Behold, I set before you this day a blessing and a curse." Moses points out the paths that lead to happiness and the ways that result in misfortune. He implies that it is up to man to choose which of the two paths to take. The Vilna Gaon explains that God continually gives us choices day by day. We may choose the good and reject the evil. Or we may choose the evil and reject the good. The good life is dependent upon our ongoing choices, not upon what we have done in the past or on what we intend to do in the future.

2. Tithing מַעֲשֵׂר. Deuteronomy 14:22 states that "you shall surely tithe all of the increase of your seed." This refers to a tenth of all the yearly produce that was to be set aside for the sanctuary.

237

Today, regarding the giving of tzedakah (charity), it is the custom for some to give one-tenth of one's gross income.

Notable Mitzvot מִצְוֹת

1. Observing the three pilgrimage festivals שָׁלוֹשׁ רְגָלִים. The Torah required that every Jew was to appear in Jerusalem on three occasions during the year—Passover, Shavuot, and Sukkot (Deuteronomy 16:16). The Torah also instructs that he should not come empty-handed, but should bring with him three animals for three different sacrifices. Today, Jews are expected to celebrate the festivals with the same flavor and gaiety as in Temple times. The only difference is that we have no sacrifices today. Donations to charity or to institutions of learning are the present-day equivalent of the traditional festive sacrifices.

Three times a year	שָׁלוֹשׁ פְּעָמִים בַּשָּׁנָה
every one of your males	יֵרָאֶה כָל זְכוּרְךָ
will appear before God.	אֶת־פְּנֵי יְהוָה אֱלֹהֶיךָ.

Deuteronomy 16:16

2. Giving charity צְדָקָה. The Torah states, "You shall not harden your heart, but you shall surely open wide your hand to him" (Deuteronomy 15:7–8). In Judaism, giving charity is considered a virtue. In assisting the poor, one must never do so grudgingly or half-heartedly. In addition to giving financial support, one must also extend a hand of wholehearted encouragement.

you will definitely open	פָּתֹחַ תִּפְתַּח
your hand to him.	אֶת יָדְךָ לוֹ.

Deuteronomy 15:8

Notable Quotations צִיטָטִים

All these words	אֶת כָּל־הַדָּבָר
which I command you,	אֲשֶׁר אָנֹכִי מְצַוֶּה אֶתְכֶם,
that you must observe and do it;	אֹתוֹ תִשְׁמְרוּ לַעֲשׂוֹת;
you shall not add to it,	לֹא־תֹסֵף עָלָיו,
nor take away from it.	וְלֹא תִגְרַע מִמֶּנּוּ.

Deuteronomy 13:1

If there be among you	כִּי־יִהְיֶה בְךָ
a pauper, one of your brothers,	אֶבְיוֹן, מֵאַחַד אַחֶיךָ,
within any of your gates,	בְּאַחַד שְׁעָרֶיךָ,
in the land	בְּאַרְצְךָ
which the Lord your God	אֲשֶׁר־יְהֹוָה אֱלֹהֶיךָ
gives to you,	נֹתֵן לָךְ,
you shall not harden your heart,	לֹא תְאַמֵּץ אֶת־לְבָבְךָ,
nor close your hand	וְלֹא תִקְפֹּץ אֶת־יָדְךָ
against your poor brother.	מֵאָחִיךָ הָאֶבְיוֹן.

Deuteronomy 15:7

There will always be poor people	כִּי לֹא־יֶחְדַּל אֶבְיוֹן
within your land.	מִקֶּרֶב הָאָרֶץ.

Deuteronomy 15:11

239

הַפְטָרַת רְאֵה

The Haftarah (Isaiah 54:11–55:5)

Summary הַסְכּוּם

This is the third of the Haftarot of Consolation. Its central promise is: "No weapon that is formed against you shall prosper. And every tongue that shall rise against you in judgment you shall condemn." Isaiah, the author of this Haftarah, speaks to the Israelite exiles in Babylon, asking them to keep the faith. God will return them to their homeland in joy and blessing.

The Haftarah Connection הַקֶּשֶׁר

The Torah portion opens with the choice presented to the Israelites between choosing right and wrong, the blessing or the curse. The Haftarah promises deliverance from Babylonian oppression if the Israelites choose the life of blessing and righteousness.

Important Concepts מוּשָׂגִים

1. Rich and poor alike are called upon to participate in the blessings of a new era by heeding the word of God.

2. Israel's victory in history is assured. No might will be capable of destroying God's Servant.

Notable Quotations   צִיטָטִים

No weapon aimed
at you will succeed,
and every tongue that accuses
you in judgment
will be repudiated.

כָּל־כְּלִי יוּצַר
עָלַיִךְ לֹא יִצְלָח
וְכָל־לָשׁוֹן תָּקוּם
אִתָּךְ לַמִּשְׁפָּט
תַּרְשִׁיעִי.

Isaiah 54:17

Bend your ear, and come to Me.
Listen, and your soul shall live,
and I will make with you
an everlasting covenant.

הַטּוּ אָזְנְכֶם וּלְכוּ אֵלַי.
שִׁמְעוּ וּתְחִי נַפְשְׁכֶם,
וְאֶכְרְתָה לָכֶם
בְּרִית עוֹלָם.

Isaiah 55:3

שׁוֹפְטִים

Shoftim (Deuteronomy 16:18–21:9)

Summary הַסְכּוּם

1. Government.
    a. Judiciary system.
    b. The king.
    c. Priests and Levites.
2. False prophets.
3. Criminal law.
4. Laws of warfare.
5. Laws pertaining to unsolved murders.

Key Concepts and Values מוּשָׂגִים

1. Prohibition of wastefulness. The prohibition in Judaism against the waste or unnecessary destruction of anything that might be useful to humans is derived from the injunction against the destruction of fruit trees in territory captured from an enemy (Deuteronomy 20:19). This precept, referred to by the rabbis as *bal taschit*, served as the basis of the talmudic law which prohibits intentional destruction of natural resources, or any kind of vandalism, even if the act is committed by the owners of the property themselves. According to this law, one must not destroy anything that may prove useful to others. A person who tears his clothing or smashes household furniture in a fit of anger, or squanders money, is likened to an idolater (Talmud Shabbat 105b).

2. Doing justly. Deuteronomy 16:20 states, "Justice, justice you shall pursue." This phrase is a guiding principle in Judaism. It

242

is often interpreted to mean that in one's pursuit of just and righteous ends, the means to the end must also be just.

3. All share in society's guilt. Deuteronomy 21:7 states, "Our hands have not shed this blood." This passage deals with the biblical rite of expiation for an unsolved murder. The elders of the city nearest the scene of the slaying cooperate in the ritual cleansing of the red heifer, and they recite these words declaring their innocence. The commentator Malbim explains the intent: "The townspeople publicly proclaim that they were not even indirectly responsible for the murder. That is to say, they did not withhold food from the murderer, so he was not driven by hunger to the slaying. And they offered the victim an escort, so that he would not go unprotected into a place of danger."

Notable Mitzvot מִצְווֹת

1. Encroaching on the property of another הַסָּגַת גְּבוּל Deuteronomy 19:14 states, "You shall not remove your neighbor's landmark." In any free economy, it is usually a daily occurrence that the financially strong can devise ways of encroaching on the rights and property of the weak. The result is often that the rich become richer, and the poor become poorer. The Torah warns against *hasagat gevul*— encroaching on another's property.

2. You shall offer peace to it. The Torah instructs the Jew to issue a call for peace before engaging in war with an enemy (Deuteronomy 20:10). Sharp debate broke out among classical commentators as to whether the call for peace applied only to optional wars or also to mandatory wars, such as those with the Amalekites. According to Maimonides, the obligation to offer peace to the enemy applied to all wars. According to Rashi, only optional wars required that a call for peace should precede hostilities.

Notable Quotations   צִיטָטִים

You shall not misuse the law,	לֹא־תַטֶּה מִשְׁפָּט,
you shall not be partial to anyone,	לֹא תַכִּיר פָּנִים,
neither shall you take a bribe.	וְלֹא־תִקַּח שֹׁחַד.

Deuteronomy 16:19

Justice, justice shall you pursue.	צֶדֶק צֶדֶק תִּרְדֹּף.

Deuteronomy 16:20

Only by the testimony	עַל־פִּי
of two witnesses	שְׁנַיִם עֵדִים
or of three witnesses	אוֹ שְׁלֹשָׁה עֵדִים
shall a condemned person die.	יוּמַת הַמֵּת.

Deuteronomy 17:6

הַפְטָרַת שׁוֹפְטִים

The Haftarah (Isaiah 51:12–52:12)

Summary הַסִּכּוּם

This is the fourth of the Haftarot of Consolation. Israel shall be redeemed from exile, and be the means of extending God's salvation to all humankind. The Haftarah sets out a program of religion— to plant heaven and establish the earth for the children of humanity. Isaiah informs the exiled Israelites that they must begin to prepare for a happy return to the Promised Land. God and Israel will soon be reunited, and all of the nations will be witness to their reunification.

The Haftarah Connection הַקֶּשֶׁר

The Torah portion, in its opening command "Justice, justice, shall you pursue," gives the fundamental requisite for all human living on earth. As one of the Haftarot of Consolation, the Haftarah provides a comforting message to the dispersed Jewish people after the destruction of the Temple and their banishment to Babylonia.

Important Concepts מוּשָׂגִים

1. Israel was chosen and preserved by God, in order that through Israel God might plant heaven, i.e., righteousness and mercy, in the soul of humanity.

2. Jerusalem will arise from its present degradation.

245

Notable Quotations צִיטָטִים

Awake, awake,	עוּרִי, עוּרִי,
clothe yourself in strength, Zion;	לִבְשִׁי עֻזֵּךְ, צִיּוֹן,
put on your richest garments	לִבְשִׁי בִּגְדֵי
of your glory, Jerusalem,	תִפְאַרְתֵּךְ: יְרוּשָׁלַָם,
the holy city.	עִיר הַקֹּדֶשׁ.

Isaiah 52:1

The Lord will go in front of you,	כִּי־הֹלֵךְ לִפְנֵיכֶם יְהֹוָה,
your rear guard shall be	וּמְאַסִּפְכֶם
the God of Israel.	אֱלֹהֵי יִשְׂרָאֵל.

Isaiah 52:12

246

כִּי תֵצֵא

Ki Tetze (Deuteronomy 21:10–25:19)

Summary הַסִּכּוּם

1. Laws pertaining to marriage and family relationships.

2. Miscellaneous ritual laws.

3. Agricultural laws

4. Moral and humane laws.

Key Concepts and Values מוּשָׂגִים

1. Kevod hamet: reverence for the dead כְּבוֹד הַמֵּת. Judaism insists on respect for the dead. According to Jewish law, the dead must be buried at the earliest possible moment. Deuteronomy 21:23 states that "a person's body shall not remain all night upon the tree, but you shall bury him the same day."

2. Restoration of lost property הֲשָׁבַת אֲבֵדָה. Deuteronomy 22:1–3 asserts that one must return a straying ox or donkey. The law here has been widened to include other lost articles that require restoration to their owners.

3. Kindness to animals צַעַר בַּעֲלֵי חַיִּים. Biblical law was very concerned about the treatment of animals. Deuteronomy 22:10 forbids the yoking of a donkey with an ox. These two animals differ greatly in size and strength, and it would be cruel to yoke the weaker donkey with the stronger ox. In addition, Deuteronomy 22:6–7 states that if one chances upon a bird with its eggs, one shall not take the mother bird along with its young. Here the ground of sympathy is the sacredness of the parental relationship. The mother bird is sacred because she is a mother. But if she is sent

247

away, and does not see her young ones taken, she does not feel as much pain. Interestingly, according to the Torah the reward for not taking a female bird with its young is that of length of days.

Notable Mitzvot מִצְווֹת

In addition to the mitzvot mentioned above of honoring the dead, being kind to animals, and restoring lost property, we also have the following mitzvot:

1. Making a parapet for one's roof. The Torah states that "you shall make a parapet for your roof . . . that you bring not blood upon your house" (Deuteronomy 22:8). In ancient times, people often slept or worked on the roofs of houses. Without a railing to protect them from falling off, their lives were in jeopardy. Since the Torah guides us in all aspects of our lives, it ought not to be surprising that a way of safeguarding one's home would be required by biblical law.

And you shall make a railing   וְעָשִׂיתָ מַעֲקֶה
for your roof.   לְגַגֶּךָ.
Deuteronomy 22:8

2. Writing a bill of divorce. Judaism sees marriage not only as a legal bond, but as a sanctification of the relationship between man and woman. In biblical times, if a man found fault with his wife on social, economic, or religious grounds, the Torah instructed him to issue a bill of divorcement (Deuteronomy 24:3). In the Talmud the written document is called a *get*. Around the year 1000 C.E. Rabbi Gershom of Mainz, whose authority was accepted throughout Europe, issued an edict which stated that a man may not divorce his wife except with her consent. The edict remains valid today.

248

And he shall write her   וְכָתַב לָהּ

a writ of divorce.   סֵפֶר כְּרִיתֻת.

Deuteronomy 24:3

Notable Quotations   צִיטָטִים

If you see   לֹא־תִרְאֶה

your brother's ox   אֶת־שׁוֹר אָחִיךָ

or sheep being driven away,   אוֹ אֶת־שֵׂיוֹ נִדָּחִים

do not hide yourself from them.   וְהִתְעַלַּמְתָּ מֵהֶם.

You shall bring them   הָשֵׁב תְּשִׁיבֵם

to your brother.   לְאָחִיךָ.

Deuteronomy 22:1

If yousee   לֹא־תִרְאֶה

your brother's donkey   אֶת־חֲמוֹר אָחִיךָ

or his ox falling on the way   אוֹ שׁוֹרוֹ נֹפְלִים בַּדֶּרֶךְ

do not look away from them.   וְהִתְעַלַּמְתָּ מֵהֶם

You shall lift them up   הָקֵם תָּקִים

for him.   עִמּוֹ.

Deuteronomy 22:4

You shall not have in your house   לֹא־יִהְיֶה לְךָ בְּבֵיתְךָ

two weights,   אֵיפָה וְאֵיפָה,

one great and one small.   גְּדוֹלָה וּקְטַנָּה.

Deuteronomy 25:14

Remember how   זָכוֹר אֵת אֲשֶׁר־עָשָׂה

Amalek treated you   לְךָ עֲמָלֵק

when you left Egypt.   בַּדֶּרֶךְ בְּצֵאתְכֶם מִמִּצְרָיִם.

Deuteronomy 25:17

249

הַפְטָרַת כִּי תֵצֵא

The Haftarah (Isaiah 54:1–10)

Summary הַסְכּוּם

Taken from the Book of Isaiah, the Haftarah brings a message of hope and confidence to the exiled Babylonian Judeans. Israel will soon be restored to the Holy Land, and God will once again renew His ancient covenant of peace. God's mercy will be everlasting, and never depart from the people of Israel.

The Haftarah Connection הַקֶּשֶׁר

As a Haftarah of Consolation chanted some weeks after the commemoration of the Ninth of Av, this Haftarah helps comfort the Judeans, adding new spirit and giving them confidence in a brighter future.

Important Concepts   מוּשָׂגִים

1. God's mercy and covenant are eternal.
2. God's anger is but momentary.

Notable Quotations   צִיטָטִים

Sing, O barren woman,	רָנִּי עֲקָרָה
you that did not give birth,	לֹא יָלָדָה,
break out into song,	פִּצְחִי רִנָּה,
be glad that you were not in labor.	וְצַהֲלִי לֹא־חָלָה.

Isaiah 54:1

For the mountains may depart,	כִּי הֶהָרִים יָמוּשׁוּ,
and the hills may be removed,	וְהַגְּבָעוֹת תְּמוּטֶנָה,
but My love	וְחַסְדִּי מֵאִתֵּךְ
shall not desert you.	לֹא־יָמוּשׁ.

Isaiah 54:10

כִּי תָבוֹא

Ki Tavo (Deuteronomy 26:1–29:8)

Summary הַסְכּוּם

1. Agricultural laws and the laws of first fruits.
2. Formulation of the covenant between God and Israel.
3. Third discourse of Moses.

Key Concepts and Values מוּשָׂגִים

1. Bikkurim: first fruits בִּכּוּרִים. In the ancient biblical harvest ritual, the farmer brought his first fruits to the priest (Deuteronomy 26:10). The offering of first fruits was accompanied by a declaration recited by the person making the offering. The declaration briefly reviews the origins of the Jewish people and reaffirms the belief in Divine Providence. The first part of the declaration, "My ancestor was a wandering Aramean," is quoted in the Passover Haggadah.

Blessings and curses בְּרָכוֹת וּקְלָלוֹת. Blessings and curses were closely bound to the belief in the power of speech. An entire litany of curses related to reprehensible actions (e.g., misdirecting a blind person, subverting the rights of the stranger, and so forth) is listed in our Torah portion (Deuteronomy 27:15–26). In addition, a catalogue of blessings for those who heed the word of God occurs in chapter 28 of Deuteronomy. Early rabbinic interpreters suggested that God actually does reward those who obey the Torah's commandments. Others simply believe that the intention of the Torah's listing of blessings and curses is to urge us to choose lives filled with good deeds so that we will be assured of an eternity of blessings. Still others, rather than understanding this section literally,

252

believe that it is the Bible's way of saying that all of our actions bear consequences of one sort or another, depending upon the nature of the action, and thus we ought to be careful about our actions.

Notable Mitzvot מִצְווֹת

Walking in God's ways. *Imitatio Dei* (imitation of God) is a slogan used by the early Church Fathers and popularized among Christians in the Middle Ages. To the Jew, the concept of trying to imitate God's attributes dates back to the Torah, which states, "and walk in His ways" (Deuteronomy 28:9). This has been understood to mean that just as God is compassionate, so humans ought to be compassionate. Just as God is righteous and just, so ought humans to be just and righteous. And so on.

You shall walk in His ways.   וְהָלַכְתָּ בִּדְרָכָיו.
Deuteronomy 28:9

Notable Quotations   צִיטָטִים

And the Lord brought us	וַיּוֹצִאֵנוּ יְהֹוָה
out of Egypt	מִמִּצְרַיִם
with a mighty hand,	בְּיָד חֲזָקָה,
and with an outstretched arm,	וּבִזְרֹעַ נְטוּיָה,
and with great terror,	וּבְמֹרָא גָּדֹל,
and with signs and wonders.	וּבְאֹתוֹת וּבְמֹפְתִים.

Deuteronomy 26:8

You shall rejoice in all the good	וְשָׂמַחְתָּ בְכָל־הַטּוֹב
which has been given to you by	אֲשֶׁר נָתַן־לְךָ
the Lord your God	יְהֹוָה אֱלֹהֶיךָ
and to your household as well.	וּלְבֵיתֶךָ

Deuteronomy 26:11

Blessed shall you be in the city,	בָּרוּךְ אַתָּה בָּעִיר,
blessed shall you be in the field.	וּבָרוּךְ אַתָּה בַּשָּׂדֶה.

Deuteronomy 28:3

Blessed shall you be	בָּרוּךְ אַתָּה
when you come and	בְּבֹאֶךָ
blessed shall you be	וּבָרוּךְ אַתָּה
when you go out.	בְּצֵאתֶךָ.

Deuteronomy 28:6

הַפְטָרַת כִּי תָבוֹא

The Haftarah (Isaiah 60:1–22)

Summary הַסְכּוּם

The prophet Isaiah again speaks to the exiled Babylonian Judeans, offering them an optimistic vision of life in the future. In addition, Isaiah provides them with their unique mission when he says that "nations shall walk at your light" (Isaiah 60:3). This means that one of the tasks of the Jewish people is to shine as a beacon of light for other nations less enlightened to follow.

The Haftarah Connection הַקֶּשֶׁר

Once again, the intention of this Haftarah is to console and offer encouragement to the despondent exiled people of Israel.

The Torah portion brings the second discourse of Moses to a close with the divine promise to make Israel "high above the nations." The Haftarah, the sixth of the seven Haftarot of Consolation, gives the highest spiritual interpretation of that promise ("Upon you God will arise, and God's glory shall be seen upon you").

Important Concepts מוּשָׂגִים

1. Israel's mission is to be a light unto the nations.

2. Every nation will fail unless it serves God.

3. The light of the Shechinah makes the light of the sun and moon unnecessary.

255

Notable Quotations צִיטָטִים

Arise, shine,	קוּמִי, אוֹרִי,
for your light is come,	כִּי־בָא אוֹרֵךְ
and the glory of the Lord	וּכְבוֹד יְהֹוָה
rises to shine upon you.	עָלַיִךְ זָרָח.

Isaiah 60:1

Nations shall flock to your light,	וְהָלְכוּ גוֹיִם לְאוֹרֵךְ,
and kings	וּמְלָכִים
to your brightness.	לְנֹגַהּ זַרְחֵךְ.

Isaiah 60:3

The smallest becomes	הַקָּטֹן יִהְיֶה
a thousand,	לָאֶלֶף,
and the least a mighty nation,	וְהַצָּעִיר לְגוֹי עָצוּם,
and I the Lord will	אֲנִי יְהֹוָה
speed its time.	בְּעִתָּהּ אֲחִישֶׁנָּה.

Isaiah 60:22

נִצָּבִים

Nitzavim (Deuteronomy 29:9–30:20)

Summary הַסְכּוּם

1. Third Discourse of Moses.

   a. God will make a covenant with the Israelites.

   b. The people are told to choose life.

2. Free will.

Key Concepts and Values מוּשָׂגִים

1. Commitment for the future. In this Torah portion we are told that God is making a covenant both with those who are present and those who are not present. This implies that the present does commit future generations. The people of Israel as a whole are forever eternally bound to God and God's covenant. Thus Jews must always act in keeping with their historic character. They are not permitted to deny their past.

2. Teshuvah: repentance תְּשׁוּבָה. Deuteronomy 30:2 states that "you shall return to the Lord your God." The Hebrew word *teshuvah* (repentance) means "to return." In the first ten phrases of Deuteronomy 30, the Hebrew word *shuv* ("turn") appears seven times. If Israel turns back to the God it has forsaken, God will graciously receive it back in turn.

Notable Mitzvot מִצְווֹת

None

Notable Quotations צִיטָטִים

Not with you only	וְלֹא אִתְּכֶם לְבַדְּכֶם
do I make	אָנֹכִי כֹּרֵת
this covenant	אֶת־הַבְּרִית הַזֹּאת
and this oath,	וְאֶת־הָאָלָה הַזֹּאת:
but also with him who is	כִּי אֶת־אֲשֶׁר יֶשְׁנוֹ פֹּה
not yet here today.	עִמָּנוּ עֹמֵד הַיּוֹם

Deuteronomy 29:13–14

For this commandment	כִּי הַמִּצְוָה הַזֹּאת
which I command you	אֲשֶׁר אָנֹכִי מְצַוְּךָ
this day is not too difficult	הַיּוֹם לֹא־נִפְלֵאת הִוא
for you,	מִמְּךָ
neither is it far off.	וְלֹא־רְחֹקָה הִוא:

Deuteronomy 30:11

The word is very close to you,	כִּי־קָרוֹב אֵלֶיךָ הַדָּבָר מְאֹד
it is in your mouth	בְּפִיךָ
and in your heart,	וּבִלְבָבְךָ
to do it.	לַעֲשֹׂתוֹ:

Deuteronomy 30:14

Today I call as witnesses	הַעִדֹתִי בָכֶם הַיּוֹם
heaven and earth that	אֶת־הַשָּׁמַיִם וְאֶת־הָאָרֶץ
life and death	הַחַיִּים וְהַמָּוֶת
have I set before you—	נָתַתִּי לְפָנֶיךָ
the blessing as well as the curse.	הַבְּרָכָה וְהַקְּלָלָה.
Therefore, you must choose life,	וּבָחַרְתָּ בַּחַיִּים,
that you may live,	לְמַעַן תִּחְיֶה,
and your seed as well.	אַתָּה וְזַרְעֶךָ.

Deuteronomy 30:19

הַפְטָרַת נִצָּבִים

The Haftarah (Isaiah 61:10–63:9)

Summary הַסִּכּוּם

This is the last of the seven Haftarot of Consolation. It is invariably read on the Sabbath before Rosh Hashanah. From the Book of Isaiah, the prophet speaks to the exiled Judeans in Babylon and predicts the future glories of Zion. Never again will the Israelites be forsaken, for God will always be their Protector. The exiles must now prepare for their return to the Promised Land.

The Haftarah Connection הַקֶּשֶׁר

The opening words of the Haftarah reflect the spiritual exaltation which possesses the souls of loyal and God-fearing Jews at the season of Rosh Hashanah: "I will greatly rejoice in God, my soul shall be joyful to my God."

Important Concepts מוּשָׂגִים

1. God's rejuvenation of Israel will be witnessed by all the nations.

2. God will always be Israel's Protector.

Notable Quotations צִיטָטִים

I will greatly rejoice in the Lord,	שׂוֹשׂ אָשִׂישׂ בַּיהֹוָה
and my soul shall be joyful	תָּגֵל נַפְשִׁי
to my God.	בֵּאלֹהַי

Isaiah 61:10

As a groom rejoices with a bride,	וּמְשׂוֹשׂ חָתָן עַל־כַּלָּה,
so shall your God rejoice with you.	יָשִׂישׂ עָלַיִךְ אֱלֹהָיִךְ.

Isaiah 62:5

259

וַיֵּלֶךְ

Vayelech (Deuteronomy 31:1–30)

Summary הַסְכּוּם

1. Moses commits the law to the priests and the Levites
2. Moses chooses Joshua as his successor.

Key Concepts and Values מוּשָׂגִים

1. Study of the law תַּלְמוּד תּוֹרָה. It is not sufficient to listen to readings from the law from time to time. In this Torah portion we are told to "hear" the law, then to "study" it, and then to "observe" it (Deuteronomy 31:12). This implies that there can be no true observance without thorough and regular study.

2. Passing on the mantle of leadership. In this Torah portion Moses has reached the age of 120 and is about to die. He calls Joshua and "in the sight of Israel" transfers the powers of leadership to him. Moses tells him, "Be strong and resolute, for it is you who shall go with this people into the land . . . and it is you who shall apportion it to them. . . . Fear not, and do not be dismayed" (Deuteronomy 31:1–8). Many commentators wonder why Moses did not choose one of his sons, either Gershon or Eliezer, as his successor. They suggest that his two sons, unlike Joshua, were not students of Torah. Joshua was probably chosen because of his demonstrated commitment to Moses and his loyalty to the Israelites.

Notable Mitzvot מִצְווֹת

Assembling the entire people to hear the Torah read every seven years. On the first of the intermediate days of Sukkot, trumpets were sounded to proclaim to everyone who had come to celebrate the festival in Jerusalem that they should assemble (Deuteronomy 31:12). The ceremony was known as the mitzvah of *hakhel* ("gathering together"). Because of its unique setting, the ceremony was likely to increase the interest of the people in the Torah and in all that the Torah stood for.

Gather the people together:	הַקְהֵל אֶת הָעָם:
the men, the women	הָאֲנָשִׁים וְהַנָּשִׁים
and the children.	וְהַטַּף.

Deuteronomy 31:12

Notable Quotations צִיטָטִים

Be strong and of good courage,	חִזְקוּ וְאִמְצוּ,
have no fear;	אַל־תִּירְאוּ;
do not be frightened of them.	וְאַל־תַּעַרְצוּ מִפְּנֵיהֶם.

Deuteronomy 31:6

Gather the people together:	הַקְהֵל אֶת הָעָם:
the men, the women	הָאֲנָשִׁים וְהַנָּשִׁים
and the children, and	וְהַטַּף,
your stranger within your gates,	וְגֵרְךָ אֲשֶׁר בִּשְׁעָרֶיךָ,
so they may hear,	לְמַעַן יִשְׁמְעוּ
and so they may learn,	וּלְמַעַן יִלְמְדוּ
and fear the Lord your God,	וְיָרְאוּ אֶת־יְהוָה אֱלֹהֵיכֶם
and be sure to perform	וְשָׁמְרוּ לַעֲשׂוֹת
all the commandments	אֶת־כָּל־דִּבְרֵי
of this Torah.	הַתּוֹרָה הַזֹּאת:

Deuteronomy 31:12

261

הַפְטָרַת וַיֵּלֶךְ

The Haftarah
(Hosea 14:2-10, Micah 7:18–20, Joel 2:15–27)

Summary הַסְכּוּם

This Haftarah is made up of selections from the writings of three prophets: Hosea, Micah, and Joel. It is assigned for the reading on the Sabbath that falls between Rosh Hashanah and Yom Kippur, called the Sabbath of Repentance (Shabbat Shuvah) because repenting is its theme.

Hosea pleads with the people of the Northern Kingdom to change their ways and return to God. Micah was the prophet who pleaded for the poor, assuring the people that God would forgive those who turned from their mistakes.

The prophet Joel speaks to his people of the impending dooms that threaten them. The people must repent with great conviction. Then the shofar may be blown and they will be brought back together again, becoming once more a sanctified nation.

The Haftarah Connection הַקֶּשֶׁר

The theme of this Haftarah is returning to God and doing sincere repentance. Each of the three prophets of repentance in this Haftarah sets the mood for the Sabbath between Rosh Hashanah and Yom Kippur, the days that are meant to move and encourage us to change our ways.

Important Concepts מוּשָׂגִים

1. God's love and mercy are unending.
2. God wants us to return and change our evil ways.
3. God pardons iniquity.

Notable Quotations צִיטָטִים

Return, O Israel,	שׁוּבָה יִשְׂרָאֵל,
to the Lord your God,	עַד יְהֹוָה אֱלֹהֶיךָ,
for you have stumbled	כִּי כָשַׁלְתָּ
because of your iniquity.	בַּעֲוֹנֶךָ.

Hosea 14:2

Who is a God like You,	מִי־אֵל כָּמוֹךָ,
that pardons the iniquity?	נֹשֵׂא עָוֹן?

Micah 7:18

Blow the shofar in Zion,	תִּקְעוּ שׁוֹפָר בְּצִיּוֹן,
order a fast,	קַדְּשׁוּ־צוֹם,
announce a solemn assembly.	קִרְאוּ עֲצָרָה.

Joel 2:15

הַאֲזִינוּ

Ha'azinu (Deuteronomy 32:1–52)

Summary הַסְכּוּם

1. The song of Moses, providing a final review of Israel's history.

2. Moses is told to climb Mount Nebo, from which he will be able to see the Land of Israel. There he will die, without entering the land.

Key Concepts and Values מוּשָׂגִים

1. Remember the days of old. In his poetic declaration to the Israelites, Moses tells the people to remember the days of old, and consider the years of ages past (Deuteronomy 32:7). Rashi suggests that we should remember and consider history in order to be conscious of what may happen in the future. Others suggest that studying history and remembering it will help us to shape future events in a way that will not repeat the disasters of the past. As George Santayana once wrote: "Those who cannot remember the past are condemned to fulfill it."

2. Tzidduk hadin צְדוּק הַדִּין. Moses declares that all the ways of God are just and righteous (Deuteronomy 33:4). This means that suffering and even death must be accepted as demonstrations of God's righteousness. A declaration to that effect (called *tzidduk hadin*) is part of the Jewish funeral service.

Notable Mitzvot מִצְווֹת

None.

Notable Quotations ציטטים

I proclaim the Name of God;	כִּי שֵׁם יְהֹוָה אֶקְרָא,
tell of the greatness to our God.	הָבוּ גֹדֶל לֵאלֹהֵינוּ.

Deuteronomy 32:3

Remember the days of old,	זְכֹר יְמוֹת עוֹלָם
ponder the years of each generation.	בִּינוּ שְׁנוֹת דֹּר וָדֹר

Deuteronomy 32:7

הַפְטָרַת הַאֲזִינוּ

The Haftarah (II Samuel 22:1–51)

Summary הַסְכּוּם

Taken from the Second Book of Samuel, the Haftarah is a song of thanksgiving and a farewell song by King David. David traces Divine Providence in his own amazing escapes from persecution and renders thanks to God for his deliverance and victories.

The Haftarah Connection הַקֶּשֶׁר

The theme link between the Torah portion and the Haftarah is that of thanksgiving to God. Just as David traces his victories in life to God, so too does Moses impress upon the Israelites the importance of keeping one's loyalty for God and faith in God's infinite mercies and kindness.

Important Concepts מוּשָׂגִים

1. God is a rock, dependable and a deliverer.
2. God delights in mercy and goodness.

Notable Quotations צִיטָטִים

The Lord is my rock	יְהֹוָה סַלְעִי
and my fortress;	וּמְצֻדָתִי;
He is my deliverer.	וּמְפַלְטִי־לִי

II Samuel 22:2

Then did I crush them	וָאֶשְׁחָקֵם
like the fine dust of the earth.	כַּעֲפַר־אָרֶץ

II Samuel 22:43

A tower of salvation of His king;	מִגְדּוֹל יְשׁוּעוֹת מַלְכּוֹ
who shows mercy to His anointed,	וְעֹשֶׂה־חֶסֶד לִמְשִׁיחוֹ
to David and to his heirs forever.	לְדָוִד וּלְזַרְעוֹ עַד־עוֹלָם:

II Samuel 22:51

This verse was chosen to conclude the Birkat Hamazon, the Blessing after the Meal.

267

וְזֹאת הַבְּרָכָה

Vezot Ha'berachah (Deuteronomy 33:1–34:12)

Summary הַסְכּוּם

1. The blessing of Moses to the twelve tribes.

2. God, the abiding source of Israel's security, prosperity, and victory.

3. The death of Moses.

Key Concepts and Values מוּשָׂגִים

1. Torah: the heritage of the congregation of Jacob תּוֹרָה. The Torah is a heritage for the people of Israel (Deuteronomy 33:4). It must remain in the family of the Jews, handed down from parent to children, from generation to generation. The rabbis emphasize the importance of transmitting this heritage from age to age, from generation to generation, so that it is never forgotten. Sifre of Deuteronomy 32:29 said that "if not for Torah, the people of Israel would not at all differ from the nations of the world." The Baal Shem Tov stated that "the purpose of the whole Torah is that each person should become a Torah."

2. Moses as "ish ha'elohim": man of God אִישׁ הָאֱלֹהִים. Moses was a man—with all the virtues and failings of a human being. Moses was also referred to as *ish ha'elohim* (Deuteronomy 33:1), a man of God. We are told that unlike the other prophets he knew God with a special degree of intimacy. In Jewish tradition Moses has come to be known as *Mosheh rabbenu*—Moses our teacher. Indeed, Moses set the standards for future prophets to come.

Notable Mitzvot מִצְווֹת

None

Notable Quotations צִיטָטִים

Moses commanded Torah to us;	תּוֹרָה צִוָּה־לָנוּ מֹשֶׁה,
an inheritance for	מוֹרָשָׁה
the congregation of Jacob.	קְהִלַּת יַעֲקֹב.

Deuteronomy 33:4

Since then, there has not arisen	וְלֹא קָם
another prophet in Israel	נָבִיא עוֹד בְּיִשְׂרָאֵל
like Moses,	כְּמֹשֶׁה,
whom the Lord knew	אֲשֶׁר יְדָעוֹ יְהֹוָה
face-to-face.	פָּנִים־אֶל־פָּנִים.

Deuteronomy 34:10

YOU HAVE NOW FINISHED THE BOOK OF DEVARIM

חֲזַק חֲזַק וְנִתְחַזֵּק

Masoretic Notes:

The Book of Devarim contains:	
	955 verses
	34 chapters
	11 Sidrot

הַפְטָרַת וְזֹאת הַבְּרָכָה
The Haftarah (Joshua 1:1–18)

Summary הַסְכּוּם

The Haftarah from the Book of Joshua tells of the beginning of his career as leader of Israel. He proceeds to carry out his leadership responsibilities and instructs Israel in the strategy to be used in order to conquer the Land of Canaan. The Israelites respond with total loyalty, saying, "All that you have commanded us we will do, and wherever we are sent we will go" (Joshua 1:16).

The Haftarah Connection הַקֶּשֶׁר

This Haftarah is meant to provide the transition from the leadership of Moses, who dies in the Torah portion, to the successor of Moses, Joshua. Though Moses has died, his work will now be assumed by his chosen leader, Joshua.

Important Concepts מוּשָׂגִים

Good leaders are called upon to be strong and of great courage.

Notable Quotations צִיטָטִים

Be strong and of good courage,	חֲזַק וֶאֱמָץ
for you will cause	כִּי אַתָּה
this people to inherit	תַּנְחִיל אֶת־הָעָם הַזֶּה
the land which I swore	אֶת־הָאָרֶץ אֲשֶׁר־נִשְׁבַּעְתִּי
to your ancestors to give them.	לַאֲבוֹתָם לָתֵת לָהֶם:

Joshua 1:6

This book of the law	לֹא־יָמוּשׁ
shall not depart	סֵפֶר הַתּוֹרָה הַזֶּה
from your mouth,	מִפִּיךָ,
you shall study it	וְהָגִיתָ בּוֹ
day and night,	יוֹמָם וָלַיְלָה
that you may observe and do	לְמַעַן תִּשְׁמֹר לַעֲשׂוֹת
all that is written in it.	כְּכָל־הַכָּתוּב בּוֹ.

Joshua 1:8

All that you have commanded us	כֹּל אֲשֶׁר־צִוִּיתָנוּ
we will do,	נַעֲשֶׂה,
and wherever you send us	וְאֶל־כָּל־אֲשֶׁר תִּשְׁלָחֵנוּ
we will go.	נֵלֵךְ.

Joshua 1:16

READINGS
and
HAFTAROT

FOR SPECIAL SABBATHS,

FESTIVALS, AND FAST DAYS

שַׁבָּת רֹאשׁ חֹדֶשׁ

Haftarah for the Sabbath of Rosh Chodesh
(Isaiah 66)

Summary and Connection   הַסִכּוּם וְהַקֶּשֶׁר

This Haftarah, taken from the Book of Isaiah, is read on a Sabbath coinciding with the beginning of a new Jewish month, called Rosh Chodesh. It was chosen for this purpose because of its reference to the new moon in verse 23: "And it shall come to pass that from one new moon to another, all humans shall come to worship Me."

The Second Temple is nearing completion, and the prophet Isaiah reminds the people that Temple worship must lead to ethical living. Sacrifices are only a means to an end.

Notable Quotations   צִיטָטִים

The heaven is My throne,	הַשָּׁמַיִם כִּסְאִי,
and the earth is My footstool.	וְהָאָרֶץ הֲדֹם רַגְלָי.

Isaiah 66:1

And it shall come to pass that	וְהָיָה
from one new moon to another,	מִדֵּי־חֹדֶשׁ בְּחָדְשׁוֹ
and from one Sabbath to another,	וּמִדֵּי שַׁבָּת בְּשַׁבַּתּוֹ
all people will come	יָבוֹא כָל־בָּשָׂר
to bow down before Me,	לְהִשְׁתַּחֲוֹת לְפָנַי,
says the Lord.	אָמַר יְהֹוָה.

Isaiah 66:23

275

מָחָר חֹדֶשׁ

Haftarah of Machar Chodesh
(I Samuel 20:18–42)

Summary and Connection הַסִּכּוּם וְהַקֶּשֶׁר

This Haftarah, from the First Book of Samuel, tells of the amazing friendship between David and Jonathan. After David slays Goliath, King Saul, Jonathan's father, becomes suspicious of David and jealous of his ever growing popularity. He seeks to destroy David, thus forcing him to go into hiding. David places himself in the power of his good friend Jonathan, who by means of a code warns David when it will be safe for him to return.

When the new moon arrives, King Saul notices David's absence. He becomes angry with his son Jonathan, accusing him of disloyalty. Jonathan warns David to flee for his life.

The Haftarah is read on the Sabbath immediately preceding Rosh Chodesh because it commences with the opening theme in verse 18: "Tomorrow is the new moon, and you will be missed, because your seat will be empty."

Notable Quotations צִיטָטִים

Tomorrow is the new moon,	מָחָר חֹדֶשׁ
and you will be missed,	וְנִפְקַדְתָּ
because your seat will be empty.	כִּי יִפָּקֵד מוֹשָׁבֶךָ.

I Samuel 20:18

But if I say to the boy:	וְאִם־כֹּה אֹמַר לָעֶלֶם:
"The arrows are ahead of you	"הִנֵּה הַחִצִּים מִמְּךָ
go your way,	וָהָלְאָה לֵךְ,
for the Lord has sent you away."	כִּי שִׁלַּחֲךָ יְהוָה."

I Samuel 20:22

Go in peace,	לֵךְ לְשָׁלוֹם
for we have both sworn	אֲשֶׁר נִשְׁבַּעְנוּ שְׁנֵינוּ
in the name of the Lord, saying,	אֲנַחְנוּ בְּשֵׁם יְהוָה לֵאמֹר:
"The Lord shall be	"יְהוָה יִהְיֶה
between me and you,	בֵּינִי וּבֵינֶךָ,
between my seed and your seed	וּבֵין זַרְעִי וּבֵין זַרְעֲךָ
forever."	עַד־עוֹלָם."

I Samuel 20:42

ראשׁ הַשָּׁנָה יוֹם רִאשׁוֹן

Torah Portion and Haftarah for First Day of Rosh Hashanah
(Genesis 21; I Samuel 1:1–2:10)

Torah Reading Summary הַסְכּוּם

The Torah portion tells of the birth of Isaac to Abraham and Sarah. Ishmael, born to Hagar and Abraham is a wild child and a bad influence on Isaac. Sarah urges Abraham to send Ishmael and Hagar away. Although Abraham is at first reluctant to do so, he ultimately acquiesces, receiving divine assurance that it is all for the best. Hagar and Ishmael are saved from starvation, and Ishmael becomes a man of war.

This passage contains the incident of God remembering Sarah. Since one of the themes of Rosh Hashanah is that of remembering, it makes for a good choice to be read. In addition, since Rosh Hashanah commemorates the birthday of the universe, the birth of Isaac provides yet another connection with the festival of Rosh Hashanah.

Haftarah Summary and Connection הַסְכּוּם וְהַקֶּשֶׁר

Taken from the First Book of Samuel, the Haftarah deals with the birth of a child, and depicts Hannah fulfilling her vow of "lending" her son Samuel, whose life was to be consecrated to the service of God. Eventually Samuel becomes a prophet and a judge of the Israelites.

As in the Torah reading, where God remembers Sarah and blesses her with a child, so in the Haftarah Hannah is remembered and blessed with her child, Samuel.

Notable Quotations צִיטָטִים

It came to pass,	וְהָיָה
as she continued	כִּי הִרְבְּתָה
to pray before God,	לְהִתְפַּלֵּל לִפְנֵי יְהֹוָה,
that Eli watched her mouth,	וְעֵלִי שֹׁמֵר אֶת־פִּיהָ,
for Hannah was speaking	וְחַנָּה הִיא מְדַבֶּרֶת
from her heart;	עַל־לִבָּהּ;
only her lips moved,	רַק שְׂפָתֶיהָ נָּעוֹת,
but her voice could not be heard.	וְקוֹלָהּ לֹא יִשָּׁמֵעַ.

I Samuel 1:12–13

I also have loaned him	וְגַם אָנֹכִי הִשְׁאִלְתִּהוּ
to God.	לַיהֹוָה.
As long as he lives	כָּל־הַיָּמִים אֲשֶׁר הָיָה
he is lent to God.	הוּא שָׁאוּל לַיהֹוָה.

I Samuel 1:28

The Lord impoverishes	יְהֹוָה מוֹרִישׁ
and enriches,	וּמַעֲשִׁיר,
He humbles and also lifts up.	מַשְׁפִּיל אַף־מְרוֹמֵם:

I Samuel 2:7

רֹאשׁ הַשָּׁנָה יוֹם שֵׁנִי

Torah Portion and Haftarah
for Second Day of Rosh Hashanah
(Genesis 22; Jeremiah 31:2–20)

Torah Reading Summary הַסְכּוּם

Abraham is commanded to sacrifice on the altar his precious son Isaac. This was a supreme test of Abraham's faith in God. At the last moment, as Abraham is about to put his knife to his son Isaac's neck, an angel of God forbids him to go through with the sacrifice. Instead, Abraham substitutes a ram offering. It is clear that God does not want human sacrifices.

Haftarah Summary and Connection הַסְכּוּם וְהַקֶּשֶׁר

The Haftarah is taken from the Book of Jeremiah. The prophet brings a message of hope to the exiled Judeans in Babylon. With poetic fancy, he portrays mother Rachel weeping for her homeless children. God comforts her with the assurance that her children will yet return to Zion after sincere repentance. Ephraim, as Israel is called, is pictured as the prodigal child whom God loves with great compassion, and whom God takes to His heart when he expresses deep remorse for his wrongdoing. Legend says that when the Jewish exiles passed by the grave of Rachel on the way to Babylon, she cried so bitterly that God Himself was deeply moved by her tears.

In the Haftarah Jeremiah urges the people of Israel to repent. Repentance is one of the major themes of Rosh Hashanah, thus providing the theme link with the festival.

Notable Quotations   צִיטָטִים

So says God:	כֹּה אָמַר יְהֹוָה:
"Those who have found pardon	"מָצָא חֵן
in the desert	בַּמִּדְבָּר
are those who survived the sword."	עַם שְׂרִידֵי חָרֶב„.

Jeremiah 31:1

A voice is heard in Ramah,	קוֹל בְּרָמָה נִשְׁמָע,
mourning and weeping bitterly:	נְהִי בְּכִי תַמְרוּרִים:
Rachel weeping for her children.	רָחֵל מְבַכָּה עַל־בָּנֶיהָ.

Jeremiah 31:14

Is Ephraim a darling son unto Me?	הֲבֵן יַקִּיר לִי אֶפְרַיִם?
Is he a beloved child?	אִם יֶלֶד שַׁעֲשׁוּעִים?
For as often as I speak of him,	כִּי־מִדֵּי דַבְּרִי בּוֹ,
I earnestly remember him.	זָכֹר אֶזְכְּרֶנּוּ עוֹד.
Therefore my heart yearns for him;	עַל־כֵּן הָמוּ מֵעַי לוֹ.
I will certainly pity him.	רַחֵם אֲרַחֲמֶנּוּ

Jeremiah 31:19

יוֹם כִּפּוּר שַׁחֲרִית

Torah Reading and Haftarah of Yom Kippur Morning (Leviticus 16; Isaiah 57:14–58:14)

Torah Reading Summary הַסְכּוּם

The Torah reading recalls the ancient sacrifices that were brought on the Day of Atonement. To impress the people with their communal responsibility for sin and their need for forgiveness, two goats were brought to the Temple. Lots were cast to designate one goat for God and the other for Azazel, symbol of wickedness. The first was offered in the prescribed manner as a burnt sacrifice. Upon the other goat, the high priest placed his hand and confessed the sins of the people, after which the goat was sent away into the wilderness.

This ceremony vividly dramatized the casting away of the sins of the Israelites. The ancient rite is read each year because of its theme of asking for forgiveness and atonement, the theme of Yom Kippur.

Haftarah Summary and Connection הַסְכּוּם וְהַקֶּשֶׁר

Taken from the Book of Isaiah, the Haftarah makes it very clear that fasting is not the only thing that God wants. In order to truly change us, fasting must lead us to strengthen our moral fiber. Fasting must help to arouse sympathy for the plight of the hungry and the oppressed. This is the true and authentic type of fast that God wants of all people.

The theme of fasting provides the connection between this Haftarah and the Day of Atonement.

Notable Quotations צִיטָטִים

Cry aloud, spare not,	קְרָא בְגָרוֹן אַל־תַּחְשֹׂךְ
lift up your voice like a horn,	כַּשׁוֹפָר הָרֵם קוֹלֶךָ
and declare to My people	וְהַגֵּד לְעַמִּי
their misdeed.	פִּשְׁעָם

Isaiah 58:1

Is this the fast that I have chosen?	הֲלוֹא זֶה צוֹם אֶבְחָרֵהוּ?
To loose the fetters of wickedness,	פַּתֵּחַ חַרְצֻבּוֹת רֶשַׁע,
to undo the bands of the yoke,	הַתֵּר אֲגֻדּוֹת מוֹטָה
and to let the oppressed go free?	וְשַׁלַּח רְצוּצִים חָפְשִׁים?

Isaiah 58:6

. . . if you turn away	אִם־תָּשִׁיב מִשַּׁבָּת רַגְלֶךָ
from doing business	עֲשׂוֹת חֲפָצֶיךָ
on My holy day	בְּיוֹם קָדְשִׁי
and call the Sabbath a delight . . .	. . . וְקָרָאתָ לַשַּׁבָּת עֹנֶג

Isaiah 58:13

יוֹם כִּפּוּר מִנְחָה

Torah Reading and Haftarah for
Afternoon of Yom Kippur
(Leviticus 18; Jonah 1:1–4:11, Micah 7:18–20)

Torah Reading Summary הַסְכּוּם

The Torah reading condemns adultery and other immoralities.
It was selected to impress upon the people the need to maintain
Israel's high standard of chastity and family morality. Impurity in
marriage, incestuous promiscuity among near relations, and other
abominations, were condemned and regarded as unpardonable sins.
The use of this passage on the afternoon of Yom Kippur was likely
prompted by the desire to inculcate on this most sacred day the
duties of self-control and domestic fidelity.

Haftarah Summary and Connection הַסְכּוּם וְהַקֶּשֶׁר

The entire Book of Jonah and several verses from chapter 7 of
the Book of Micah are read on the afternoon of Yom Kippur. The
prophet Jonah is sent by God to Nineveh, the capital of Assyria, to
inform its people of the punishment that would soon come upon
them because of their wrongdoings. Jonah, afraid of his mission
tries to run away, taking a ship headed for Tarshish. A powerful
storm breaks forth, and the sailors cast lots to see who might be
responsible. The lot falls on Jonah, who is thrown overboard. A
giant fish swallows him, but after three days he is spewed forth
onto dry land. Again God commands him to go to Nineveh. This
time Jonah goes as instructed; when they hear his message, the

Ninevites repent and are saved from God's wrath and punishment. Jonah is unhappy with the outcome. He had not wanted to save the people of Nineveh because they are pagans and enemies of Israel.

We learn from the story that God is interested in the repentance of everyone. God is the God of the whole universe, and all people are God's people. Jonah's flight from God's Presence was as futile as our attempts to escape from our conscience and from our duties toward our fellow human beings.

Three verses from the Book of Micah conclude the Haftarah. They form a tender appeal to the God of mercy and forgiveness. These same verses are also read on the Sabbath of Repentance (Shabbat Shuvah).

Notable Quotations צִיטָטִים

Jonah rose up to flee	וַיָּקָם יוֹנָה לִבְרֹחַ
to Tarshish	תַּרְשִׁישָׁה
away from God.	מִלִּפְנֵי יְהֹוָה

Jonah 1:3

The Lord summoned a big fish	וַיְמַן יְהֹוָה דָּג גָּדוֹל
to swallow up Jonah,	לִבְלֹעַ אֶת־יוֹנָה,
and Jonah stayed in its belly	וַיְהִי יוֹנָה בִּמְעֵי הַדָּג
for three days	שְׁלֹשָׁה יָמִים
and three nights.	וּשְׁלֹשָׁה לֵילוֹת.

Jonah 2:1

God saw	וַיַּרְא הָאֱלֹהִים
their good deeds;	אֶת־מַעֲשֵׂיהֶם,
they turned from their evil ways.	כִּי־שָׁבוּ מִדַּרְכָּם הָרָעָה.
And God relented	וַיִּנָּחֶם הָאֱלֹהִים
from the harm that	עַל־הָרָעָה
He had said He would do to them,	אֲשֶׁר־דִּבֶּר לַעֲשׂוֹת־לָהֶם.
And He refrained.	וְלֹא עָשָׂה.

Jonah 3:10

You will cast into	וְתַשְׁלִיךְ
the depths of the sea	בִּמְצֻלוֹת יָם
all their sins.	כָּל־חַטֹּאתָם:

Micah 7:19

This verse is the basis of the Tashlich service on the afternoon of the first day of Rosh Hashanah, when we take bread crumbs symbolizing our sins to a river and cast them into it.

סֻכּוֹת יוֹם רִאשׁוֹן־יוֹם שֵׁנִי

Torah Reading for First and
Second Days of Sukkot
(Leviticus 22:26–23:44)

Haftarah for First Day of Sukkot
(Zechariah 14)

Torah Reading Summary   הַסִּכּוּם

The Torah portion deals with the details of the holy Sabbath, and the festivals.

Haftarah Summary and Connection   הַסִּכּוּם וְהַקֶּשֶׁר

Taken from the last chapter of the Book of Zechariah, the Haftarah is a vision of God's judgment upon the enemy nations. Israel will finally be redeemed from the hands of its many enemies. At that time the nations will be converted to the worship of the one God of Israel, and Jerusalem will be elevated into the religious center of the world.

Tradition has it that the final judgment described in this Haftarah will take place on the festival of Sukkot, and thus its link to the holiday.

Notable Quotations צִיטָטִים

Behold, the Lord's day is coming,	הִנֵּה יוֹם־בָּא לַיהוָה
when your spoils will be taken	וְחֻלַּק שְׁלָלֵךְ
from you.	בְּקִרְבֵּךְ.

Zechariah 14:1

In that day there will be	בַּיּוֹם הַהוּא יִהְיֶה
inscribed upon the bells of horses	עַל־מְצִלּוֹת הַסּוּס
"sacred to the Lord,"	„קֹדֶשׁ לַיהוָה,
and the kettles in the Lord's house	וְהָיָה הַסִּירוֹת בְּבֵית יְהוָה
shall be like the bowls	כַּמִּזְרָקִים
before the altar.	לִפְנֵי הַמִּזְבֵּחַ.

Zechariah 14:20

סֻכּוֹת יוֹם שֵׁנִי

Haftarah for the Second Day of Sukkot
(I Kings 8:2–21)

Haftarah Summary and Connection הַסִכּוּם וְהַקֶּשֶׁר

The Haftarah tells of the dedication of the Jerusalem Temple by King Solomon in the tenth century B.C.E. The consecration of the Temple was celebrated by festivities extending over fourteen days, of which the last seven were the festival of Sukkot. Thus the choice of this passage.

Notable Quotations צִיטָטִים

They brought up the ark of the Lord,	וַיַּעֲלוּ אֶת־אֲרוֹן יְהֹוָה
and the tent of meeting,	וְאֶת־אֹהֶל מוֹעֵד
with all the holy vessels	וְאֶת־כָּל־כְּלֵי הַקֹּדֶשׁ
that were in the Tent.	אֲשֶׁר בָּאֹהֶל

I Kings 8:4

I have surely built for You	בָּנֹה בָנִיתִי
a dwelling,	בֵּית זְבֻל לָךְ
a place for You to live in forever.	מָכוֹן לְשִׁבְתְּךָ עוֹלָמִים:

I Kings 8:13

סֻכּוֹת שַׁבָּת חוֹל הַמּוֹעֵד

Torah Reading and Haftarah for the Intermediate Sabbath of Sukkot
(Exodus 33:12–34:26; Ezekiel 38:18–39:16)

Torah Reading Summary הַסְכּוּם

The episode of the golden calf created a rift between God and the Israelites. Moses begs for God's forgiveness. God instructs Moses to hew another set of stone tablets to replace the first which he had broken. At the second revelation God makes known His thirteen attributes, which include mercy, graciousness, patience, generosity, truth, and forgiveness.

God renews His covenant with the Israelites, reminding them that they must reject idolatry and worship only Him.

Haftarah Summary and Connection הַסְכּוּם וְהַקֶּשֶׁר

Taken from the Book of Ezekiel, the Haftarah is a prophecy of the messianic time to come. Ezekiel foretells that the restoration of Israel to the land of its ancestors will include battles and invasions under the leadership of Gog, an apocalyptic figure of unknown identity. The enemy shall suffer defeat. An old tradition to the effect that this battle will be waged during Sukkot determined the choice of this Haftarah for the Intermediate Sabbath.

Notable Quotations צִיטָטִים

It shall come to pass in that day, וְהָיָה בַּיוֹם הַהוּא
when Gog will attack בְּיוֹם בּוֹא גוֹג
the land of Israel . . . עַל־אַדְמַת יִשְׂרָאֵל

Ezekiel 38:18

My holy Name is known וְאֶת־שֵׁם קָדְשִׁי אוֹדִיעַ
among My people Israel. בְּתוֹךְ עַמִּי יִשְׂרָאֵל

Ezekiel 39:7

שְׁמִינִי עֲצֶרֶת

Torah Reading and Haftarah
for Shemini Atzeret
(Deuteronomy 14:22–16:17; I Kings 8:54–66)

Torah Reading Summary הַסִכּוּם

The Torah reading for Shemini Atzeret deals with a variety of laws, including the following:

1. Tithes. One-tenth of the yearly farm produce was to be set aside for the sanctuary.

2. Year of release. In every Sabbatical year (i.e., seventh year), money loans were cancelled to allow the poor a chance to move out of their poverty.

3. Release of Hebrew slaves. Slaves were given their freedom after six years of continuous service.

4. Observance of the three pilgrimage festivals. Passover, Shavuot, and Sukkot.

Haftarah Summary and Connection הַסִכּוּם וְהַקֶּשֶׁר

The first section of I Kings 8, describing the dedication of the Temple, is the Haftarah for the second day of Sukkot. The closing part of the chapter is the Haftarah for Shemini Atzeret. In verse 66, there is a specific reference to the "eighth day," and thus its connection to Shemini Atzeret, the so-called eighth day of the festival of Sukkot.

Notable Quotations   צִיטָטִים

Blessed be God,	בָּרוּךְ יְהוָֹה
Who has given rest	אֲשֶׁר נָתַן מְנוּחָה
to His people Israel	לְעַמּוֹ יִשְׂרָאֵל
according to all that He promised.	כְּכֹל אֲשֶׁר דִּבֵּר

I Kings 8:56

On the eighth day	בַּיּוֹם הַשְּׁמִינִי
he sent the people away	שִׁלַּח אֶת־הָעָם
and they blessed the king,	וַיְבָרְכוּ אֶת־הַמֶּלֶךְ
and went unto their tents joyful	וַיֵּלְכוּ לְאָהֳלֵיהֶם שְׂמֵחִים
and glad of heart for all the goodness	וְטוֹבֵי לֵב עַל כָּל־הַטּוֹבָה
that the Lord had shown	אֲשֶׁר עָשָׂה יְהוָֹה
to David His servant	לְדָוִד עַבְדּוֹ
and to Israel His people.	וּלְיִשְׂרָאֵל עַמּוֹ:

I Kings 8:66

293

שִׂמְחַת תּוֹרָה

Torah Reading and Haftarah
for Simchat Torah
(Deuteronomy 33:1–34:12, Genesis 1:1–2:3;
Joshua 1:1–18)

Torah Reading Summary   הַסְכּוּם

Simchat Torah marks the completion of the Torah-reading cycle, which concludes with the final parts of Deuteronomy. The reading of the story of creation from Genesis marks the renewed cycle of the year ahead.

Haftarah Summary and Connection   הַסְכּוּם וְהַקֶּשֶׁר

The Haftarah for Simchat Torah takes us to Joshua, the prophetic book that comes directly after the Five Books of Moses. There is a close connection in subject matter. The Torah reading concludes with the death of Moses. The Haftarah tells of God's charge to Joshua, his successor. Joshua proceeds to carry out his leadership responsibility and tells the Israelites of his strategy for defeating the Canaanites. In turn, all of the tribes of Israel pledge their loyalty to Joshua.

294

Notable Quotations צִיטָטִים

Every place where shall tread	כָּל־מָקוֹם אֲשֶׁר תִּדְרֹךְ
the sole of your foot,	כַּף־רַגְלְכֶם
I have given it to you,	בּוֹ לָכֶם נְתַתִּיו
as I told Moses.	כַּאֲשֶׁר דִּבַּרְתִּי אֶל־מֹשֶׁה:

Joshua 1:3

שַׁבָּת חֲנֻכָּה

Maftir and Haftarah of the First Sabbath of Hanukkah (Numbers 7; Zechariah 2:14-4:7)

Summary of Maftir Reading הַסְכּוּם

The maftir (concluding Torah reading) for the first Sabbath of Hanukkah relates to the offerings brought by the tribal princes. The presentation took place at the time when Moses anointed and sanctified the tabernacle as well as the altar and all of the vessels connected with it. The offerings consisted of gifts for the transport of the tabernacle, and golden and silver vessels for the service of the sanctuary, with sacrificial animals for the dedication ceremony.

Haftarah Summary and Connection הַסְכּוּם וְהַקֶּשֶׁר

The Haftarah tells of the prophet Zechariah urging his fellow exiled Israelites to sing and rejoice, for God is among them. At its conclusion he has a vision of a candelabrum, the seven-branched Temple menorah. This serves as the special link to Hanukkah, which has as its symbol the *hanukkiah*, or eight-branched Hanukkah menorah.

Notable Quotations צִיטָטִים

Sing and rejoice, O daughter of Zion,	רָנִּי וְשִׂמְחִי בַּת־צִיּוֹן
for lo, I come,	כִּי הִנְנִי־בָא
and I will dwell in the midst of you,	וְשָׁכַנְתִּי בְתוֹכֵךְ,
says the Lord.	נְאֻם־יְהֹוָה.

Zechariah 2:14

Not by might, nor by power,	לֹא בְחַיִל וְלֹא בְכֹחַ,
but by My spirit,	כִּי אִם־בְּרוּחִי,
says the Lord of Hosts.	אָמַר יְהֹוָה צְבָאוֹת.

Zechariah 4:6

And he said to me:	וַיֹּאמֶר אֵלַי:
"What do you see?"	„מָה אַתָּה רֹאֶה?
And I said: "I have seen,	וָיֹּאמַר: "רָאִיתִי
and behold a candlestick all of gold	וְהִנֵּה מְנוֹרַת זָהָב כֻּלָּהּ
with a bowl on the top of it,	וְגֻלָּהּ עַל־רֹאשָׁהּ
and its seven lamps thereon."	וְשִׁבְעָה נֵרֹתֶיהָ עָלֶיהָ״.

Zechariah 4:2

שַׁבָּת שְׁנִיָּה חֲנֻכָּה

Haftarah for the Second Sabbath of Hanukkah
(I Kings 7:40–50)

Haftarah Summary and Connection   הַסְכּוּם וְהַקֶּשֶׁר

The Haftarah describes the various objects used in King Solomon's Temple. They were carefully designed by the master artist Hiram.

This Haftarah is read during Hanukkah because it was after the Maccabee defeat of Antiochus that the Jerusalem Temple was again dedicated.

Notable Quotations   צִיטָטִים

Hiram made	וַיַּעַשׂ חִירוֹם
the ash pots and the shovels	אֶת־הַכִּירוֹת וְאֶת־הַיָּעִים
and the sprinkling basins.	וְאֶת־הַמִּזְרָקוֹת

I Kings 7:40

Solomon made	וַיַּעַשׂ שְׁלֹמֹה
all the vessels	אֶת כָּל־הַכֵּלִים
that were in the house of the Lord.	אֲשֶׁר בֵּית יְהֹוָה

I Kings 7:48

298

שַׁבָּת שְׁקָלִים

Maftir and Haftarah of Shabbat Shekalim
(Exodus 30:11–16; II Kings 12:1–17)

Summary of Maftir Reading   הַסִכּוּם

When a census was taken, every adult Israelite was required to contribute a half-shekel toward the maintenance of the sanctuary. The half-shekel was a form of ransom for the soldiers, who were potential although unwilling takers of human life. The Torah portion also emphasizes that poor and rich alike are equal in the eyes of God, and that both must donate the same amount.

Haftarah Summary and Connection   הַסִכּוּם וְהַקֶּשֶׁר

When Jehoram, king of Judah in the ninth century B.C.E., died, his widow, Athaliah, became the ruler. She promoted idolatrous worship, leading to a revolt against her. She eventually was removed from the throne, and her grandson Jehoash succeeded her, cleaning the Temple of all of its idolatry.

This Haftarah is always read on the Sabbath of Shekalim, when we are reminded of the half-shekel given to maintain the tabernacle. The Haftarah describes Jehoash instructing the priests to gather money for the Temple's repair.

Notable Quotations צִיטָטִים

Jehoiada made a covenant	וַיִּכְרֹת יְהוֹיָדָע אֶת־הַבְּרִית
between God and the king	בֵּין יְהֹוָה וּבֵין הַמֶּלֶךְ
and the people	וּבֵין הָעָם
that they should be God's people.	לִהְיוֹת לְעָם לַיהֹוָה

II Kings 11:17

Jehoash said	וַיֹּאמֶר יְהוֹאָשׁ
to the priests:	אֶל־הַכֹּהֲנִים,
"All the money of the holy things	"כֹּל כֶּסֶף הַקֳּדָשִׁים
brought into the house of God	אֲשֶׁר־יוּבָא בֵית־יְהֹוָה
even the money for	עוֹבֵר אִישׁ כֶּסֶף
the persons for whom	נַפְשׁוֹת
each person is assessed,	עֶרְכּוֹ,
all the money that	כָּל־כֶּסֶף אֲשֶׁר
a person's heart prompts him	יַעֲלֶה עַל־לֶב־אִישׁ
to bring into the house of God."	לְהָבִיא בֵּית יְהֹוָה.„

II Kings 12:5

שַׁבָּת זָכוֹר

Maftir and Haftarah of Shabbat Zachor (Deuteronomy 25:17–19; I Samuel 15:1–34)

Summary of Maftir Reading   הַסְכּוּם

This additional portion, read on the Sabbath before Purim (Shabbat Zachor), deals with the injunction to remember (*zachor*) the horrendous attack of Amalek upon the Israelites. Its connection to Purim is related to the fact that Haman was related to the Amalekites, who were archenemies of Israel.

Haftarah Summary and Connection   הַסְכּוּם וְהַקֶּשֶׁר

The Haftarah of the Sabbath of Remembrance deals with Amalek's aggression against Israel during the time of King Saul. The prophet Samuel tells Saul to retaliate against Amalek for all of the cruelties perpetrated upon the Israelites. According to tradition, Haman, who wished to destroy the Jews of Persia, was a descendant of Amalek. Hence, the special reading on the Sabbath before Purim.

Notable Quotations   צִיטָטִים

I remember what Amalek did	פָּקַדְתִּי אֵת אֲשֶׁר־עָשָׂה
against Israel,	עֲמָלֵק לְיִשְׂרָאֵל,
when he set himself against them	אֲשֶׁר־שָׂם לוֹ
on the way, as they came up	בַּדֶּרֶךְ בַּעֲלֹתוֹ
out of Egypt.	מִמִּצְרָיִם.

I Samuel 15:2

שַׁבָּת פָּרָה

Maftir and Haftarah of Shabbat Parah
(Numbers 19:1–22; Ezekiel 36:16–38)

Summary of Maftir Reading   הַסְכּוּם

The additional maftir reading lays down the regulations for bodily purification. It relates to the mysterious rite of the red heifer, whose burnt ashes helped to remove defilement resulting from contact with the dead. The theme of purification and the lengthy preparation of the red heifer provide a sound connection with the forthcoming festival of Passover, whose theme is one of preparation and purity.

Haftarah Summary and Connection   הַסְכּוּם וְהַקֶּשֶׁר

Moral purification is likewise the theme of the Haftarah, taken from the Book of Ezekiel. God justly sent Israel into captivity, says the prophet. To vindicate His honor, God will restore the Israelites, not so much because they deserve it, but rather to vindicate His own honor. The restoration will be accompanied by a moral renewal. On the one hand, God will implant "a new heart and a new spirit" into the nation. On the other hand, Israel's soul will be swept away by sincere repentance that will cause it to be ashamed of its evil past. The theme of purification provides a theme link with the festival of Passover, and that is why this Haftarah was chosen to be read several weeks before the festival.

Notable Quotations צִיטָטִים

I will sprinkle on you,	וְזָרַקְתִּי עֲלֵיכֶם
clean water	מַיִם טְהוֹרִים
and you shall be clean;	וּטְהַרְתֶּם
from all your uncleanliness	מִכֹּל טֻמְאוֹתֵיכֶם
and from all your idols	וּמִכָּל־גִּלּוּלֵיכֶם
I will cleanse you.	אֲטַהֵר אֶתְכֶם.

Ezekiel 36:25

A new heart also will I give you,	וְנָתַתִּי לָכֶם לֵב חָדָשׁ,
and a new spirit	וְרוּחַ חֲדָשָׁה
I will imbue in you.	אֶתֵּן בְּקִרְבְּכֶם.
I will take away the stony heart	וַהֲסִרֹתִי אֶת־לֵב הָאֶבֶן
out of your body,	מִבְּשַׂרְכֶם,
and I will give you a heart of flesh.	וְנָתַתִּי לָכֶם לֵב בָּשָׂר.

Ezekiel 36:26

שַׁבָּת הַחֹדֶשׁ

Maftir and Haftarah of Shabbat Hachodesh
(Exodus 12:1–20; Ezekiel 45:16–46:18)

Summary of Maftir Reading   הַסְכּוּם

The Sabbath before the beginning of the Hebrew month of Nisan is called Shabbat Hachodesh. The additional maftir reading especially chosen for this occasion describes the paschal sacrifice of the first Passover in Egypt, as well as the rules and preparation of the perennial celebration of the festival.

Haftarah Summary and Connection   הַסְכּוּם וְהַקֶּשֶׁר

The Haftarah, like the maftir Torah reading, touches upon the Passover sacrifices in the course of Ezekiel's description of the restored Temple in Jerusalem. This provides the connection between the Haftarah and its being read a couple of weeks before the start of the festival of Passover.

Notable Quotations צִיטָטִים

On the first day of the first month,	בָּרִאשׁוֹן בְּאֶחָד לַחֹדֶשׁ,
you shall take a young bullock	תִּקַּח פַּר־בֶּן־בָּקָר
without blemish,	תָּמִים,
and you shall purify the sanctuary.	וְחִטֵּאתָ אֶת־הַמִּקְדָּשׁ.

Ezekiel 45:18

You shall prepare a yearling	וְכֶבֶשׂ בֶּן־שְׁנָתוֹ
without blemish	תָּמִים
for a daily burnt offering	תַּעֲשֶׂה עוֹלָה לַיּוֹם
to God.	לַיהוָֹה.

Ezekiel 46:13

שַׁבָּת הַגָּדוֹל

Haftarah for Shabbat Hagadol
(Malachi 3:4–24)

Haftarah Summary and Connection   הַסְכּוּם וְהַקֶּשֶׁר

The Sabbath preceding the festival of Passover is designated as the Great Sabbath (Shabbat Hagadol) in commemoration of the great miracle that occurred on the Sabbath preceding the exodus from Egypt. It is based on the tradition that when God ordered the Israelites to prepare lambs on the tenth of Nisan for the paschal offering, the Egyptians were paralyzed with fear and could not prevent them from doing so, even though the lamb was an Egyptian deity.

The Haftarah is taken from the Book of Malachi, who is preaching to a despondent generation. The Temple has now been rebuilt, but Malachi is not satisfied with the faith of the Israelites. Not until the people reach a more mature state of religiosity can they expect to have a complete redemption. Only then will Elijah the prophet come and announce the beginning of the Messianic Era.

Because Elijah was traditionally regarded as the advance messenger who would appear at Passover time and announce the dawn of a new era, this Haftarah, with its Elijah reference, was chosen to be read on the Sabbath immediately preceding Passover.

Notable Quotations צִיטָטִים

Will a man rob God?	הֲיִקְבַּע אָדָם אֱלֹהִים
Yet you rob Me.	כִּי אַתֶּם קֹבְעִים אֹתִי

Malachi 3:8

Behold, I will send you	הִנֵּה אָנֹכִי שֹׁלֵחַ לָכֶם אֵת
Elijah the prophet	אֵלִיָּהוּ הַנָּבִיא
before the coming of	לִפְנֵי בּוֹא
a day of the Lord,	יוֹם יְהוָה
great and terrible.	הַגָּדוֹל וְהַנּוֹרָא.
And he shall turn	וְהֵשִׁיב
the heart of the fathers	לֵב־אָבוֹת
to the children,	עַל־בָּנִים
and the heart of the children	וְלֵב בָּנִים
to their fathers.	עַל־אֲבוֹתָם.

Malachi 3:23–24

פֶּסַח יוֹם רִאשׁוֹן

Torah Reading and Haftarah for
the First Day of Passover
(Exodus 12:21–51; Joshua 5:2–6:1, 6:27)

Summary of Torah Reading   הַסְכּוּם

Moses instructs the elders of Israel in all of the laws of Passover. All generations to come are to observe the Passover traditions. In addition, the children of succeeding generations are to be instructed at Passover as to the origin and significance of the festival.

The Torah reading concludes with the last of the ten plagues, the slaying of the Egyptian firstborn sons. Pharaoh summons Moses and Aaron, and tells them that he wants them out of Egypt as soon as possible. Moses and Aaron comply, and the children of Israel begin to make a quick exit, not allowing time for their bread to rise.

Haftarah Summary and Connection   הַסְכּוּם וְהַקֶּשֶׁר

The Haftarah for the first day of Passover is taken from the Book of Joshua. In it is a description of the historic Passover which the Israelites observed at Gilgal after they had crossed the Jordan River. It was the first celebration of Passover in the Holy Land. In preparation for the Passover observance, all of the Israelite males were circumcised. They then ate the first matzot made from wheat in the Holy Land. This Haftarah is read on the first day of Passover because it describes the first Passover celebration to take place in Israel.

Notable Quotations צִיטָטִים

Make knives of flint,	עֲשֵׂה לְךָ חַרְבוֹת צֻרִים,
and circumcise	וְשׁוּב מֹל
the children of Israel again.	אֶת־בְּנֵי־יִשְׂרָאֵל שֵׁנִית.

Joshua 5:2

The children of Israel encamped	וַיַּחֲנוּ בְנֵי־יִשְׂרָאֵל
at Gilgal	בַּגִּלְגָּל
and kept Passover	וַיַּעֲשׂוּ אֶת־הַפֶּסַח
on the fourteenth day	בְּאַרְבָּעָה עָשָׂר יוֹם
of the month at evening	לַחֹדֶשׁ בָּעֶרֶב
in the plains of Jericho.	בְּעַרְבוֹת יְרִיחוֹ.

Joshua 5:10

פֶּסַח יוֹם שֵׁנִי

Torah Reading and Haftarah for
the Second Day of Passover
(Leviticus 22:26–23:44; II Kings 23:1–9, 21–25)

Summary of Torah Reading הַסְכּוּם

In this reading Moses instructs the Israelites in the observance of the Sabbath and festivals. This reading presents a comprehensive description of the sacred seasons of the Jewish year, including Passover, Shavuot, Rosh Hashanah, Yom Kippur, and Sukkot.

Haftarah Summary and Connection הַסְכּוּם וְהַקֶּשֶׁר

This Haftarah was chosen because of its account of the great Passover celebrated after King Josiah's reformation. In the eighteenth year of his reign (621 B.C.E.), during the course of repairs to the Temple, a scroll of the Torah (possibly the Book of Deuteronomy) was discovered. Josiah was so stirred by its message that he proceeded vigorously to cleanse the Temple of all idolatry. Part of the account of his reform prefaces the description of his celebration of Passover in the Haftarah, and thus its selection as the Haftarah of the second day of Passover.

Notable Quotations צִיטָטִים

And the king stood on the platform,	וַיַּעֲמֹד הַמֶּלֶךְ עַל־הָעַמּוּד
and made a covenant	וַיִּכְרֹת אֶת־הַבְּרִית
with God	לִפְנֵי יְהֹוָה
to walk after Him	לָלֶכֶת אַחַר יְהֹוָה
and keep His commandments,	וְלִשְׁמֹר מִצְוֹתָיו
testimonies and statutes.	וְאֶת־עֵדְוֹתָיו וְאֶת־חֻקֹּתָיו

II Kings 23:3

And the king commanded	וַיְצַו הַמֶּלֶךְ
all the people, saying:	אֶת־כָּל־הָעָם לֵאמֹר
"Keep Passover	"עֲשׂוּ פֶסַח
for the Lord your God,"	לַיהֹוָה אֱלֹהֵיכֶם„
as it is written	כַּכָּתוּב
in this book of the covenant.	עַל סֵפֶר הַבְּרִית הַזֶּה.

II Kings 23:21

שַׁבָּת פֶּסַח חוֹל הַמּוֹעֵד

Maftir and Haftarah for the Intermediate Sabbath of Passover
(Exodus 23:12–34:26; Ezekiel 37:1–14)

Summary of Maftir Reading   הַסְכּוּם

After Israel worshipped the golden calf, Moses shattered the first set of tablets. Now he again ascends Mount Sinai in order to receive the new set of tablets. Moses pleads for God's assurance of support. God reassures Moses, and also reveals His thirteen divine attributes. Moses then brings down a new set of tablets with the Ten Commandments.

Haftarah Summary and Connection   הַסְכּוּם וְהַקֶּשֶׁר

The Haftarah is taken from the Book of Ezekiel. The prophet finds himself in a valley of dry bones. Under the vivifying effect of God's spirit, the bones knit together and become covered with flesh. Ezekiel understands this vision to mean that the people of Israel, having been exiled to Babylon, will again be reborn as a nation.

Both the fact that Passover, recalling past deliverances, looks forward to future redemption, and an old tradition that the resurrection of the dead will take place during Passover, determined the choice of this passage as the Haftarah for the Intermediate Sabbath of Passover.

Notable Quotations צִיטָטִים

The hand of God was upon me,	הָיְתָה עָלַי יַד־יְהֹוָה
and the Lord carried me on a spirit,	וַיּוֹצִאֵנִי בְרוּחַ יְהֹוָה
and set me down	וַיְנִיחֵנִי
in the midst of the valley,	בְּתוֹךְ הַבִּקְעָה
and it was full of bones.	וְהִיא מְלֵאָה עֲצָמוֹת:

Ezekiel 37:1

So I prophesied as God commanded	וְהִנַּבֵּאתִי כַּאֲשֶׁר צִוָּנִי
and the breath came into them,	וַתָּבוֹא בָהֶם הָרוּחַ
and they came to life	וַיִּחְיוּ
and stood up upon their feet,	וַיַּעַמְדוּ עַל־רַגְלֵיהֶם
an exceedingly great host.	חַיִל גָּדוֹל מְאֹד־מְאֹד:

Ezekiel 37:10

פֶּסַח יוֹם הַשְּׁבִיעִי

Torah Reading and Haftarah for the Seventh Day of Passover
(Exodus 13:17–15:26; II Samuel 22)

Summary of Torah Reading הַסִכּוּם

The Torah reading describes Israel's experiences following the exodus. Pharaoh mobilizes the Egyptian army and begins his pursuit of the fleeing Israelites. When Moses and the children of Israel reach the Red Sea, Moses raises his rod, the waters split apart, and the Israelites miraculously are saved. When the Egyptians reach the water, they become bogged down, sink to the bottom, and drown. Moses and the children of Israel sing a magnificent song of thanksgiving.

Haftarah Summary and Connection הַסִכּוּם וְהַקֶּשֶׁר

The Haftarah connects to the theme of the song of thanksgiving. In the Haftarah, David composes his own song of thanksgiving to God for all of his victories and deliverances from the enemy.

Notable Quotations צִיטָטִים

The Lord is my rock	יְהֹוָה סַלְעִי
and my fortress,	וּמְצֻדָתִי
and my deliverer.	וּמְפַלְטִי־לִי:

II Samuel 22:2

A tower of salvation of His king;	מִגְדּוֹל יְשׁוּעוֹת מַלְכּוֹ
who shows mercy to His anointed,	וְעֹשֶׂה־חֶסֶד לִמְשִׁיחוֹ
to David and to his heirs forever.	לְדָוִד וּלְזַרְעוֹ עַד־עוֹלָם:

II Samuel 22:51

פֶּסַח יוֹם הַשְּׁמִינִי

Torah Reading and Haftarah for
Eighth Day of Passover
(Deuteronomy 15:19–16:17; Isaiah 10:32–12:6)

Summary of Torah Reading הַסְכּוּם

The Torah reading for the eighth day of Passover deals with a variety of laws, including those related to tithes, the year of release, release of slaves, and a comprehensive description of the three pilgrimage festivals.

Haftarah Summary and Connection הַסְכּוּם וְהַקֶּשֶׁר

The Haftarah, from the Book of Isaiah, begins with a prediction that Assyria will be defeated. This prophecy indeed comes true. The Haftarah continues with Isaiah's message of hope that the Israelites will again be gathered together from lands of exile and return to Israel.

The Haftarah also contains the famous great vision of the Messianic Era when peace and harmony will reign supreme among all people. Because the Haftarah contains several allusions to the redemption from Egypt (vv. 11, 15, 16), it was chosen for the last day of Passover.

Notable Quotations   צִיטָטִים

A shoot will come out	וְיָצָא חֹטֶר
from the stock of Jesse, and	מִגֵּזַע יִשָׁי
a twig shall grow out of his roots.	וְנֵצֶר מִשָּׁרָשָׁיו יִפְרֶה:

Isaiah 11:1

The Lord will utterly destroy	וְהֶחֱרִים יְהֹוָה אֵת לְשׁוֹן
the tongue of the Egyptian sea,	יָם־מִצְרַיִם
and God will sweep his hand	וְהֵנִיף יָדוֹ
over the river	עַל־הַנָּהָר
with His scorching wind	בַּעְיָם רוּחוֹ

Isaiah 11:15

The wolf shall dwell with the lamb,	וְגָר זְאֵב עִם־כֶּבֶשׂ
and the leopard	וְנָמֵר
will lie down with the kid.	עִם־גְּדִי יִרְבָּץ

Isaiah 11:6

Behold, God is my salvation.	הִנֵּה אֵל יְשׁוּעָתִי
I will trust and not be afraid.	אֶבְטַח וְלֹא אֶפְחָד

Isaiah 12:2

שָׁבוּעוֹת יוֹם רִאשׁוֹן

Torah Reading and Haftarah for
First Day of Shavuot
(Exodus 19:1–20:23; Ezekiel 1:1–28, 3:12)

Summary of Torah Reading הַסִּכּוּם

The Torah reading describes the preparation for God's revelation at Mount Sinai. The major portion of the Torah reading is the enumeration of the Ten Commandments. Shavuot is the festival which commemorates the revelation at Mount Sinai, and thus these passages were chosen for inclusion on the first day of Shavuot.

Haftarah Summary and Connection הַסִּכּוּם וְהַקֶּשֶׁר

The Haftarah describes a remarkable vision of God by the prophet Ezekiel. It is the vision of the Divine Throne-Chariot, whose main feature is a group of four-faced living creatures. This amazing appearance of a manifestation of God connects the Haftarah to the Torah reading, where again God reveals His will at Mount Sinai.

Notable Quotations צִיטָטִים

Out of the midst thereof	וּמִתּוֹכָהּ
came the shape of four creatures.	דְּמוּת אַרְבַּע חַיּוֹת.
And this was their appearance:	וְזֶה מַרְאֵיהֶן:
they had the likeness of a man.	דְּמוּת אָדָם לָהֵנָּה.

Ezekiel 1:5

Then a spirit lifted me up,	וַתִּשָּׂאֵנִי רוּחַ,
and I heard behind me	וָאֶשְׁמַע אַחֲרַי
the voice of a great rushing:	קוֹל רַעַשׁ גָּדוֹל:
"Blessed be the glory of God	"בָּרוּךְ כְּבוֹד־יְהֹוָה
from His place."	מִמְּקוֹמוֹ.„

Ezekiel 3:12

שָׁבוּעוֹת יוֹם שֵׁנִי

Torah Reading and Haftarah for Second Day of Shavuot (Deuteronomy 15:19–16:17; Habakkuk 2:20–3:19)

Summary of Torah Reading הַסִכּוּם

The reading deals with the laws of tithing, release of debts in the seventh year, the release of slaves every seventh year, and a description of the three pilgrimage festivals of Passover, Shavuot, and Sukkot.

Haftarah Summary and Connection הַסִכּוּם וְהַקֶשֶׁר

In the Haftarah, Habakkuk pleads with God to intervene on behalf of his people. He visualizes his petition as granted in a graphic picture of the march of God and God's retinue to overthrow the enemy. Now God will redeem Israel from persecution.

As in the case of the Haftarah for the first day of Shavuot, this too is a description of a manifestation of God. For this reason, and also because the language in places recalls the revelation at Sinai, it was chosen as the Haftarah for the second day of Shavuot.

319

Notable Quotations צִיטָטִים

A brightness appears as the light.	וְנֹגַהּ כָּאוֹר תִּהְיֶה
He has beams ready at His side.	קַרְנַיִם מִיָּדוֹ לוֹ
And there is the hiddden source	וְשָׁם חֶבְיוֹן
of God's power.	עֻזֹּה:

Habakkuk 3:4

Yet I will rejoice in God,	וַאֲנִי בַּיהֹוָה אֶעְלוֹזָה
and I will exult	אָגִילָה
in the God of my salvation.	בֵּאלֹהֵי יִשְׁעִי.

Habakkuk 3:18

יְמֵי צוֹם

Torah Reading and Haftarah for Fast Days
(Exodus 32:11–14, 34:1–10; Isaiah 55:6–56:8)

Summary of Torah Reading הַסְכּוּם

Moses pleads for forgiveness for the people of Israel, asking God never to forsake the covenant He made with our ancestors Abraham, Isaac, and Jacob. God favorably responds to Moses' plea.

The theme of God's forgiveness for transgressions is appropriate for fast days that remind us of God's displeasure with the Israelites and the catastrophes that resulted.

Haftarah Summary and Connection הַסְכּוּם וְהַקֶּשֶׁר

The Haftarah is from the Book of Isaiah. Even as fasting is designed to bring people into a mood of repentance, Isaiah calls on us to change our ways and return to God's ways. Isaiah promises that in return for authentic repentance (which includes doing justly and being righteous), God will bring about the redemption of Israel.

Notable Quotations צִיטָטִים

Seek God while God may be found,	דִּרְשׁוּ יְהוָה בְּהִמָּצְאוֹ
call upon God while God is near.	קְרָאֻהוּ בִּהְיוֹתוֹ קָרוֹב:

Isaiah 55:6

Thus says God:	כֹּה אָמַר יְהוָה
Keep justice and do righteousness,	שִׁמְרוּ מִשְׁפָּט וַעֲשׂוּ צְדָקָה
for My salvation is near to come.	כִּי־קְרוֹבָה יְשׁוּעָתִי לָבוֹא

Isaiah 56:1

תִּשְׁעָה בְּאָב

Torah Reading and Haftarah for the Ninth of Av (Deuteronomy 4:25–40; Jeremiah 8:13–9:23)

Summary of Torah Reading   הַסְכּוּם

Moses prophesies that there will come a time when Israel will forsake God and turn to idolatry. God in His anger will disperse the Jews throughout the lands. But if Israel sincerely wishes to repent, Moses assures them, God is prepared to listen to prayers.

The theme of this Torah reading, Israel's punishment for its sins and a chance for redemption, makes it an appropriate one for Tisha B'Av, the day commemorating the destruction of both Temples in Jerusalem.

Haftarah Summary and Connection   הַסְכּוּם וְהַקֶּשֶׁר

The prophet Jeremiah tells of the despair of the Israelites due to their dishonesty and their betrayal of their neighbors, brothers, and sisters. For this they must suffer the consequences, namely, Jerusalem becoming a wasteland of destruction.

Notable Quotations צִיטָטִים

I will utterly consume them,	אָסֹף אֲסִיפֵם,
says God.	נְאֻם־יְהוָֹה.
There are no grapes on the vines	אֵין עֲנָבִים בַּגֶּפֶן
nor figs on the fig tree.	וְאֵין תְּאֵנִים בַּתְּאֵנָה

Jeremiah 8:13

Is there no balm in Gilead?	הַצֳרִי אֵין בְּגִלְעָד
Is there no physician there?	אִם־רֹפֵא אֵין שָׁם
Why then is not the health	כִּי מַדּוּעַ לֹא עָלְתָה
of the daughter of my people	אֲרֻכַת
recovered?	בַּת־עַמִּי?

Jeremiah 8:22

Let not be proud	אַל־יִתְהַלֵּל
the wise one in his wisdom	חָכָם בְּחָכְמָתוֹ
Let not be proud	וְאַל־יִתְהַלֵּל
the mighty in his strength	הַגִּבּוֹר בִּגְבוּרָתוֹ
Let not be proud	אַל־יִתְהַלֵּל
the rich one in his wealth.	עָשִׁיר בְּעָשְׁרוֹ.

Jeremiah 9:22